W9-CUK-654

1-
st

TK

Ex Libris

Natalie Snyder

THE BEDSIDE 'GUARDIAN'

11

A Selection from the
GUARDIAN

1961 - 1962

with a Foreword by
JAMES MORRIS

COLLINS
ST JAMES'S PLACE, LONDON
1962

ACKNOWLEDGEMENTS

The publishers wish to express their thanks
to George Allen & Unwin *Limited* for
permission to reproduce an article by Francis
Chichester which will appear in the forthcoming book *Crossing the Atlantic Alone* by
Francis Chichester.

© *The Manchester Guardian and*
Evening News Ltd., 1962
Printed in Great Britain
Collins Clear-Type Press
London and Glasgow

Foreword

THIS book is, as the Americans would neatly have it, "instant newspaper". The whole point and pungency of the *Bedside Guardian* lies in the fact that it consists entirely of extracts from one year's issues of a daily paper: it was written in bits and pieces, in a hurry, sometimes indeed reluctantly, sometimes in all the heady exhilaration that seizes the newspaperman at the very last moment, when the story is hot and sizzling in his mind, and the cable office is just preparing, with an incomprehensible reference to national holidays, to close down until Thursday evening. We were writing for the hour when we wrote these pieces, for the late edition, for the influence we fondly thought our reports might exert, for the fun of our incomparable trade, and sometimes, to be frank, just for the money.

Instant newspaper, but more pertinently instant *Guardian*. I must not sound complacent, and it is difficult enough anyway to write an introduction to a book in which you are yourself represented—not unlike compiling your own obituary, with a selection of tributes from your wide circle of intimates: I think it undeniable, though, that not many daily newspapers could extract, year after year, enough suitable material from their files for an annual collection of this sort. This is not all brag, for the *Bedside Guardian* reflects, to my mind, both the faults and the merits of its irrepressible parent. Other papers might well produce a more logical essence of the year's news, a more disciplined response to contemporary history, a more provocative crossing of t's or dotting of i's. We would not claim to be unexcelled in every branch of our calling, as many an intrusive purple passage proclaims. We can, however, reasonably claim

5

this, with a mock-modest and ingratiating bow: that no other daily journal in our language can beat the enthusiasm, range and variety that this book is able to present.

Enthusiasm I offer first, for it is the salt of the *Guardian's* flavour. The great thing about this paper, at least from the writer's point of view, is the pleasure of writing for it. It may not make you rich, or even fearfully famous, but it leaves you free, unhampered, even footloose. It does not brainwash you. It tries hard not to edit you. It pursues the theory that the reporter is at his best when he is enjoying himself, and while this may sometimes raise a wry sneer amongst us when we are engaged in some unspeakable chore of reportage, nevertheless there are all too often moments in the service of the *Guardian*, as Neville Cardus recorded long ago, when you pinch yourself with disbelief, so unlikely does it seem that you are actually being paid for having such a wonderful time.

This sense of pleasure inevitably shows, in the posh pages of this anthology as in the fish-and-chips wrapping of yesterday's paper. It shows in the *Guardian's* celebrated profusion of styles, subjects, approaches and interpretations. It shows, sometimes perhaps too blatantly, in the intensely personal idiom of it all, and in the licence always shown to individual quirks and mannerisms. Finding myself in Reykjavik one day when nothing in particular was happening there, I sent a dispatch to the *Guardian* reporting that, so far as I could see, nothing in particular was happening. I cabled it off in a moment of cheerful idleness, and scarcely expected even so genial an employer to print it. But print it the *Guardian* did, with only the dryest flicker of a smile, at the top of a column on a dull day, and beneath the flaming headline: " *No News From Iceland* ".

It is just this empirical and imperturbable taste that makes this paper, though the most famous of all provincial journals, still the least parochial of publications. C. P. Scott decided, years ago, that his *Guardian* was to be not simply a local paper, nor even a national paper, but a paper of international meaning. This it is. Its standards are the standards of humanity, and it has always

6

looked every man, whatever the colour of his skin or the state of his loyalties, straight, frankly and often caustically in the eye. (This has led, over the generations, to one or two paradoxes of sympathy: during the Boer War the *Guardian* was burnt on the Stock Exchange for supporting the Boers, but half a century later it was a Boer spokesmen who, asked to comment upon the *Guardian's* reporting of South African affairs, observed witheringly that it was " accurate, but of a liberal bias "). The *Guardian's* flexibility of opinion, though not of conviction, means that there is nothing stuffy, monolithic or parish-pump about its reputation. Its corporate image is rather of the prismatic kind, changing colour in the eye of the beholder: as one with a resilient strain of old-school patriotism in me, I have never quite forgotten the Jordanian dissident who, describing to me some new Anglo-Arab perfidy, added as a kindly afterthought: " Of course, I don't mind telling *you* this, Mr. Morris, because I know the *Guardian* is anti-British! "

But no, the values that our paper tries to honour are values that any intelligent Englishman covets for his country and its friends: variety of thought and expression, honesty of judgement, humour in the right place, the duty to criticise when a critic is required, decency as a way of life, beauty as an end in itself. Tall talk, for journalism, but then the *Guardian* has never been afraid to aim high. I sometimes think, on its more elaborate mornings, that a positively Baroque flavour informs its columns. Certainly it is far from Bauhaus, far from Socialist Realist, far from anything cold, hard or arrogantly functional. This book is instant newspaper indeed: but to those of us who write the *Guardian*, it offers us day by day the aspiration of producing, if you will forgive a high-faulutin' finale, something approaching instant literature.

James Morris

John Maddox

CROSSING THE CHANNEL

THE HISTORY

The prospect of some kind of link between England and France across the English Channel now seems to be immediate. Recent experience with engineering works of many kinds has for one thing shown that the physical problems of linking the two countries in this way are not nearly as severe as they seem at first sight—and as, indeed, they were in reality a few decades ago. On the other hand some of the less technical objections to the various schemes which have been proposed have been shown by recent events to have become empty of real content: there is, for example, not even a trace of substance in the argument that any physical link would undermine British island military strategy.

The melting away of some of the old technical obstacles to the construction of a physical link across the Channel has not, unfortunately, been an unmixed blessing. For if in the thirties it was difficult to decide whether any kind of link could be established, the problem has now become that of knowing what kind of link would be best to build. Should it, for example, be a bridge or a tunnel?

Unfortunately the recent polemical clash between the Channel Tunnel Study Group and the Société d'Etude du Pont sur La Manche has not done a great deal to make these issues clearer than they were. The trouble is that it is necessary to balance the costs of the various schemes which are being proposed against the revenues which the completed engineering ventures are likely to earn from passenger and goods traffic carried between England and France. The estimates of cost are necessarily somewhat in error at this stage. Still more serious errors affect the calculation of how much money a bridge or a tunnel would earn in a year.

But even this does not complete the list of problems to be solved. For it is by no means certain the bridge and the tunnel exhaust the list of feasible means for connecting the two countries. Why not, for example, build a barrage across the Channel, and use this not merely for the transport of people but also for the generation of enormous quantities of electrical power?

Against this background of an increasing variety of technical possibilities the British and French Governments will soon have to decide which scheme to favour. In these circumstances there is much to be said for knowing what technical considerations are likely to be most important in each of the schemes.

THE TUNNEL

Historically this is the oldest of the schemes for a permanent link between Britain and Europe. Its conception goes back to one of Napoleon's engineers, who suggested that a tunnel should be bored beneath the Channel in 1802. The first serious proposals for an engineering construction were put forward a century ago, and in 1872 the French Channel Tunnel Company was formed to exploit them. The British Government appears to have been most closely involved with these projects under Ramsay MacDonald, who in 1930 arranged for the publication of an official study estimating that a rail tunnel beneath the Channel would cost £30 millions.

The Channel Tunnel Study Group was formed in 1957 by the Channel Tunnel Company, a similar group in Paris, the financial holding company left behind after the nationalisation of the Suez Canal, and an American technical study organisation known as Technical Studies Incorporated. In the last three years this organisation has made more detailed surveys of the

Channel bed and of the rock formations beneath it than those which were possible in the old days, even with the help of trial tunnels bored out beneath the Channel from Shakespeare Cliff (near Dover) and Sangatte (near Calais).

Two different schemes for linking Britain and France by tunnel have been considered by the group. On the one hand there is a proposal for a subterranean tunnel bored in the cenomanian or lower chalk formation running continuously beneath the Channel. The integrity of this formation, whose thickness varies from 262 feet (on the English side) to 213 feet has now been established. The Channel Tunnel Study Group has suggested that boring a tunnel in this formation would be feasible, but that the need to keep well above the rock formation underlying the chalk would " seem to exclude the possibility of a tunnel with a very large diameter such as would be required to contain both a road and a railway line."

The boring of a tunnel in a solid chalk stratum would be much easier—mile for mile—than the work now under way in the hard igneous rock beneath Mont Blanc, and easier than the boring of tunnels in the treacherous strata beneath the Thames. It has been estimated that progress could be made at a rate of one mile every three months. With the accumulation of experience from other tunnel projects now under consideration, the chances are that this speed could be considerably enhanced.

The alternative scheme is for a tunnel laid in a trench cut in the surface of the Channel bed, continuously beneath the water. Such an immersed tube would have the drawback that dredging out the trench in the rough waters of the Channel would be difficult, though the study group has pointed out that oil drilling rigs would be of great service here. One great virtue of the arrangement would be that it would enable a tunnel big enough for rail and road traffic to be built.

With all tunnel schemes ventilation becomes a problem if road traffic is to be considered. The schemes which the Channel Study Group have put forward involve one or two artificial

islands for ventilating inlets in mid-Channel if a road tunnel is
to be provided as well as a rail tunnel. If the scheme for boring
through the chalk is considered, a road tunnel would have to
be separate from a rail tunnel. Otherwise, in a covered tube
construction, a double-deck construction could be used.

THE BRIDGE

Schemes for bridges across the Channel have been in currency
for nearly a century, but those put forward in the last few years
have been blessed with a greater air of reality than earlier schemes,
mainly because improved methods of construction have become
available.

Other bridge-building schemes started since the war have
also shown what can be done to span great expanses of water
with steel structures. The bridge now being built across the
Chesapeake Bay in the United States, so as to connect two
previously separated pieces of Virginia (and in the process to
provide a coastal route south to Florida), will be 11 miles long.
The needs of heavy sea traffic will be met by leading the
bridge into a tunnel at two places along the path planned for
it.

A scheme of comparable magnitude is being considered to
link together the Danish islands of Fyn and Sjaelland. This
structure will be twelve miles long in one of its proposed forms.
The spans of the Forth Bridge now nearing completion in
Scotland will in fact be greater than those of the bridge whose
building is being urged by the Société d'Etude du Pont sur
La Manche.

In this scheme the bridge proper would be 20.3 miles long,
running between Dover and Calais. The deck of the bridge
would have room for rail traffic in each direction and for seven
lanes for road traffic of various kinds. Altogether there would
be 164 piers anchored in the bed of the Channel, the deepest of
which would lie 184 ft. below the surface of the sea. There
would be ten spans of 1390 feet—sufficient it is claimed for

the largest ships—other spans of the bridge would be 740 feet long.

The construction of a bridge of this type differs from the construction of a shorter bridge merely in the greater amount of work needed. The problems to be solved are not specially difficult, and indeed the depth of the water in which properly sited piers would have to be anchored is less than the depth of some of the channels in which other large bridge schemes have already been built.

In this proposal, piers would be anchored by floating out to the chosen sites great elliptical caissons of concrete, sinking these at the appropriate places and then filling them with concrete and rubble. No great difficulty is entailed in this operation. The building of the steel superstructure to be erected on these piers would, it is claimed, be simplified to some extent by floating out prefabricated sections of the bridge from ports to be established on the coast. It is certain that the design of this superstructure has been immensely simplified and cheapened by the present availability of steel alloys of high strength and reasonable cost. These have made possible marked reductions of the cost of the metal needed to provide given strength.

The stability of part of the bridge structure has already been tested in wind tunnels, and in the process it has been possible to show how the speed of winds on the surface of the traffic decks might be reduced to reasonable proportions. It would seem prudent to carry out more comprehensive studies of the bridge structure as a whole before construction began, but there is no cause to fear for the structural integrity of the bridge as a whole.

THE DAM

By comparison with the tunnel and the bridge, the notion of a dam across the Channel which would serve both as a means of transport and as a source of electrical power, has received comparatively little attention. A French engineer, M. C. C. M. Hardy, does appear to have made extensive studies of the feasibility of such a project, and has been good enough to provide details of some of the conclusions at which he has arrived. Other arguments in favour of a Channel dam have also recently appeared in lay publications.

The feasibility of a dam across the English Channel can no longer be in doubt. Many of the dikes recently built in Holland to enclose reclaimable land have been laid in water every bit as deep as that between England and France. M. Hardy has pointed out that one of these dams is 31 km. long (that across the Yssel Sea). He also argues that the scheme being worked out in France to obtain tidal power from an artificial lagoon built around Mont St. Michel will entail a dam the same size as the one that would be necessary to separate the English Channel from the North Sea.

The technique of dam building as worked out by Dutch engineers entails the excavation of some of the surface material from the bed of the Channel, and the construction in this of a gently sloping dike made largely of local materials. In a dam across the Channel, of course, locks would be provided at various intervals for ocean-going vessels. It is to be supposed that the width across the top of the dam would be sufficient for any demands likely to be made for transport between England and France.

The special feature—and the special attraction—of a dam is that this would make it possible to generate vast quantities of electrical power. The tidal flow in the Channel is certainly sufficient to account for all the electricity at present used in Britain. The chance that this supply would also suffice for the whole of Europe is possible.

M. Hardy has suggested that the problem of ensuring that this supply of electricity was uniform, in time should be solved by building an artificial lagoon by means of a Y-shaped dam with—in his scheme—two arms of the dam resting on the French coast. The idea is that the lagoon would be filled up from the tidal flow in the Channel and discharged through turbines when electricity was in greatest demand.

A further point which has not been adequately discussed concerns the effect which a continuous dam would have on the flow of water in the North Sea. It seems likely that the interference with free tidal flow through the Strait of Dover would cause a comparatively rapid silting in of some of the low-lying areas off the Dutch coast. Not only would the building of a Channel dam take the pressure off the existing coastal defences in northern Europe, it might even provide a welcome and very large supply of reclaimable land.

Though there have been no detailed estimates of the cost of building a dam across the Channel, the chances are that it would not be very different from the costs of a bridge or a tunnel. A figure in the region of £100 millions, or some small multiple of this, would seem to be reasonable. The dam would, however, have the economic virtue that further investments of capital in generating equipment might produce enormous dividends in terms of electrical power.

It is not of course possible to make accurate estimates of the profitability of these different schemes without much more accurate estimates of the demand for traffic facilities than have already become available. In the comparison between the bridge and the tunnel it seems to be accepted that the bridge would cost nearly twice as much as the tunnel, but that this extra cost would be offset by the extra traffic which could be carried. A more important point, perhaps, is that a bridge offers greater flexibility than a tunnel, and thus some greater hope of meeting unpredictable demands likely to be made in the future.

The danger is that one or other of these schemes might be mounted by accident, as it were, merely because its proponents were best able to win financial support, or conceal some of the administrative difficulties of handling traffic in the completed scheme. It would therefore seem that the best administrative course would be for the governments of Britain and France to agree in principle that some crossing of the Channel is necessary, and for them to mount a more searching and dispassionate inquiry than has yet taken place into the best way of doing this.

Though it may easily be that the scheme for a Channel dam is not really practicable, its feasibility indicates that any inquiry should be wider than may at first sight have seemed possible. If there is to be a link across the Channel it should be a symbol of the future and not a monument of the past.

Norman Shrapnel

ENTRY INTO THE COMMON MARKET

In marked contrast to his gloomy hesitancy earlier in the week Mr. Macmillan looked and sounded yesterday like a man leading a nation into the next stage of its history. It was a vigorous and imaginative speech in which he invited the Commons to endorse the Government's decision on the Common Market.

It was also a diplomatic speech in the domestic sense, for he told the House—and particularly those behind him who are deeply worried about sovereignty—that we should contemplate not so much a federated Europe, on United States lines, as a "confederation" of individual nations.

He was sharply taken up on this by Mr. Gaitskell, who mentioned an earlier Government prospect, offered by the President of the Board of Trade, of political federation as the likely outcome. The country, Mr. Gaitskell was convinced, would not have that at any price.

Federation or confederation—that was the distant scene. What the House was concerned with now was the first step— and it was a step too many for some who were still sombrely wondering where it was all going to end. Making Mr.

Macmillan grasp this nettle was Mr. Gaitskell's most telling moment. For the rest, he was in the shadow of this resurgent Prime Minister, an unusual state of affairs these days.

Mr. Gaitskell had, of course, put himself in a position in which it was hard to shine. He had to celebrate hesitancy—to erect a statue, as it were, to a man sitting on a fence. He did it as well as could be expected, and his supporters appeared loyal.

The official Labour Party sat stolidly in their seats with the look of total abstainers to a man, although the virtuous expression on a number of faces—or did one imagine it?—seemed slightly uneasy. This abstaining look was not shared, needless to say, by Mr. Sydney Silverman or by a whole cellarful of potentially rebellious Conservatives who might, it was thought, just possibly be flushed out into the lobby if Mr. Silverman decided to force a division on the Government's motion.

Mr. Silverman had the air of a man who intended to force anything he could, beginning by holding up the Prime Minister for several minutes with the bayonet of a Silverman point of order—a weapon usually feared by all.

Nothing discomposed this revitalised Mr. Macmillan. He was completely in command, and the House listened heavily, and for the most part silently, but with the deepest attention. The Liberals could be excused from attending very hard. They looked like early Christians being preached to by a bishop who had been converted late, and Lord Hinchingbrooke—who thinks Mr. Macmillan the victim of a shot-gun marriage ordered by President Kennedy—scowled a good deal. Mr. Macmillan was not, however, going to be put off by things like that.

He spoke of this idea that had " gripped men's minds," and sounded at last as though it had really gripped his own. He spoke of our long tradition of isolation, and drew his first cheer by insisting that security in isolation is a thing for which we can no longer hope. That would have been a platitude if he had not gone on to utter a warning to any " Little Europeans " who may be thinking in terms of an inward-looking and self-

STEP BY STEP

sufficient Europe. Little Europeans, to Mr. Macmillan, are as dated as Little Englanders.

Our Commonwealth remains precious and unique to Mr. Macmillan, and he underlined his pledge to do nothing that might endanger it. Our agriculture will have to face change anyway, and he thinks it would do well to take a hand in shaping its future in wider fields. Our industry, too, he said, will have to face intense competition whether we go into the Common Market or stay out. Many people, Mr. Macmillan remarked in passing, thought we had enjoyed too much shelter.

While re-emphasising that " the moment of decision " has not yet come, the Prime Minister was frank and forceful about the way he wants it to go. " We have much to gain and much to contribute," he said finally. "And much to lose," a voice put in, but interruptions were few and there was a strong cheer at the end. As for Lord Hinchingbrooke, he scowled on.

If the depth of the split running through both parties on this issue has been underestimated, it is not through any lack of any effort on Lord Hinchingbrooke's part. When he stopped scowling and started speaking it turned out to be an extraordinary performance. He put in his wedge, first on one side and then on the other, and whacked it as hard as only he knows how.

Then, scorning all middle-way Conservatives, he moved purposefully beyond the extreme Right and shook hands with the extreme Left. There are Conservatives, Lord Hinchingbrooke said scornfully, who would sooner be ruled by European bureaucracy than by British Socialism. Not Lord Hinchingbrooke.

What he wanted was to find a new grouping, drawn from both sides, which would exorcise the spirit now at large. It is an evil spirit, the noble lord is convinced, as evil as the Jabberwock, and he let the House into the Wonderland logic of all his thoughts.

"A most remarkable speech," Miss Jennie Lee commented —and well she might.

Peter Jenkins

HERO'S WELCOME FOR MAJOR GAGARIN

"I am still an ordinary mortal," Major Yuri Gagarin said at his mammoth Press conference at Earl's Court yesterday. But London took a different view. It greeted the Soviet space hero with enthusiasm bordering on hysteria: a genuinely warm welcome combined with the sort of excesses of behaviour normally reserved for visiting royalty and film stars.

His open Rolls arrived at Earl's Court to the roar of police motor-cycles and shrieks of feminine pleasure. Just after one o'clock, half an hour late because of the traffic and the crowds, he was swept into the forecourt of the exhibition hall, where a large crowd had been gathering all morning. Stepping from the car on to the red carpet he looked the prototype Russian hero—the Soviet equivalent of the " all-American boy."

He is smallish, dark, upright, clean-cut. He wore a waisted khaki jacket, air force blue trousers, a khaki cap with blue band, the Gold Star of the Soviet Union and a permanent, good-natured smile. A bouquet of red carnations, white michaelmas daisies and orange gladioli was thrust into his arms as he was embraced and shaken by the hand. " The most kissed man in Europe," said a man in the crowd.

Police linked arms to keep back the crowd. Foreign students chanted " Gagarin, Gagarin, Gagarin." A Soviet photographer was struck in the chest by a policeman when he moved forward to get a shot; he did not appear greatly surprised. Then the spaceman was hustled by police through the hundreds in the foyer; he reached the lift and safely ascended to lunch.

But this was nothing to what happened later. Reporters had to fight their way to the stairs to the fashion theatre where the Press conference was held at three o'clock. By 4.15, when Gagarin emerged to attempt his tour of the exhibition, thousands had gathered around the stairs, in the Cosmic Hall and along the route he was to follow. Repeated announcements were made asking the public to clear the way but no attention was paid.

Gagarin was mobbed on appearance. A path was forced into the Cosmic Hall where a large model sputnik toppled above the heads of the crowd. Luckily it was righted before anyone was hurt. He saw nothing of the exhibition. It soon became clear that a tour was impossible and he was hustled out, still smiling, by a dozen grim-faced constables standing head and shoulders above him.

As a result of this hurried exit his car was not ready and the police had to force his way across the forecourt and lift him bodily into the vehicle. Then they set about pushing it through the mob until it managed to get under way along the Warwick Road back to the peace of the Soviet Embassy. Helmets had been shed, frightened children were crying, shins were bruised, and feet trodden on.

By comparison, the Press conference which intervened between these turbulent scenes was a quiet affair. Not much information came out of it: there were too many journalists, from too many countries, interested in too many special "angles." Only two questions of scientific interest managed to get asked; for the rest it was how he felt, what about women in space, what his wife said, could he speak English, what did he think of England? Obviously a serious young man, he must have been surprised by the trivia which the reading public was deemed to want to know about the first man in space.

The personality of the man emerged, however, under this treatment. He is not given to speculative thought, not a very imaginative man, a pleasant sense of humour but not a master of repartee. A down-to-earth fellow one might almost say had not the march of science made the expression entirely inappropriate.

What were his personal feelings in space? He was too busy to have personal thoughts. What did he think of science fiction? He had read a lot but regretted the authors made supermen of their astronauts; they were just ordinary men; it was "just a case of thorough training and a certain amount of knowledge." Did he have nightmares after his experience? No; he had never been "much of a dreamer." Did he experience a "sense of eternity"? asked an oriental journalist thinking of his readers. He experienced no sense of infinity or anything of the kind—"Perhaps I fail to understand it."

He is a firmly but naturally modest man. He refused to be

regarded as a celebrity and looked forward to the day when his profession would number enough to escape the glare of publicity. His Gold Star of the Soviet Union was numbered 11,175, he pointed out. This meant 11,174 accomplished something notable before him.

When given a chance to speak about the practical aspects of space flight he was much more in his element. He explained carefully that he had landed inside the rocket although an alternative system was available by which he could have been ejected to descend by parachute. He told a questioner that a spaceman could not be an observer only. He was bound " to take an active part and to direct the flight." He was hoping for another trip if he was again " entrusted."

The spaceman was welcomed at the airport, when his silver Aeroflot TU 104 touched down just after eleven o'clock, by Mr. Francis Turnbull, secretary of the office of the Ministry for Science, Sir Ronald Lees, Deputy Chief of the Air Staff and Lord Drogheda, chairman of Industrial and Trade Fairs, the company organising the exhibition. Mr. Turnbull said: " I have the honour on behalf of Her Majesty the Queen to welcome you on your first arrival to Britain. Your courage and daring in undertaking the first manned space flight has been greatly admired by the people of Britain."

At the lunch given for Major Gagarin at the exhibition by its organisers, Mr. Julian Amery, Air Minister, said, "I know I shall be expressing our unbounded admiration of the coolness, skill, and yet modesty with which, like some new Columbus, you ventured out into the unknown and returned."

Mr. Amery said that Britain too proposed to launch out into space and follow the trail that Major Gagarin had blazed. He referred to proposals to form a space club with France and other European countries around the Blue Streak rocket. Although this was a long way from the stage reached by Russia and America there were many young men in the Royal Air Force who were only waiting for a chance to follow his example.

Last night, to complete perhaps the second most hectic day in his career, Gagarin attended a reception given in his honour at the Soviet Embassy.

Alistair Cooke

GLENN'S ROCKET TAKES OFF

The morning of Colonel Glenn's eleventh date with an orbit dawned without clouds over Cape Canaveral and without high waves off Bermuda. And so at last the eighteen tracking stations around the globe, the recovery ships, the 1500 expert watchers were alerted for a " Go," the syllable the American people have been waiting to exhale since the middle of December.

A few miles away, on Cocoa Beach, 5000 people, hundreds of whom had slept in their cars by the seashore, set up radio and antennae, focused telescopes, rocked babies, and faced the rocket and his escape tower and saw the colonel wave and waddle aboard.

At nineteen minutes after eight a hatch bolt broke and was quickly replaced. Twenty-two minutes before the zero hour there was a failure in one of the loading valves that feed liquid oxygen from the ground tanks into the rocket itself. In a rare burst of tact, Mercury Control did not report the slip until it was within a minute of being repaired. At thirteen and a half minutes to go, the helicopters at Canaveral began to spin their blades against the extreme possibility of an instantaneous recovery if the flight was aborted right after the take-off.

At eight minutes, the last assurances squawked over the public address system: " All Systems Go." At six and a half minutes, an electrical power failure in the computer system at Bermuda was reported as restored.

Two and a half minutes to go, the escape tower swung off. Twenty seconds from the word, the umbilical cord dropped away and Mercury Control intoned the countdown in seconds. There was the deep low frequency rumble modulating to an enormous woosh of sound and a vicious tongue of flame. Soon the Atlas was a fiery keyhole, and then an acorn and then a snowflake.

Within a minute or so the army of workers at Canaveral and the 500-odd reporters had lost all visible connection with their personal project and were at one with the silent crowds on the Florida beaches, in railroad stations and airports from New York to Seattle: gaping in extraordinary silence at giant television screens and hearing the elated exchange between Glenn and Mercury Control: " On trajectory . . . booster engines off . . . tower gone . . . go, baby, go . . . 5.8 cabin pressure holding."

He was already 500 miles down range, in contact with Bermuda, and off again across the Atlantic. More soaring waves of sound and static and the bright baritone again: " I can see the booster turning around. I feel fine, the view is tremendous." The next interval, and the Goddard Space Control Centre unscrambled the telemeter chatter and Mercury Control announced: " All Systems Go. Colonel Glenn is at the proper orbit angle."

This, to Canaveral and the tracking stations, was the first crisis passed, since the tiniest error in the lift-off could distort the orbit angle many thousands of times. In a now reassuring official tone, Colonel John Powers, the chief information officer at Mercury Control, announced that Glenn's velocity was 17,545 m.p.h., that he would orbit between a perigee of 100 miles and an apogee of 160 miles.

For the next eighty minutes we learned to attach a precious value to the regular assurances on cabin pressure and oxygen. He mentioned some " severe vibration " after take-off but he plainly survived it, and by the time he was over Africa we had heard that all the systems were in shape to sustain the theoretical seven orbits. "All systems," he crowed, "go and I am go . . . the capsule is in fine shape."

The first and almost flawless recorded tape between Glenn and a tracking station was taken at Kano in Nigeria. He was "very comfortable, all systems O.K. . . . a beautiful view of the African coast." Nine minutes later he had made contact with Zanzibar, and ten minutes later was high over the Indian Ocean.

At Muchea, in Australia, the same thing, and again at Woomera. He had been up an hour and fifteen minutes when he was commanded to take a deep breath. He did so and must have been relieved to hear, from a doctor on the other side of the earth and the ionosphere, that "your medical status is excellent." He had already celebrated this suspicion by pumping some fruit paste and meat paste into his gullet from the tooth-paste tubes they developed to overcome the problem of eating outside gravity.

By the time he had completed the first orbit, in 1 hour 36 minutes and 40 seconds, we heard a tape recorded as he had gone over Mexico. He was having some "minor difficulty with the attitude control." It takes only one pound of thrust, delivered by a hydrogen peroxide exhaust, to keep the capsule yawing and rolling according to plan. The automatic control evidently failed, but he announced, with no audible concern, that he was successfully using a combination of manual and electrical control known as "fly by wire." This mild concern began to nag both Colonel Glenn and Mercury Control as he took off on the second loop.

And throughout that orbit Mercury Control was contacting the tracking stations and getting the same reassuring, but slightly sinister, story from the astronaut. His automatic system was definitely out but he was handling the capsule's attitude with the greatest of ease. A momentary pause from this fearful item was filled by the flashing word from Auburn,

25

Maine, that it had named a street in his honour, and from St. Paul, Minnesota, that its latest school will be known as the John H. Glenn Junior High School.

There were two frantic, but well-disciplined, minutes at Mercury Control when the decision had to be made to bring him down or let him go into the third orbit. They let him go and the drama began to move to a tidy end as he spanned the Atlantic for a third time, and the North Atlantic Recovery Fleet disbanded. The curiosity now was all about the place of his landing, and while the tracking tapes discussed nothing but the time to fire the three retro-rockets that would diminish his speed and bring him down, we were already hearing a cavernous cheer go up from the crew of U.S.S. *Randolph*, which had been plotted as the probable rescue ship.

Back in the capsule, Glenn was counting his chickens with jocular confidence. He told a groundling astronaut to "get the cake ready": a 980 lb. invitation to gastritis, exactly the dimensions of the capsule (9 feet by 6 feet), that had been baked for the 27th January attempt and been embalmed in an air-conditioned truck ever since. Over Muchea again he delivered a solemn message: "Hey, Gordon, get this to General Shoop, the marine commandant—I have four hours' required flight time. Request flight chit be prepared for me." All fliers get a bonus for four hours' flying time a month. Colonel Glenn undoubtedly will be rewarded, at the usual rate of pay: three times round the globe—$215.

There was only one other jolting moment before the smooth descent, the succession of parachutes, and the rescue by the destroyer *Noa*. Over the Pacific he was having trouble deploying the heat shield which pushes away the 3000 degrees of heat when the rockets fire. This agony lasted for about four minutes, when he said, over Hawaii, that the switch had worked, it was the signal that was out. Then the rockets fired, no doubt about it: "I felt it was going to send me clear back to Hawaii."

The *Randolph* spotted the big parachutes through the clouds.

The U.S.S. *Noa* was only six miles away. The helicopters went off like flying lobsters and they saw him and the capsule in a rippling sea with a water temperature of 81 degrees. After that we switched to Washington to the well-tempered President, then to the ecstatic parents, and to Grand Central Station and the dissolving crowds, and strong men blowing their noses. John Glenn inscribed his name after the Wright Brothers and Lindbergh: " I am go."

Alistair Cooke

JET CRASH MOCKS GLENN'S DAY

A flawless day, with a whistling cold wind and a sky as crystalline as Capri, rose out of a week of fog and rain to welcome Colonel John Glenn to his New York triumph. The colonel and his family and the team of astronauts were half-way between Washington and La Guardia field when this beautiful bowl of sky was cracked by a huge explosion and smeared by trails of smoke that are still winding up this evening from 15,000 gallons of fuel and the blown wreckage of a 707 Astrojet that fell into Jamaica Bay.

At 10.18 this morning when the canyons of downtown New York were crammed with a million happy people, and the ticker tape was already mimicking a sizeable blizzard, American Airlines flight No. 1, its first jet non-stop flight of the day to Los Angeles, wheeled from its take-off pattern to begin the five-hour run and shot down into the bay. Its engines cracked, it fired into innumerable hunks of plastic and metal, and there was never a chance that any of the eighty-seven passengers and eight crew members could survive.

The New York police had spared from Glenn's route only skeleton crews for the patrol and maintenance of the rest of the city. The television networks had all their mobile units stationed strategically between La Guardia, where his plane came in; the East River drive, which he would ride down to Bowling Green; the route to City Hall Plaza, to which bands and marching units of the army, air force, navy, and marine corps would lead him; and the long trek north up Broadway and Fifth Avenue to the Waldorf Astoria, where the city would pay its homage at a luncheon and the mayor would pin on him a Medal of Honour, a token hitherto reserved for heads of state.

Mercifully, few of the hundreds of thousands of milling citizens had any way of knowing about the senseless horror that was to mock and haunt the roaring gaiety of Glenn Day. But the police and television crews knew. And there was a slimmer bodyguard and single camera to spot the Washington party when it touched down at La Guardia. The police and the networks had diverted their La Guardia crews five miles away to Idlewild and the rim of the runway that gives on to the marshes and waters of Jamaica Bay.

Within twenty minutes the tension of Glenn's arrival was suspended while we went out to the bay and watched policemen wading the shallow waters, the firemen and the coastguards fishing bodies into rowboats, priests and nurses stacking gruesome packages under blankets. From then on, for the three hours it took for the colonel to crawl through the cow path the vast crowds had left for him, we were always going back to the dishevelled scene by the bay: the cameras roving the horizon over the rising tide and the smudged rescuers and the mounting parapets of bodies, and then cutting to the universal grins and the cheerful hysteria of two million New Yorkers, and the colonel's shining face and the snowstorm of ticker tape and streamers.

It was like a brilliant and infuriating sequence in a film by Fellini. Neither scene had any connection with the other,

28

except by way of hammering home a crude irony, a gross and gratuitous contrast between the man who circled the globe three times and was plucked safe and sound from alien space, and eighty-seven non-aviators who flew two minutes in the true and tried Astrojet and were snuffed out in a wink.

The only bearable way to enjoy this parade, and wallow in the simple pride for this gay and modest hero was to be on the streets, oblivious of the other scene, tending a wounded rib, or waving a flag, or warning the pedlars (who are illegal in New York) that a cop was coming at a clip.

The motorcade went pretty much according to plan. At the last minute it was decided, by the White House no less, that Vice-President Johnson, who is the head of the President's Committee on Outer Space, should be in the parade. He sat up with the colonel and his lady in the lead car, the only political reminder that this Administration had asked and got another third of a billion dollars towards the thirty billions it will take in the next decade to try and get a man on the moon.

For the whole eighteen miles of the tour after the colonel had crossed the Triboro Bridge, the scene varied only according to the background of its architecture. Not a horizontal ledge of overhanging apartment buildings, not a set back or terrace of the downtown and midtown skyscrapers was empty of jumping midgets. And from Bowling Green to the Waldorf the skies were flailing with incalculable tons of paper. The trees along the route were bare when the tour began and newly leaved when it ended with deposits of torn telephone books and weaving branches of stock prices.

New York, let us just say, did the colonel proud according to a mad, tumultuous tradition which in its time has done honour to the Marquis de Lafayette, to the returning warriors of the First World War, and the Second, to Ike and Bradley and MacArthur and the shockingly skinny Wainwright from Bataan. And to-day to the man from outer space. But the sweet smell of success will always be soured by the acrid odour from Jamaica Bay and the tasteless mistiming of whatever gods preside over the art and science of human flight.

Alistair Cooke

BERLIN: INSIDE THE HURRICANE'S EYE

The United States Navy aeroplanes that duck into the Caribbean hurricanes often take a breathing spell in the very middle of them, in that floating centre of dead calm where it is possible to read the instruments and calculate the direction and speed of the encircling storm. The Brandenburg Gate is such an " eye." Its monumental design is of another age and makes it seem to be the most permanent thing about this beleaguered city. Its sauntering police and guards, exchanging pleasantries with the daily workers from West Berlin and the tourist bus-drivers, are operetta extras likely as not to line up on the hour and let loose a lively baritone chorus: " We are gentlemen of East Berlin, Wi-ith many a bow and grin." Their perfunctory screening of visitors suggests we are about to visit a royal park.

Along the Stalinallee there are coffee stalls where seedy youths in faded jeans and angry haircuts bend over transistor radios, wolf hot-dogs, and spark the girls. There are bookstalls that make a sort of *sportsfest* display of the Olympic champions: heroic, potted lives of Mao Tse-tung, of Castro, of Nkrumah and Sukarno, and sets of free postcards of Berlin *en fête* for, of all people, Paul Robeson. The newspapers are thin pep-sheets of the sort handed out at Salvation Army or anti-vivisection rallies. They reprint brief, ecstatic sermons on well-worn texts from Khruschev and Ulbricht and Professor Bernal.

"After all, it's just a matter of balance…"

LOW

BRINK

" The West German General Staff is openly pressing for the whole gamut of nuclear and missile weapons . . . the Bonn generals, who all served under Hitler, are demanding military bases throughout Western Europe . . . the generals' demands have the full backing of the Federal Government . . . (they) would subordinate the West German economy to the plans of the militarists. . . . But there is a way to defeat this plot . . . it is that of the complete renunciation by both German States of every sort of nuclear and missile weapon, the limitation and eventual abolition of the arms and armed forces of

31

both under mutual control, their withdrawal from military alliances, and the conclusion of a peace treaty."

There are squibs about new goods available in the H.O. (State-owned) stores and dead-pan proclamations that in the Democratic Republic there is no unemployment—a needless reminder of the labour pinch that is relieved by the 30,000 West Berliners whose daily work is in the Eastern sector. There is nothing at all about the serious food shortages in East Germany, which you have read about in the West Berlin papers, or the wide and worrisome resentment among Eastern farmers of the collectivisation of the farms. There are compensating reassurances—perhaps a clue to the truth of these Western reports—about the progress of negotiations for a new trade pact with West Germany, which have been going on continuously since last winter. But the sight of a West German patrol, the report of a field exercise in England that includes German troops, fires up the headlines again with their "flashes" and " bulletins " pounding home the grisly theme of the magazines, of Ulbricht's weekly warnings, of the propaganda pamphlets you can pick up in the little " reception building " just inside the gate. This theme, broadly stated above in the quotation from Professor Bernal, is the stage thunder that rattles and rumbles over the life of the East Berliner. We of the West have paid it too little attention, but it is as ubiquitous and maddening as rock 'n' roll in every dance hall from Los Angeles to Bath.

After a day or two in East Berlin you begin to wonder how seriously it is possible for the East Germans, and their castaways in East Berlin, to take it. My own hunch is that it bores the East Berliners, who can check in person on the other lurid tales of the aggressive, decadent life of the West, but that it unites in fear the grumbling farmers of East Germany and the evangelical clergy and their parishioners, whom the Russians have failed to split or seduce.

It is most forcefully stated in an alarming pamphlet called

32

" Check German Militarism," issued by " the German Peace
Council " (no other identification supplied, or needed, since
it is a highly inflammatory summary of the arguments rehearsed
by the Presidium of the World Peace Council at its Bucharest
session last November). Its thesis may be absurd and negligible
to us, but it was sung by Mr. Krushchev to President Kennedy
in Vienna, and it is as familiar to the lowliest provincial gauleiter
as " The Vicar of Bray " to a church choir.

"It is a fact," the story begins, "that Bonn militarism,
supported by the leading N.A.T.O. Power, has to-day started
with the peaceful annexation of France and would like to begin
to-morrow with the peaceful ' invasion ' of England. For the
same purpose Bonn militarism has again taken up contact with
the Franco régime. . . . It will (soon) clear the West European
rear as a springboard for the implementation of war plans, the
individual stages of which become already apparent: . . . first
stage, the ' liberation ' of the G.D.R. by means of a small
atomic *blitzkrieg* meant as a police action. Second stage,
' peaceful ' blackmail actions and after their inevitable failure
an attack on the Polish People's Republic and the C.S.S.R. to
restore the old German aggression frontiers. Third stage, main
thrust against the U.S.S.R. Along with the launching of these
war preparations . . . goes a colonialism carried on in the most
varied forms and with unprecedented violence, of which Bonn's
participation " [*sic!*] " in the Algerian war is characteristic, and
the policy of interventionist ' aid ' in Africa, in the Arab countries, in Latin America, and in wider spheres of Asia. This
development is marked ideologically and politically, as in the
time of Hitler and Goebbels, by an unrestrained anti-com-
munism proclaiming a special German world mission—this
time for the salvation of the Christian Occident from the Red
devils."

It does not take an extreme susceptibility to the political
atmosphere of a city to begin to believe, not that this thesis is
true but that it is the thing to argue about it, that it is the issue
to debate, like the Common Market in London and the threat

of Castro's régime in Washington. It sounds criminally malicious, you say to yourself, but so did Dr. Paul Roa's tiresome charge before the Security Council that the United States was preparing an invasion of Cuba!

Before you entered the Brandenburg Gate, this grievance was as remote and paranoid as Hitler's rampage about the Sudetenland in, say, 1936. Now you see, or think you see, a sullen population—one third of the isolated city—obsessed by it. Unhappily, in the last week or two this booming propaganda has at last served its turn. The East German headlines grow blacker still at the news from Washington that President Kennedy is sending over new divisions and urging the American population to have always on hand two weeks of emergency food. The "plot" of the "Bonn generals" can easily be made to seem like a true prophecy of the moves that Washington is in fact preparing.

After a day or two this whirling nightmare and the eerie contrast of the calm at its centre begins to get you down. So you retreat through the Gate to recover your reason and watch the genial West Berliners reading the dispatches from Washington through the monocular rim of their beer-steins. They lift an eyebrow, confess to boredom with the "new crisis," and go about their brisk business and their pleasures.

But after this brief brainwashing in East Berlin you find yourself sitting down and taking stock, and wondering why a new crisis has arisen, who provoked it, and what in fact are the Western military plans for a showdown.

Wesley Boyd

THE ROAD TO BUCHENWALD

The road to Buchenwald is busy again. The coaches roar up the steep hill out of Weimar, past the Soviet Army camp sheltering behind the trees on the lower slopes of the Ettersberg. Near the top of the plateau they swing left into a side road which curves away gently through the beech and pine trees. A smooth, strong road through the silent forest, it stops suddenly in a clearing on the very top of the Ettersberg.

The coaches pull into a well-disciplined car park in front of the neat crescent of barracks which once housed the S.S. The passengers step down and stand waiting, unsurely, in mumbling groups. A guide comes forward to receive us. He is a short, wiry man, his face lined and tanned, his hair thick and grey. As he shepherds us into one of the barracks he explains that all the guides at Buchenwald are former inmates of concentration camps; he spent his years of suffering at Sachsenhausen.

On the ground floor a large and detailed model of Buchenwald as it was has been constructed. "This," he reminds us with a casual sweep of his arm, "was only one of 1100 concentration camps which the Nazis built all over Europe. Here 56,000 people were exterminated." He tells the story of the camp quietly, without emotion, all the time fingering unconsciously the round badge of the Socialist Unity Party in his buttonhole.

"... here in the German Democratic Republic we are keeping the memory of this Fascist barbarity alive so that it will not happen again. We have learned the lesson of the mistakes in German history. Unfortunately this cannot be said of another part of our homeland. In West Germany all this is being systematically forgotten. People who share the responsibility for places like Buchenwald have been promoted to high office under Adenauer. In West Germany the past is the present again. Already we can hear the militarists crying for the return of the old lands in Poland. . . ."

Outside the children and the tourists queue at the post office to buy picture postcards. Our guide leads us down to the camp still enclosed by the high barbed wire and watch-towers. We file, uneasily, through the heavy ornamental wrought-iron gates with their bitingly cynical motto of welcome: JEDEM DAS SEINE ("To each what he deserves"). "What would be the fate of the Nazis who again hold high positions in West Germany if each got what he deserved?" our guide asks.

We stand in the soft winter sunshine on the barren ground where thousands stood in sun and rain for hour after endless hour and where even yet only a few tufts of coarse grass find courage to grow. Most of the buildings have gone. The land runs bare and uneven down to the barbed wire. Even in the sunshine there is an air of darkness and desolation about the place.

We see the punishment poles on which prisoners were suspended for agonising hours until their wrists and shoulders were dislocated. We see the "Chariot of the Singing Commandos," the poetic title given by the S.S. to the heavy, ugly cart laden with stones which they made prisoners pull round the camp and sing as they ran. We see the underground cell where fine men were foully killed. We see the reconstructed house of death, its floors and walls painted red as in the days of blood, where prisoners were stood against a slit in the wall to be "measured" and shot in the back of the neck by a concealed executioner.

We see the lead-lined trolleys in which the bodies were trundled away and tipped down a chute into the crematorium. We see the crude ovens where men were reduced to ashes to be used as fertiliser on the surrounding farms. We see the cheap little surgery where S.S. doctors turned human heads into decorative paper-weights. We see the ghastly photographs and exhibits in the museum.

In the Communist ritual Buchenwald is an important ceremony. It was here that many leading German Communists, Ernst Thälmann among them, were interned and murdered. Communists, too, played the major role in organising the illegal resistance movement among their fellow-prisoners which was strong enough to rise up and liberate Buchenwald as the American forces advanced on Weimar.

"Buchenwald," our guide says proudly and frequently, "was the only concentration camp able to liberate itself. Here you had a great example of international solidarity with people from many countries working together against Fascism for peace and liberty." He tells us of the group of British and Canadian parachutists who were brought to Buchenwald for execution. The camp resistance movement managed to conceal and save four of them. A memorial stone to the others has been laid down in the square. It testifies, in German, Russian, and English, that " the lives of four British patriots were saved by the solidarity of German anti-Fascists."

Away from the camp on the other side of the Ettersberg a huge memorial has been erected around the sites of three mass graves. Its dominant piece is a tall bell tower which frowns down on Weimar and the lovely, hazy woods of Thuringia. "Here on this beautiful hill only a few miles from what was once the most civilised town in Germany, here not far from the graves of Goethe and Schiller there are other graves," our guide recites.

He leads us down the Avenue of Stones with its seven large rectangular concrete blocks. Each carries a relief and a verse recounting the history of Buchenwald from the construction of the camp:

A camp of death is built up here,
    Enclosed with miles of wire, a deadly cage.
Grey rows of barracks filled with fear.
    The searchlights play, a symbol of the age,
And through the dark we see a gallows rear.
    Oh time of shame! Recall this time with rage!
Remember, when the name of Buchenwald you hear!

From the Avenue of Stones the Avenue of Nations runs, linking the three circular graves. It leads through the Freedom Gate into the Avenue of Liberation which ascends to the bell tower. Beside the mass graves there is one small cemetery. It lies to the right of the bell tower, almost hidden from view by the bushes and the natural rise of the land. The guides do not go there and the path is not easy to find. Yet it is well cared for and there are flowers on some of the graves. This is the place where the American troops who came to Buchenwald buried the dead they found in the camp.

Inside the square bell tower we stand, head bowed, round the bronze plate in the centre of the floor. Under the plate the ashes of the dead brought from many scenes of Nazi horror lie buried. Vile names like Auschwitz, Lidice, Ravensbruck, and Oradour have been scraped roughly into the bronze so that they should be without beauty. Our guide nods silently towards the wall. In German, Russian and French, there is inscribed part of the Buchenwald Oath: " Our slogan is the destruction of Nazism with its roots. Our aim is the construction of a new world of peace and liberty."

The bell tolls solemnly in its high tower. Our pilgrimage is over. The coach takes us back along the road that was made by men who now lie buried in three circular graves. It is smooth and strong as befits a road that was washed with tears and bonded with blood. It takes us back through the silent

forest away from the hill where the bones of the dead are called
upon to testify that Fascism is evil and Communism good. It
is a road we travel gladly.

Alan Paton

SOUTH AFRICA'S BLACK STALLION

One of Mr. Luthuli's [1] famous countrymen, the poet Roy
Campbell, wrote thus of his own determination not to write
obscurely:

> I will go stark, and let my meanings show
> Clear as a milk-white feather in a crow
> Or a black stallion on a field of snow.

This is Luthuli—the black stallion. His standing on a white
field is an image not to be laboured. But the other part of the
image is perfect—the blackness, the strength, the pride that
makes him no man's plaything, and a certain solitariness, partly
imposed by the harsh bans of authority, partly a quality of his
own nature.

Mr. Luthuli understands deeply the dominant role that white
fear plays in South African politics, and the way in which the
Christian Afrikaner has become more a believer in historical
determinism than in Christian redemption. He writes:

" The tendency to see oneself perpetually as a victim will lead
to the evasion of responsibility and the condoning of evil."

That goes right to the heart of it. Many Africans to-day are
no longer willing to believe that the evil actions of authority

[1] *Let My People Go*, by Albert Luthuli (Collins, 25s.).

39

are inspired by fearful motives. Mr. Luthuli is still willing to believe it, and he states that this belief has possibly protected him against hatred and bitterness. But under no circumstances does he say to white South Africa: I know you are afraid, I know you want to do justice; therefore, we shall wait upon your conversion. On the contrary, he expects no such conversion, although he always notes and welcomes the conversions of individual white South Africans and speaks warmly of the white Congress of Democrats and the non-racial Liberal Party, even though he thinks the time for non-racial parties is after liberation, not before. As for his own demands for his own people, he does not modify them by one jot or tittle; his demand is full participation in government, that cry of " one man one vote " which is both the pride and the terror of the West.

Mr. Luthuli describes a meeting with Mr. Harry Oppenheimer, who, after declaring that he understood the African point of view, took Mr. Luthuli and his friends to task, because the extreme nature of their demands (the vote) and their methods (the boycott) made it difficult for him (Mr. Oppenheimer) to convince others of the justice of such demands. Mr. Luthuli's reply was characteristic; he said they were real demands, and that

" it was far better that white South Africa should here and now know their nature than be constantly taken by surprise by being admitted to our thoughts instalment by instalment."

That says a great deal about the South African situation in which there is no provision for political concession and adjustment. It also says a great deal about Mr. Luthuli himself. What he is, in fact, saying to white South Africa is this: our democratic ideals are as high as yours, and you will have to trust yourself to them, for power will be in our hands; but we cannot wait for your change of heart, because you will not have one. To this he adds grave words:

40

". . . we should have no illusion about the price which he (the white man) will exact in African blood before we are admitted to citizenship in our own land."

Mr. Luthuli demands one qualification of white South African co-workers: they must believe unreservedly in African liberation. It would be misleading to say he is uncompromising in this goal; it would be correct to say he cannot conceive of any other.

Is Mr. Luthuli an African Nationalist? Of course he is. His love of Africa and all things African is manifested in these pages. But he states categorically that the slogan " Africa for the Africans " means Africa for all those who love her and make her their home. This reassurance is sometimes nullified because he speaks of "my people," meaning his own indigenous fellow-Africans. It is this which leads some white people to doubt him and to turn for safety—even with heavy hearts—to the Afrikaner laager. Mr. Luthuli never minces words in speaking of white supremacy: he talks damningly of white rule, white domination, white arrogance, white callousness. He does not use nice words like Western, foreign, alien, imported; he just uses " white." This is characteristic of him, but it repels those white South Africans who were reaching out timid and tentative fingers to touch him.

Compounded with this ruggedness and uncompromisingness is a deep religious faith. Mr. Luthuli makes it clear that, at Groutville, conversion to Christianity meant the creation almost of a new kind of people; his faith was deepened at Adams College, under Edgar Brookes. But this did not prevent him from being a critic of South African Christianity and of the way in which the Church tended to accommodate itself to the general secular pattern of the country. Mr. Luthuli condemns apartheid utterly as a corruption of Christian standards, an attempt to pour back this new kind of people into the old mould of tribalism.

He was, therefore, bound to question the duty of a Christian

41

towards the State. With full understanding of what he was doing, he, as head of the African National Congress in Natal, and at the same time Chief of the Umvoti Mission Reserve, took a leading part in the defiance campaign of 1952, which aimed to break openly certain apartheid laws. Of this he writes that "what we have aimed to do in South Africa is to bring the white man to his senses, not to slaughter him."

Because of these actions he was summoned to Pretoria, where Dr. Eiselen, who could make and unmake chiefs, asked him how he, an officer of the law, could encourage people to defy the law. The outcome of it all was that Mr. Luthuli was deposed. He made a public statement which contained a famous passage:

"Who will deny that 30 years of my life have been spent knocking in vain, patiently, moderately, and modestly at a closed and barred door?"

He concluded: "The road to freedom is via the Cross, Mayibuye! Afrika! Afrika! Afrika!"

Mr. Luthuli states more than once that his faith sent him into politics and sustained him through the interminable treason trial. He concludes his book by saying that if God gives him strength he will die, if need be, for the cause. That Mr. Luthuli is a convinced Christian there can be no doubt; but his Christianity is unrecognisable to the great majority of white South African Christians. That is the state of our nation.

The question is often asked: how does this Christian man co-operate so warmly with Communists? Mr. Luthuli's answer has always been the same. He is not a Communist; he believes communism to be "a mixture of a false theory of society linked to a false religion." He himself tends towards socialism, and he is no worshipper of the State. His main purpose is African liberation, and resistance movements cannot afford the luxury of McCarthyism. Once he put the matter pithily to me. He said: "If a man is working with me for liberation I do not inquire into his lesser politics."

Mr. Luthuli's willingness to co-operate with all led to the Congress Alliance, the Freedom Charter, the treason trial, and his several bannings. It is this invincible resolution that is portrayed without adornment in this unadorned book. Strength, pride, integrity, they show in his book, as they show in his strong rugged face.

Is Mr. Luthuli representative of the people? Do they share his high ideals, his abhorrence of totalitarian power, his magnanimity? He does not pose this question but he answers it. He says he does not for a moment entertain the idea of Africans turning into race oppressors, he says the Master Race concept is not theirs. The trouble is that the great majority of white South Africans do not believe him; why should black men be more magnanimous than they?

The great strength of Mr. Luthuli's book, its unadorned picture of courage and integrity, is also its great weakness. There is no echo of Luthuli the orator here; the tone is too flat and even. Poetry he does not permit himself. When his second ban expired he waited for the bans to expire of his devoted associates Conco and Yengwa, so that they could travel together. "We decided," he says, "to give ourselves a shake in the air of freedom." But such touches are rare. Nor does Mr. Luthuli permit himself much emotion, except occasionally, when he speaks of his wife or mother, or of some close associate such as Dr. Conco, or of some admired white friend, such as Bishop Ambrose Reeves, to whom he pays more than one deserved tribute.

This artistic and dramatic deficiency, or alternatively this emotional austerity and modesty, deprives us of much of the *feeling* of some of these events; and it applies to the description of the home life also, so that we do not know what it was like to live in Groutville. Nor do we know what it was like to belong to the African National Congress, and to attend its conferences, and to know that one's course was dangerous.

43

The autobiography in fact reads like a statement of basic material for a biography that should certainly one day be written.

Yet as the great strength is the great weakness, so is the weakness the strength. Quite clearly this story is the truth, set down by a man to whom truth comes so naturally that he does not think to adorn it and dramatise it. In his epilogue, Mr. Luthuli, in a passage less austere than most, grieves over those whose good and honourable desires led to banishment, deportation, and gaol, while their families suffered poverty and acute distress. One may well grieve over them and over South Africa. And one may grieve over the noble writer of this book, whose life has been spent in brave struggle and resistance and suffering, when it could have been spent more fruitfully and creatively in the service of South Africa.

Arthur Miller

A NATION TALKING TO ITSELF

A good newspaper, I suppose, is a nation talking to itself. Anybody who has talked to himself knows that events themselves quickly fade away, leaving behind their underlying themes and principles; we do not ask ourselves what happened but stare at the why and how. The Bedside Guardian 10,[1] a selection of pieces from the Guardian, 1960-1, is, of course, not the work of one man, but reading it at one lope it begins to seem that way—an Englishman of stable temperament yet lively and amused, having a look around. Not that the styles are unvaried or the attitudes altogether consistent, but that a certain connective tissue of basic premises underlies the whole,

[1] The Bedside Guardian 10 (Collins, 13s. 6d.).

so much so that a foreigner, and basically an amateur about England, does come away with the sense of having read the varying moods of a monologue, or more precisely a chorus remarkable for its individual voices.

A man's character can be surmised by the kinds of challenges he feels he must accept, and the kinds that leave him oblivious. A nation's too. The *Guardian* seems most aroused when it perceives the need for just appraisal. I imagine that a collection of pieces from any American paper or magazine would give off much more that is frenetic, alarmed, uncertain, and in many cases bellicose. At the same time, though, one would feel perhaps that the Americans were " in " the cross-tides of the time and hounded by the need to decide, while this collection of British reporting is strangely removed, even though the writers and the *Guardian* and the British themselves are quite as concerned as the Americans; it is simply that in these pieces they seem not to have to keep telling themselves that they are. Withal, the nation here seems oddly confident of itself. Confident and peculiarly without a future challenge.

It is not, however, the confidence of those who know they will win—indeed, it would be hard to tell from these pages that we are all in a struggle for the world, or civilisation, or whatever. It is rather a sense that the struggle is very old, that it is imbedded in the walls of our era, that alien seeds have shot up strange new plants in our garden which might just be trained and made to look decent since it is not possible to root them all out. An American collection would be filled with rooting-out instructions; the *Guardian* writers go on the premise that it is a very old garden which for some not quite knowable reason will probably survive indefinitely. The American vision is apocalyptic in comparison.

When Alistair Cooke reports on American politics, for instance, I am charmed into the feeling that the subject may still be written about with wit and yet with serious concern, that one does not have to assume a cynicism or an alarm as though in the Last Days in order to show that an election of a President

45

is both important and ephemeral. Mr. Cooke, an Englishman, makes one feel that there is something steady underneath even us.

The same sort of security emanates from Norman Shrapnel's report on the debate in the House of Lords on censorship. Our would-be suppressors are quite as determined as yours but not many of their libertarian opponents know how to laugh at the absurdities any more. Possibly it is that one does not believe that the English censorship, when it triumphs, is really going to overwhelm the entire publishing industry, while here, from time to time in the past, just such an air of general emergency seems justified. I emphasise " seems," for the fact is it hasn't happened and probably won't.

The nature of the future is oddly different than it is here, too. Mark Gapper's description of the new railroad train from Manchester to London, the Midland Pullman's first trip, exactly fits my observations about British amateurism. The management distributed free plastic luggage label holders and pen-knives to the first passengers, for one. For another, the writer's own attitude is that of a wry amusement at this " celebration " for the inception of a new set of cars. In America a new train, if it were to be celebrated, which is doubtful, would have twenty or so six-foot starlets aboard, an endless flow of liquor for the reporters, some full-page advertisements in the Press, and at least one official statement containing a challenge to all other railroads, open or implied. So modest a victory for progress as the Midland Pullman would verge on a defeat. Maybe Art Buchwald could bring such an event down to size, but few others, and those not amiably.

There is not much evidence in this collection of the England that is " Wasteland," the England of the Angry Young Men, the England split between Establishment and the Displaced. So that Betty Thorne's *Life in our street* seems to threaten the rest of the pieces with a danger from the underground. The children suffocating with television, the used-up father, the chore-devoured mother, and the conformist neighbours—one

46

reads this feeling at home at last. And it prompts one to ask whether or not—(and I am genuinely asking a question, not making a statement in question form)—the collection is not too well-unified and overly reassuring. And the reason I am uncertain about this is my inability to ever tell when an Englishman is disturbed. Christopher Driver, for instance, is probably accurate in describing the anti-Polaris demonstration as a rather wet event, not particularly unsettling to either the American submarine commander, the reporters, or the demonstrators themselves. At least it seemed to me that, as described, it did not disturb anyone very deeply. I can only wonder, however, if an English reader would feel the same quietism, or whether his cues for passion are in fact in this report and simply escape my probably inflamed sensibilities.

The world, in short, as this collection sees it, lacks imminence. Or rather, it is made to appear that way. Possibly it is as much as anything a product of the literacy of the pieces; when sentences are as complete as these, urgency is squeezed out more often than in. Cooke is an exception, and Bill Weatherby, who tries to speak for the subject of his interviews, as he should, instead of using his man to make his own fortune in quips and journalistic quackery. The strength in the *Guardian* spirit is that it may generate just attitudes; its weakness is that it may unknowingly avoid confronting whatever cannot yet be weighed, whatever is still forming, whatever is only germinal and not in being. For while the book as a whole is far from the merely polite, it lacks the crudeness of life which I am sure underlies England as it does everywhere. I should like its writers to look into your newer emotions towards negroes coming into the country; into the attitudes of your peace demonstrators, of which you have more than any other country, evidently; and even into the reasons why your cars, so well-built, have so often to be repaired—and I own two, and love and curse their sturdiness and unreliability.

Having appeared to call the paper on its surface inoffensiveness, it is now time to remark on its blank-staring acerbity, as

47

for instance in the leading article on the attempted invasion of Cuba, or Anthony Hartley's straightforward arraignment of Sartre's logic-spinning, Patrick Keatley's irreverent description of how the television people sealed the visiting Dr. Banda's lips, and especially James Morris's vivid history of the town of Huddersfield. Here again I am home, for the process of civilising the industrial town is high on the American agenda. These pieces, and others in the book, are more than journalism, for they place a phenomenon in the stream of historical development.

I began this review by noting the seeming unity in the collection. Something more noteworthy should be added, namely the clear individuality of each writer, his unobstructed personal quality. If one's hand never shakes while reading the book one is nevertheless held by its many-pronged probing for those acts of men and the accompanying emotions which hold him together, rather than those that demonstrate his flying apart. Altogether it is a conservationist collection, plausibly decent—like a young man rather than an old bitter lady, uneasily antic, espousing virtue rather than morals, appreciation rather than enthusiasm. It is almost as though these were writers on the lookout for our best rather than our worst, the human rather than the unhuman, a surprising predilection these days. I can never visit England without wondering what this severed head of empire will come to; at her most modern she seems like a hesitating self-conscious imitation of America, at her most antique a museum full of proud and useless things. Yet I have nowhere felt as safe nor as certain of a people's common sense, on which everything ultimately rests after all. It is a similar feeling that rises from these pages—not the ring of prophecy, perhaps, but a sense of bread.

Letters

"THE MAN WHO PUTS THE MISPRINTS IN"

SIR,—So at last you are to print in London and your ace humorist, the man who puts the misprints in the London edition, will be out of work. I foresee many a damp eye in Dorking, not to mention lumps in throats at Loughton and Throgmorton Street. Could you not give him a job writing humorous leaders? When I read recently in your paper, "arter he left the building, Mr. X . . .", I nearly wrote to applaud your pioneering spirit in printing the London edition in the vernacular. Yet all too soon, alas, it is to be no more.

However, the above is mere digression. This letter is one of protest; most violent protest. Last week, sir, you overdid it. Ventilating the Channel Tunnel may well be "bereco etao," but even if it is "cwmfyvbgkq," you had no right to say so, at least not in print. But to go on and call the whole thing "mfwy mfwm"—really, sir, these filthy four-letter Cambrian words should be left unprinted.

If I were a man of principle I would cancel my subscription to your obscene paper and take the "Daily Distress" instead. However, the salutary shock of knowing that one of your faithful readers has even contemplated such drastic action will, I feel sure, make you pull your socks up and never again print such pornographic tirades. "Mfwy mfwm" indeed! O tempora! O mores!—Yours, etc.   B. HINCHLIFFE

[It is indeed our intention to pension off our misprints man, but it is not quite clear at the moment whether he has yet reached pensionable age.—ED. *Guardian*.]

Vladimir Dedijer

DECLINE OF ENGLISH FOOTBALL

Football is my first and lasting passion. It started with a red ball sent home by my father during the First World War, from which he never returned; and I learned the art of ball control from my Uncle Drago, my mother's youngest brother, who died when he was sixteen and I was ten. And so my tuition was finished.

Our home in Belgrade was near the football ground and although my mother, a strict disciplinarian, did not allow me to go to matches, the roar of the crowds on a Sunday afternoon only increased my longing for the game. When, later, my younger brother went to live in England with a Quaker family, he discovered that the English also played football and he began to write regularly describing the fortunes of various favoured teams. His choice was Aston Villa; mine was Huddersfield Town, and I remember being unable to eat my supper when a letter came describing how their goalkeeper was pushed into the net in the first minute of the Cup Final. One day when an expected letter did not arrive I bought an English paper. I was able to pick out the league results, but to get at the stories I had to use a dictionary, which showed me that the English even used our words *korner, faul, bek,* and so on in describing the game. Soon I had in my note-book over three hundred words about games which I used without knowing that they were English.

Seven years later, soon after I had arrived in London as a journalist, I saw Huddersfield play Arsenal at Highbury.

I did not forget my passion for football even in the grimmest days of the war. In May 1942 I played in the team of the Partisan Supreme Command at a little town in Bosnia, while the roar of the guns of the advancing Italian divisions echoed over our heads. Later on I discovered that this was not the first time partisans had played football while the guns were rumbling. In *Illyrian Letters*, a book made out of articles which he contributed to the *Manchester Guardian*, young Arthur Evans, defying Disraeli and visiting Bosnia in 1876 during the insurrection against the Turks, describes how he played football at the insurgents' headquarters with a ball made of soldiers' caps knotted together. He ends his account of the game: "I believe that there is no other people in Europe endowed so largely with the English love of field sports as these much-maligned Southern Slavs."

I remembered this when I was next at Highbury, this time for the Yugoslavia-England international match in 1950, as president of the Yugoslav Sports Association. In the dressing-room, before the game, our captain, Mitic, was giving final advice to his team. English play, he said, followed a regular and predictable pattern. If they could only slow down the game, control the centre of the ground with short passes, and initiate unorthodox attacks, they could hold the English. "Watch them, and they'll give the game away; they always signal beforehand where the ball is going."

At this point I was asked to say a few words. I knew what they should be: "Three tons of coal and a suit of English worsted for every one of you if you draw," I shouted.

We were quickly two goals down. For a while the mist, the unearthly noise of the pipe band's overture to the game, and the Highbury roar drove everything Mitic and I had said out of their minds. In the second half, however, Mitic managed to pull our men together and with the help of unexpected attacks we equalised.

This result at Highbury was the beginning of the decline of British football. Later there was to be defeat: 3–6 and 1–7 against Hungary, and 0–5 against Yugoslavia. (Yugoslavia shares with Hungary the best overall results against England: three victories, two games drawn, and only one defeat. How happy Sir Arthur Evans would have been!)

During the last two years I have been watching English football and trying to discover the reasons for this decline. Tactically, it follows two predictable patterns, and the innovators like Winterbottom, Busby, or Nicholson can make little headway amid the generally prevailing conservatism. The players' status at last has been improved, but England still lags behind most other football powers in this respect. Above all, England's international players are trained less scientifically than those of her main competitors, because the clubs put their interests before the interests of the national team.

Recently I watched the match between Manchester United and West Bromwich Albion at Old Trafford with my friend Professor Max Gluckman. The visiting team crudely imposed the traditional W-system of play on their more sophisticated opponents, and as we deplored the tedious football which resulted I began to see a connection between what was wrong with British football and what I have felt increasingly to be wrong with British life as a whole to-day.

The traditional strength of the British has been the power to adapt themselves to changing conditions; even Marx conceded these empirical skills, this sense of timing. But to-day, British improvisation has become slow and fumbling. At a time when her future depends entirely on making the most of her know-how, not only in industry but also in sport and the arts, she seems half-sunk in a complacent doze.

What I find lacking most in Britain to-day are new ideas. In politics the Labour Party to my sorrow appears as barren of inspiration as the Government. Just as the Football League was the last in Europe to concede better conditions for players, so this Government has been the last to appreciate the advantages of planning. Even unilateralism, the only visible exception to this prevailing apathy, is no adequate response to the problems of a rapidly changing world. " Ban the Bomb " is a slogan which narrows the scope of politics to a single issue, however important that issue may be. It deals with the consequences and not with the causes of world troubles; it does not contribute to a better understanding of the new shape of the world as the African and Asian nations begin to grow out of poverty and backwardness or of Britain's place in it.

With these glum thoughts in mind I turned my attention to the second half. For some time the play followed the same monotonous patterns, and then suddenly Charlton broke with a series of brilliant improvisations to score with a perfect shot from twenty-five yards. The terraces boiled with excitement. Thousands of closed, grey Lancashire faces, stiff with cold, opened up and glowed. The true God Football had showed himself for an instant and we worshippers rejoiced.

So I went home happy, after all. The fire in my study was burning well, and the news on the radio that Huddersfield had beaten Norwich away 2–1 completed the redemption of an unpromising day. I dozed and blinked at the fire . . . which was doing duty on this grim northern day for the winter sunshine of my native land; I thought about Charlton's glorious shot. I had seen one like that before, but that was in another country . . . in Belgrade, when Tommy Taylor was playing for that other United team in the last game before Munich.

The room was dark now, the fire was red; a red ball in the heart of it.

Eric Todd

REAL MADRID OUTPLAYED BY
MANCHESTER UNITED

At the sixth attempt—Real Madrid had won four of the five
previous meetings with one drawn—Manchester United beat
the " greatest club side in the world " 3-1 at Old Trafford last
night. They fought with magnificent spirit from start to
finish and victory flattered them not one little bit.

How far Real Madrid were affected by the absence of Puskas,
or the rain, or the heavy conditions, is a matter for idle speculation; suffice it to say they were less impressive than they
were on their last visit but let there be no mistake about it, they
played only as well as they were allowed to. Once or twice
there were flashes of the old Real notably from Gento and
Del Sol, yet the writing surely was on the wall for them when
Di Stefano and Santamaria were left behind when the teams
came out for the second half. For most of the game Real were
restricted to long-range shooting and young Gaskell scarcely
ever faltered. Real indeed were outplayed and seldom looked
like saving the game.

Hopes that United would carry on where they left off against
Fulham on Saturday were more than justified. In the light of
the side's performance one hesitates to make comments on
individuals, so splendidly did all play, but it would be wrong
not to mention Nicholson, Dunne, Giles, and Chisnall, four of
United's younger players who surely are destined to make a big
impact on the game. Considering the enormity of their task
they could not be faulted and, like Byrom and Lawther, of
Blackburn Rovers, whom one saw recently, they are here to stay.

Real Madrid soon were on the attack and, after Gaskell had

54

made a good catch when Casado lobbed the ball into the jaws of the goal, United conceded a corner under severe pressure but Tejada made a mess of the kick. United were kept on the defensive for exactly seven minutes but when at last they broke away they shaped most promisingly. Good work by Dunne paved the way for a fine centre by Charlton which Araquistain saved, and the goalkeeper was equally confident in dealing with a commendable shot by Herd from 12 yards. When Real returned to the attack they were awarded a free kick some twenty-five yards out. Distance was no object to Vidal whose hard, rising drive found a way past everyone except Gaskell, who took the ball high up and cleanly.

United's defenders were doing well, particularly in the air —Di Stefano so far had not once beaten Foulkes—and Setters suddenly fancying himself as a forward put in a worthy shot that was diverted for a corner and this led to United's going ahead in the fourteenth minute. Chisnall took the corner kick, a short one, and when Giles gave him back the ball the young outside right cut in, beat Miera and scored with a splendid shot well out of Araquistain's reach. United had played with excellent spirit and were not flattered by their lead.

Real, as it was expected they would, retaliated, but their finishing was poor and, after Vidal had volleyed far too high, Di Stefano turned the ball over the crossbar when Ruiz gave him a perfect pass. Whereupon one or two people observed, " He must be getting old," but of course players like Di Stefano and Matthews never seem to grow old. Certainly Di Stefano did his best to make up for his lapse and against a less determined defence he might have succeeded.

United, however, were calling the tune and a pretty lively one at that. Herd worrying the life out of Santamaria had a shot diverted luckily by Araquistain—Santamaria completed the clearance at leisure—and a few minutes later Herd ran brilliantly over half the length of the field and Araquistain saved a terrific drive at the second attempt. Just before the interval Chisnall and Giles confounded the Real defence and Herd, sitting on the ground, hooked the ball inches wide, but the referee not surprisingly awarded Real a free kick as Lawton in turn appeared to be sitting on Araquistain. From the free kick the ball ran loose and Di Stefano beat Gaskell with a superb shot from twenty-five yards. That was in the forty-third minute. In the forty-fourth United regained the lead with a goal no less spectacular. Nicholson pushed the ball down the left wing, Herd ran on to it, and gave Araquistain no chance with a left-foot shot. Real were not playing as well as many people thought they would, but this did not detract from the all-round merit of United's performance.

Real made several changes for the second half—why, one wonders, were they not announced over the loud-speakers?—and Di Stefano and Santamaria were not among those present. So much for reputation. The newcomers were Bueno at outside left and A. Ruiz at left half, whose arrival led to readjustments in the attack and the half-back line. United, of course, were quite satisfied, and nearly more so when Herd sent another scorcher past Araquistain, but the goal was disallowed for off-side. That at least was the only conclusion the spectators could arrive at. Still they could afford to be generous. United continued to dictate matters and Giles and Nicholson were not far off the mark with efforts that were better than anything Real had produced so far in this half.

In the seventieth minute Bueno headed the ball beautifully past Gaskell after a corner kick by Gento and even the United players looked surprised when the referee disallowed the goal for reasons not apparent—unless there had been some pushing. In the closing stages there was more excitement at both ends with Gaskell having far more to do than Araquistain, but he dealt capably with everything that came his way whereas the Real goalkeeper made a scrambling save from Herd after the latter had made another fine run. Herd, however, had the last word. One minute from the end he accepted a pass from Quixall—who had come on as substitute for Giles who had been injured—and somehow or other he found a gap between Araquistain and the near post. A great goal and an appropriate finish to a first-class display by United.

Pat Ward-Thomas

CARR RECOVERS GLORIOUSLY

J. B. Carr, golfer of Sutton and Portmarnock and citizen of Ireland, won probably the most difficult and exhausting victory of his immense career when he beat G. Francis, of New York, on the last green in the quarter-final of the United States amateur championship at Pebble Beach last evening.

Now Carr meets H. D. Wysong, a most talented young player from Texas, in the 36-hole semi-final, while Nicklaus in the opposite half of the draw plays M. C. Methvin, of Arkansas, another of the remarkable youths who emerge year by year in this championship. Not since 1936, when J. McLean lost at the thirty-seventh hole to J. Fischer in the final at Garden City, has a golfer from the British Isles progressed so far in this by far the most exacting amateur event in the world.

Throughout the years no golfer has given his friends and supporters greater agony of mind than Carr. On this afternoon, in sunlight of rare brilliance which brought an indescribable beauty to the setting, he played a match surpassing everything that had gone before it for its suspense. Francis, a young man of pleasant, stolid manner, strange grip, and abrupt short swing, was not of Walker Cup class as Carr soon was aware. He therefore knew that he should beat him, and this awareness, together with the proximity of the semi-final, was almost lethal in its effect.

Carr realised that this was his great opportunity, possibly his last in the American championship, to banish the memory of the failures on other excursions to the United States. Here, too, was the chance on behalf of the team to lessen the impact of the defeat in Seattle. Carr realised that if he could reach the 36-hole semi-final there would be no further need for defensive approach, that he could allow his normal attacking game full scope, and that he could gain infinitely more than he could lose. The outcome was a study in apprehensiveness which has had few if any parallels in modern golf on the highest level.

In all fairness and taking the most objective view possible —though this was by no means easy watching this match—it must be said that fear was abroad in the brilliant afternoon, a fear of winning which is the most destructive element in all golf. This was a classic example of handing the initiative from one side to the other. In the end Francis made the greater number of crucial errors and Carr survived, but at what cost to the nerves of his supporters, who included many Americans, can never be known.

The end of this match must be described first. When Carr, bearing in mind all that had gone before, cut his pitch to the fourteenth, took three putts and became one down it seemed that he could not possibly win. This belief became almost unbearable when, after both had sliced to the fifteenth and found a bunker with their second shots, Francis had a putt of eight feet to win the hole and become two up. His ball finished two feet past the hole and then he missed, and the game incredibly was even. The language of astonishment that was uttered among Carr's followers at this moment does not bear repeating, but the sixteenth strained incredulity even further.

Carr drove a yard into the thick rough and was unfortunate, on this course at least, to find a really heavy clinging lie. He forced the shot, with the great strength that is his, just short of the green. Francis, with the better drive, then missed the green on the right but left himself a fairly easy chip of perhaps nine

58

yards. Carr played a good chip, but the ball broke left some seven feet from the hole. Francis then chipped to two feet. It was most improbable that Carr would hole at this juncture and he did not. He was having great difficulty in making the putter move through the ball at all. It now seemed certain that he would be one down again, but astonishingly Francis gave his putt a horrid little jerk and missed. To say that Mrs. Carr and her friends breathed again would be a considerable understatement.

In the morning Carr had hit a superb stroke with his four-iron to the seventeenth green; now a powerful slice followed, and his ball came to rest in the rough of what has been called " the most famous piece of turf in California," that part of the green from which getting down in two is a fearsome exercise. Francis pulled his shot and, fortunately for him, did not strike it well enough or he would have been in the ocean. Carr played a delicate wedge shot some five yards past the hole, Francis recovered from the sand to twelve feet, Carr missed and so did Francis, and then there was a desperate suspense, believe it or not, of watching Carr hole from fifteen inches for the half.

Carr paced about the eighteenth tee, settling his nerves before driving, and one was vividly aware of what he must have been feeling. He then hit one of the few great strokes of the match. A magnificent long shot, straight as an arrow into the perfect position on the fairway just beyond the little spinney which catches so many who try to play safe. This stroke was the reward of all the years and hours of practice. Francis sliced his into a bunker, played out, but was not within range of the green for his third shot. Carr played a safe stroke with a three-iron, and then Francis hooked on to the beach; but suspense was not yet over.

Carr's pitch only just scrambled over the bunker guarding the green. Francis was on the green in five, including the penalty stroke for visiting the beach, and then—irony of ironies—Carr with two putts for the match holed his long one for a four, a round of seventy-nine, and overwhelming relief for the British team and not a few Americans besides. Their anxiety for Carr to win was in no sense directed against Francis but simply was an expression of affection for Carr and a desire that he might meet Nicklaus in the final.

From the outset it was apparent that Carr was uneasy. His first drive was sliced and the hole lost to a five. The golf thereafter was reasonably good. Francis pitched almost dead from the fifth tee and won the sixth as well after playing his second with wood from the shallow bunker on the left of the fairway and pitching to within seven feet. The American's first indication of nerves was apparent on the seventh and eighth greens, where he took three putts. At the ninth they were all square, deservedly so, and then Carr began his process of self-destruction by leaving a putt of a yard comfortably short at the eleventh.

After winning the thirteenth he failed to stay down long enough on his third shot to the fourteenth and took three putts in consequence. This is a most difficult green unless the third shot is firm enough to reach the vicinity of the hole. Then came the torture of the last hour, but when the pressure really was at its pitch it was Carr with the honour who hit the great drive to the eighteenth when, had he failed, a disappointment that would have been almost too cruel to bear would probably have awaited him.

What a game this golf can be when it reduces strong men to such depths of frustration and incompetence on the greens, and yet those watching knew well enough, or should have done, that in like circumstances they would have fared no better. Most of them, too, had some understanding of the tension that was afflicting both men. The quarter-final round is often the most taxing of a championship. Then the pressure becomes acute because reaching the semi-final means that a man's name is inscribed on the tablets of history. In the end, out of all the doubts and all the fears, this proved to be one of the triumphs of Carr's career, a conquest of suspense and anguish, and finally the fulfilment of an ambition. When it was done there was something akin to weeping, mingled with the cheers and the sighs, beneath the old cypress trees.

Pat Ward-Thomas

BOBBY JONES AT EAST LAKE

All through the summer-time and the long journeyings across the United States there was one moment I had been anticipating more than all the others. It came on a golden morning in the last days of September when the face of a coloured chauffeur appeared at my window, and I knew that R. T. Jones had come to take me to that beautiful course on the outskirts of Atlanta known as East Lake.

The meeting had been planned many months before, but in the weeks immediately preceding it Jones had been afflicted with a virus infection and this was his first day abroad. It was typical that he should make what must have been a considerable effort to avoid disappointing a visitor. We drove that morning through the cool, wooded streets of suburban Atlanta, past houses that seemed among the most beautiful in America, simple, dignified, and proud. In time we came to East Lake, which has a special place in history because it was here that a small boy began the learning of golf, and before it was done had become the greatest player the game had ever known.

Now, more than half a century later, we sat in the dining-room of the clubhouse that enshrines so much of Jones's enduring spirit and the triumphs of all his years. We did not speak of these things because Jones does not dwell in the past. He was keen to hear of Pebble Beach and its recent championship, and he talk turned on Nicklaus. There was no little emphasis in his voice when he spoke of the boy as a great golfer, and he used the adjective in its true context. His belief that Nicklaus was capable of winning any championship was clear, but he agreed with the reservation that his weight might become a handicap.

We talked of Palmer and his unbelievable six at the last hole of the Masters in the spring; of the article Jones had written, for diversion and not publication, about the way in which Palmer played the bunker shot that cost him so dear; of the professional world and the riches to be found therein; and of the great company of fine young players, Pott, Goalby, and so on. In all this talk of others there was no hint of the criticism that sometimes afflicts the conversation, however slightly, of many great elders when they discuss a new generation. There is in Jones a depth of gentleness and modesty that makes it impossible for him to speak unkindly or grudgingly of anyone. The greatness of this man cannot be expressed in terms of golf, incomparable though his record may be, unchallenged though it may remain for all time.

It had been arranged that after lunch I should play the course with Harold Sargent, the head professional at East Lake. After a few minutes in his company it was easy to understand why he had been president of the United States Professional Golfers' Association for three years recently. Such men are rare in a profession that abounds with good fellows but not necessarily balanced or intelligent ones. It seemed straight away that Sargent was an example, uncommon in sport, of a man with a keen executive mind as well as a strong sense of purpose, a deep knowledge of his profession, and withal a quiet assurance and poise that gave conviction to all that he said and did.

The time came for Jones to return home and for me to explore the course. He did not linger and thus was spared the sight of my ghastly ducking hook from the tenth tee, where we began our round. It vanished into the lake opposite the house where Alexa Stirling, who learned her golf with Jones, used to live. Happily this proved to be the last of such non-sense. The soothing presence of Sargent helped to preserve a semblance of rhythm and for once it was possible to enjoy one's golf, as well as observe the course.

The first impression of East Lake is one of graceful spaciousness. It rises and falls gently amid trees, but these never crowd in upon the holes in the manner of so many American courses. There is a feeling of freedom on the tees, but almost invariably the drive must be placed to find the best approach to the greens. At once it is evident that judgment of distance plays no little part and also that boldness, more often than not, would be rewarded and timidity punished. The severest trouble usually protected the front of the greens, and the entrances to some of these were menacingly narrow.

This round was a precious opportunity not only to tread on what seemed like sacred ground but to examine the setting of the Ryder Cup match in 1963. Then it will last three days, fourball, foursomes, and singles, an unfortunate development but one that need not be considered now. A number of alterations are planned so that the course will be an exacting enough test. Mostly these involve the creation of new bunkers to stiffen tee shots and the lengthening of some holes to bring existing bunkers into play for the first-class drivers. In one instance a bunker and pine trees are being removed to give a fairer sight of the tenth green and a bunker that is at present hidden. Bent grass is being substituted for Bermuda on the greens, and the first nine, which had been completed, were beautiful putting surfaces. The fairways were in such splendid condition that one could almost have used the small ball. In some of the wooded areas, where the sun never penetrates too strongly, fescue is being sown to give a rough of lighter texture.

When the days of the Ryder Cup match approach will be time enough to give chapter and verse of the course. For the present a few memories will suffice: of the long narrow fairway of the first and the adjacent hillock, where the house of Jones used to stand and where now there is only a cool spinney with one lonely maple tree; of the wonderful downhill sweep of the fifth, curving to the right, with its view across the lake to fairways on the back nine, mounting and falling on a distant hill-side; of the beautiful short sixth with its green almost surrounded by water; of the great plunge of the ninth with its second over the lake to a green behind which magnolias will be blooming in 1963.

Then there is the splendid tenth with its long iron to the green; the fall of the twelfth with Atlanta peeping over distant trees; the uphill fade of the fifteenth, where Jones used to swing the ball from right to left over trees which now are too tall for such adventures; the deceptive length of the shot needed from the seventeenth fairway which leans down to the lake; and the superb eighteenth, calling for one last noble stroke. All this and so much more was memorable that sunlit day in September.

Keith Gascoigne

PUSH-BALL

PIONEERS REVIVE CAVALRYMEN'S SPORT

The push-ball season had a wet and windy beginning here to-day. Lieutenant-General Sir John Cowley, Colonel Commandant of the Royal Pioneer Corps and Master-General of the Ordnance, had to skip smartly out of the way when he pushed off into the wind at Simpson Barracks, the Pioneers' depot, and the rain which drove over the open countryside on to polished buttons was enough to break a batman's heart.

It seemed right that the Pioneers, whose Latin motto claims that hard work overcomes everything, should be the corps to revive the game. Strong men have tried twenty minutes of it and felt faint at half-time, which is easily explained by a quick look at the rules.

Teams comprise "not more than ten players" whose positions are "left to the discretion of the respective captains"; that apart, the delineation of the field of play almost completes them. True, there is a saving clause forbidding "holding on to the lace of the ball, kicking or punching an opponent, jumping on or kicking the ball," but otherwise the players simply try to shove the ball, about six feet in diameter, over the other side's goal lines, preferably between the posts which mark the eight-foot wide goal.

Before the Second World War, the game was popular with the cavalry, who played it with horses, the irreverent adapted it for motor-cycles, and a London newspaper had it played as a circulation stunt on the beaches.

Looking round for something easily learned by the rawest recruit fresh from the simplicities of civilian life yet which would offer a variation on the eternal soccer, the depot commandant, Lieutenant-Colonel E. H. C. Archer, remembered the game he played before the war.

It promised the right kind of physical development—arms and thigh muscles—rather than the belly, as in its rival, tug-of-war. The problem was the ball. The Navy, Army, and Air Force Institute, over a period of months offered to make one for between £100 and £200. A newspaper provided a manufacturer's name and sets of rules.

The ball is made, along with various helmets and suits, by a London firm of rubber manufacturers and diving engineers; it is inflatable (blowing it up with an attachment to an army lorry took four hours, three gallons of petrol, and a hasty recharging of batteries); supplying it in "heavyweight rot-proof divers' dress material" cost £75, and to-day the material seemed just right. A moment or two before the general's arrival, the wind which had been threatening to whip an officer's peaked cap into the static water tank before the guard room, did so. The rain held off for the arrival, to combine with the wind for a push off.

Twenty hefty Pioneers pushing a 6-foot wide sphere of air inevitably tend to lift it, and the rules say nothing about catching it when it is being carried towards the water tank. The impact of twenty bodies hurled at the ball from a ten-yard starting line is alarming, but serious injury seemed to be avoided, and a discreetly stage-managed draw left honours even between a training company and the depot Corps of Drums.

Already interest is stirring; several local units have inquired about cost and the police ("we shoot them already," Colonel Archer said with startling military candour) are forming a team. For all that, one cannot see push-ball ever having the mass appeal of tenpin bowling.

James Morris

TO CATCH A CRAYFISH

The fresh-water crayfish season has opened on the Oxfordshire Dorn. You doubt it? You don't realise that at this very instant, on the muddy beats of Middle England's rivers, placid and weedy beneath the willows, the fresh-water crayfish are hungrily crawling and groping, like little grey lobsters down there in the ooze? You don't believe in a fresh-water crayfish season? You've never heard of a fresh-water crayfish? Well, I found it hard to credit it all myself until a few days ago; but hardly had I returned from a journey around South America, surfeited with everything exotic, when a friend rang me up with the news. " Come quickly! " he cried, his voice a'tremble. " The fresh-water crayfish season has opened! "—and there and then, with the rhythms of Rio still in my head we arranged an expedition.

He lives in a village eight or ten miles west of Oxford, and he had learnt the mysteries of the craft, he told me blandly, from Mrs. Branchflower, an elder resident of the place. It was apparently a folk-sport encrusted with many an antique usage, quirks of lore and country ritual, and embedded so deeply in Oxfordshire custom that when Mrs. Branchflower was a girl crayfishing parties on the Dorn were occasions of beribboned village festivity. It was a medieval kind of activity, my friend added with relish, like swan-upping, say, bull-baiting or Tolly-polly; and indeed, if some of the technical terms in this essay strike you as pitching it high, put it down to tradition.

This is the way to catch fresh-water crayfish. First get Mrs. Branchflower to make you half a dozen coarse string nets, called *scamblers,* each attached to a long cord traditionally known as the *gribb.* Next cut yourself a stout forked stick, the *launcher,* and buy a few kippers, the older the more effective, to be used as *lure.* Then wait till a dark night in autumn. You must fish at night, because that's when the creatures are most avidly feeding; and the darker the evening, the smellier the kippers, the oozier the Oxfordshire Dorn, the more irrepressible your instincts of English heritage, the better your ancient game will be.

In our case it was a long, soggy, squelchy walk along the water-meadows to the stream, which at that point attains a width of rather more than four feet and a depth of several inches. First went my host, all medieval energy, trundling our equipment laboriously in a wheel-barrow; then stumbled our crew of five small boys in trailing mackintoshes, brandishing torches, " Corgi " toys, and packets of " Twiglets "; finally came my hostess and I, with two bottles of wine and three packets of sausages. There was a nip in the air above the willows, and this was, they assured me, all to the good, for as an old county lay had it, " When frost be up, crayfish sup."

We lit a fire down there among the weeds, while the owls hooted and Jupiter rose with Saturn in splendid partnership, and presently our sport began. To the gribb of each scambler we attached a piece of white paper, known as *Old Nick's Tail,* to act as a marker in the dark; to the scambler itself we gingerly tied a chunk of lure; and advancing to each likely *swayle,* or fishing-station, we swung our nets gently to the river-bed with the launcher, ensuring that the lure was juicily uppermost—or, as they say in the vernacular, fastened Wootton style. "That's it, lads," cried my host with satisfaction, unfastening his gaiters. "Launch away there! Watch your scambles, now! Tighten your gribbs!"

Then we sat back and waited. We toasted some cheese at the fire, and drank a good deal of wine, and the boys made themselves some unusually repellent hot-dogs, horribly garnished with ashes, leaves and lumps of mud: and soon we had a huge old saucepan (the *scamble-pot*) bubbling there upon the sticks. My friend was eagerly whittling the prongs of the launcher, and his wife was rather obliquely explaining to me that though the flavour of fresh-water crayfish was undeniably interesting, it was not, she thought she ought to warn me, actually the kind of taste she would personally enjoy as an everyday appetiser—though of course it represented, she hastened to add, with an anxious glance towards her husband, very much a rooted sort of pleasure.

And before long it was time for the first kill. Slithering through the damp darkness in a confusion of children, we soon spied the nearest of our Old Nick's Tails, grubby white among the grasses; and delicately sliding the launching-prongs down the gribb, we raised the scambler with infinite circumspection from the river-bed. At first it was hard to see the mesh for the droppings of sludge and water-weed, but, peering through the light of our wavering lamps, presently we made out the old slice of kipper, eerily frayed and tattered around the edges, as though the ghouls had been at it; and sure enough, writhing there miraculously in the torchlight, crawling and clinging to the lure, waving their pincers impotently, were three unmistakable, unbelievable fresh-water crayfish. The season had opened on the Dorn. The boys danced an atavistic jig. My

68

host's face beamed in the fire-light. We popped those crustaceans spryly into the pot, and in a moment or two, when they were bright red and bubbling, we ate them with mess and merriment, complimenting each other upon their ineffable subtlety of texture.

I do not want to dramatise my subject, but I can only say that as the night drew on an air of immemorial English madness seemed to overcome it, infinitely improbable to recollect. Time after time we groped our way to the swayles, found our Old Nick's Tails, launched our launchers Wootton style, drew in our gribbs, hoisted our scamblers, inspected our lures, and hurled our crayfish into the scamble-pot. Pound by pound our sausages sizzled, mug by mug vanished the red wine, brighter and brighter blazed those planets in the southern sky. Many an old horned ghost hovered around us, many a jolly yeoman shade warmed its knobbly fingers at the fire, and when at last we staggered back across the fields, festooned (as ritual, so they said, demanded) with the claws of disembodied crayfish, my host burst at last, casting aside the very last of his conventional mufflers, into the exuberant verses of the " Fresh-water Crayfish Song":

> Ay, ay, the moon is high,
> Old Man Crayfish be a'nigh.
> Scour the scambler, tramp the swayle,
> Every gribb must have its Tail.
> Ting-a-ling-ling! Come warm the pot,
> Old Man Crayfish wants it hot.

I followed him through the meadows airy and bemused like a clown with an ass's head. Was it fact, fantasy, or Chateauneuf-du-Pape? Had the spell of the Incas gone to my head? Did I wake (ting-a-ling) or sleep?

Geoffrey Moorhouse

LADY BOUNTIFUL

In another age and another place Mrs. Lily MacLuskie would simply have been the toast of the town. She would, perhaps, have enjoyed her greatest local success in California during the gold rush, when thirsts were notoriously difficult to contain. As it is, her health is said to be drunk in places as far apart as Wellington (N.Z.) and Vancouver (B.C.), which may in part be due to an improvement in communications, but which almost certainly has rather more to do with the sheer expansiveness of her nature. Off-hand, one cannot think of any contemporary figure with even a fraction of her compelling zest for life, unless it be Mr. Brendan Behan.

For the past thirty years Mrs. MacLuskie has kept a public-house in a Lancashire village within spitting distance of the Lune estuary. It is a bewitching place in high summer and in winter it is as bleak as an ice-cap. This, undoubtedly, has had a strong formative influence on Mrs. MacLuskie's philosophy as a publican, though that philosophy is mostly something deep and inbred, and mysterious as an elixir. She does not despise the consumption of beer, to be sure, but it is upon her dispensation of spirits that her reputation chiefly depends. She is a woman who appreciates the value of a warming drop on a cold night.

She does indeed. The trouble (though that is hardly the proper word) with Mrs. MacLuskie is that she has a magnificent contempt for the imperial measure. When Mrs. MacLuskie pours you a drop of whisky you get rather more than the Commissioners of Customs and Excise in their wisdom intended you to get. A drop to her is no drop at all unless it exceeds the capacity of that pewter measure. It must be brimming over the top before she consents to transfer it to your glass. There is no extra charge. Not unnaturally, her customers tend to drink a disproportionate amount of spirits.

Her reason for this distribution of largesse is simple and disarming. " Spirits," she says, " are expensive enough and you want to have a proper taste of what you're paying for." Only she doesn't quite put it like that. Her conversation is invigorating, not to say startling at times; all of a piece with the notices that hang above the bar—" If you don't see what you want she's probably changed her job " and " If you need glasses, see an optician—don't take ours! " She will have no truck with the optic measures which decant a precise amount of liquor from an upturned bottle behind the bar. " They just wet the bottom of the glass," she says with a deal of scorn.

She has not, apparently, fallen foul of authority as a result of her singular and highly competitive approach to business. In any case, it is hard to conceive of any form of authority which would be equal to a dispute with Mrs. MacLuskie. " What I do in my own house is my affair," she declares, and it would take a dauntless man to quibble with her there. A woman who spent her youth as a stewardess on the boats between Heysham and Ireland during the days of Sinn Fein can be expected to hold her own in any argument. It was then, she implies with a wink, that she acquired the technique (to put it no more strongly) which she now uses to rid her bar of rowdies. No need to resort to violence at all, or even to call a policeman. A certain verbal attack has usually sufficed.

The collection of hats, which is not much less celebrated than the bounty, is merely by way of keeping up a family tradition. Her mother, she explains, used to wear a trilby when she went to milk the cows, and the habit has remained with her daughter behind the bar. It would obviously be preposterous, possibly indelicate, to ask why. Mrs. MacLuskie currently affects an Anthony Eden, which she wears indoors as well as out above

71

a smart black two-piece suit, like a buxom Vesta Tilley doing her Burlington Bertie stuff. But she has others, including a silk topper, in her wardrobe, and she brings them out for general approval " on Scotch holidays." The origin of this festival seems to be obscure even to Mrs. MacLuskie herself. But the way she perpetuates it, it will obviously be a wow.

Peter Eckersley

QUESTIONS IN THE HOUSE

At The Mount—a large public-house on a housing estate at Netherton, Liverpool, done in brewers' contemporary (a portrait of the Queen and two strident floral papers on the same wall)—a woman in the lounge bar was knitting a white cardigan when a large docker in his fifties leaned over and said: " You look like Mme. Defarge in *A Tale of Two Cities*." It was not the kind of allusion which normally crops up in Liverpool pub conversations.

The name-dropping was perhaps pardonable; other people throughout the pub were also flexing their mental muscles for the hour before closing time. Towards nine o'clock the loudspeaker system, which might have been dispensing the background music which sounds like violins playing long-forgotten melodies under water, suddenly came to life. " In what profession," it asked, " would you find an underwriter?" And: " How wide is a standard roll of British wallpaper?" " Who wrote *The Invisible Man*?" " What is the name of the sea between Italy and Yugoslavia?"

The respectful quiet normally reserved in pubs for television or a good punch-up developing at the bar came down as the first home game of the 1961–2 season of the Merseyside Quiz League (The Mount *v*. Captains Green) began.

Singing is allowed in only a couple of Liverpool pubs, which may be why the quiz-game has caught on in so many others. Merseyside at present has twenty-four quiz teams with pubs or licensed clubs as their home grounds; they have now been divided into Eastern and Western leagues to cut down the amount of travelling required for away games. Eighteen teams in Manchester have just formed three leagues. Competition in most pubs to get into the four-man team is keen; several teams have at least a dozen reserves. Mr. Jack Robinson, a quantity surveyor and public relations man for the Merseyside League, estimates that at least 5000 people in the North are taking part in pub quizzes every week, although not all of them play in official championships.

The leagues have graduated from casual general knowledge sessions with a pint at stake to well-organised affairs with large trophies and printed score-cards which are filled in and sent off to the league secretary. Teams submit questions at the beginning of the season to go into a pool; the sixty-four questions required for a match are sent in a sealed envelope to the home licensee.

The brewery which controls most of the pubs in the Merseyside League keeps a paternal eye on the proceedings, donates prizes, installs microphones, and admits that business has picked up considerably in the normally quiet first half of the week, when most of the games are played.

Mr. Jim Traynor, a Bootle docks checker, says that he started the craze in the winter of 1958–9 when, along with most of the other regulars at The Mount, he had found himself uprooted by slum clearance from his old home and put down on the housing estate. He had got the idea at his old local down by the docks. " We used to have a cultural group down there; we used to invite lecturers to talk about things like local history and the work of the National Dock Labour Board. One night a lecturer didn't turn up; we didn't want to just sit there. I'd run quizzes on troopships during the war, so we filled in the time with a quiz. When we got The Mount as our new local, we started the thing in style."

He thinks the major appeal of the quiz is the amount of audience-participation it involves: "One man in the team is asked, 'Who painted the Mona Lisa?' Somebody listening to the quiz in the saloon bar whispers the answer to his wife, then sticks his chest out when he's right."

The question-master is supplied with six supplementary questions in case involuntary promptings from the audience are overheard by the teams. Some of the younger customers at The Mount were tending to join in rather more noisily, shouting "Max Bygraves" and collapsing helplessly while an electrician in the team considered earnestly the question: "Who became famous as 'The Swedish Nightingale'?" A group of teenagers in the darts room continued to play 101-up while the quiz was on. They said they had thought of forming a junior quiz team but somehow the idea had fallen through.

The game was a serious affair, tricked out with the trappings of the television game; each contestant had his number stuck in a cork on the table in front of him among the pint glasses. The visiting Captains Green team were, in fact, also regulars of The Mount; but they had formed their team in the saloon bar. "We just do it for laughs; don't do any homework," said Frank Jones, a docker. "The Mount team all come from the lounge side, though; they do a lot of studying. The lounge always takes life more seriously than the bar, though, doesn't it?"

A microphone relayed the answers given by the contestants as the eight-round match proceeded; there was a collective groan from all over the house when one man didn't know which ocean is called the herring-pond, and another when someone else thought that Dyaks came from Iceland. The teams galloped easily through questions about the queen who said "We are not amused," the first general to cross the Alps,

74

the term of office of the American president. The general feeling was that it had been an easy night.

This new thirst for knowledge is not as great as the one which drove people a century ago to the lending libraries and the mechanics' institutes. But it has brought some fairly radical changes to the pub. Mr. John Thayer, a brewery executive who is the league president and who acted as question-master, said: "It's tending to change patterns of drinking. Before the quizzes began, a man would try to persuade his wife to come out to the pub about eight o'clock on a Monday evening.

"But she'd say she'd rather watch television than come out and just sit there, not saying anything, watching people until closing-time. The man would manage to get out on his own about half an hour before time for a few quick pints. Now they both come to the pub earlier and have a leisurely evening."

John Shields, a pipe and boiler coverer, who captained one of the teams, says that these days they tend to discuss events in the news, the international situation, and books they have read. "I go to the library a lot. My strong subjects are Greek mythology, the Bible, and geography. Before, in pubs, people never talked; they just had long, pointless arguments about darts and football. The kind of arguments that have no answers; the ones that just go on all night. Now we talk about things that have answers. It stops trouble. I mean, you can't really keep on arguing all night about what George Gershwin's negro folk-opera was called, can you?"

Norman Shrapnel

... AND THE FRENCH AT BRIGHTON

" All they want is jazzing and jiving and having a good time," a woman resident said with a touch of spite in her voice, as though enjoying yourself in an English holiday resort—even Brighton—were some kind of perversion anyway. But the really astonishing thing was that she was talking about the French.

What French? Surely not those staid and civilised family parties pottering round the Lanes, the town's more elegant Flea Market, discreetly comparing curio prices in the softest voices ? Surely not those voluminous mammas, establishing themselves at the beachhead with a day's supplies like some last outpost of the cold peace? Surely not those richer and more disenchanted visitors who, having eaten as well as they can, show blank faces on the balconies of the seafront hotels—sundials to catch whatever rays may emerge?

Not these, of course. It was the students the woman meant, boys and girls who now come in their thousands to Brighton and other South Coast towns, having fun and learning English —in that order of priority, and why not? The antagonism of a section of the townspeople, quite a big section by all accounts, seems deplorable and, from the material viewpoint, extremely shortsighted. For these students, already measurable in the local economy, are potentially vital. They are P.R.O.s for the tourist imports of the future, a trade which will have to grow as the home market dwindles—and in that respect the writing is already on the wall, or in the registers of the hotels and boarding-houses. London may now go to Venice or Seville or Majorca, but a surprisingly large part of Paris is willing to come to Brighton.

Undoubtedly these coastal resorts should attend more to the French. Common Market or no Common Market, here is one branch of the English family that scarcely needs to be dragged kicking and screaming into Europe, for in spite of all discouragements Europe is more than willing to come to it. Brighton is still the English town above all others that the French want to love, and you can scarcely walk a hundred yards through its streets without hearing their language. Superficially it is easy to see why. Brighton is the one resort that has an air as well as just air. This makes a Parisian feel at home, even though so many of the natives welcome him with folded arms.

Grudgingly or not, what do they have to offer him? Well, the most central direction sign is in French as well as English, and it shows the way—a little pointedly as it may seem—to the railway station. There are a French Protestant Church, an occasional French film, and at least one restaurant where they serve *escargots* (properly dished up with garlic butter) and also bouillabaisse (" twenty-four hours' notice, please ") for 10s. 6d., which is flamboyantly cheap by Marseilles standards.

Whether or not they have the patience to wait all that time for a patriotic meal, I suspect that most of the French tourists and visitors now coming over, many of whom are relatives of the students, would be willing to skip the bouillabaisse and the octopus provençale and settle for some good home cooking and a few friendly smiles. They certainly admire the clothes and the prices charged for them, and young Frenchwomen can be seen any hour of the day crooning over sweaters. Other aspects of contemporary British shopping baffle and alarm them: the gift shop vulgarities (sexy mementoes and " the exciting ball pen shaped like a lady's leg "), or the comic postcards, some of which have touched a new low in obscenity.

The French, it has to be faced, are a bit frightened by the moral standards of the contemporary British, and they approach the uninhibited beaches with a certain *pudeur*. This is an ironical reversal of traditional attitudes, but it is easy to see why. Utterly motionless, the promenade-watchers lean on the railings and

77

gaze fixedly at the roasting or shivering flesh below. Even to the pure things can be a bit murky. He, or she, that toucheth pitch shall be defiled therewith: OIL (TAR) CLEANSING STATION says a prominent notice near the Lost Children Bureau. WAIT YOUR TURN is the instruction inside to the oily (or tarry) revellers. Unnerved by this hazard as much, perhaps, as by the beach behaviour of some of the home tribes, the French tread gingerly over the stones towards the sea itself. I suspect that they find it chilly, but none would admit to staying out for that reason. Most of them, anyway, swim not in the sea but in the sea-water baths.

They like the Lanes. They like the air, in both senses of the word. Perhaps they even enjoy such surprises as the invitation to " Meet the Wax Man who shakes hands " (a Louis Tussaud enterprise) a few feet from another notice saying that " William Ewart Gladstone often stayed at this hotel." They like the ambience of the place, even though Brighton gives the impression nowadays of a town battling hard and successfully against its own surviving elegance.

Yet in spite of the march of bingo, in spite of the bulldozing of the property speculators, in spite of the new moral laxity which shocks the French, the English South Coast resorts remain spiritually clad in hooped Edwardian bathing costumes. They do not take kindly to foreigners. They do not much like being loved.

So the French, having explored Battle Abbey and Arundel and Hurstmonceux, and spent more time in London than they intended—having even, who knows, gone on a homesick day excursion (" Over Four Hours on the French Coast ") to Dieppe—now tend to go farther afield. They visit the Lakes. They push on into Scotland. No doubt this was inevitable, though one cannot help feeling that Brighton, if it went out of its way a bit, could hold many more of them for far longer. Will the South Coast eventually become a frontier which people are always crossing both ways, and at which nobody ever stops?

W. J. Weatherby

DEAR MARIE:

Although this will seem to justify all your prejudices about the British, I feel honour bound to explain what happened to that book you gave me before I left Paris.

How harmless it seemed when you bought it for me at Brentano's, yet you might as well have filled my pockets with those feelthy peectures which were pressed into our hands as we crossed the Rue de Rivoli. You chose Jean Genet's *A Thief's Journal* because you said it would help me to understand a difficult French writer. You said—and your words came back to haunt me when I landed in Birmingham—" Genet romanticises criminals and his homosexuality is a bore, but the book is an eloquent self-portrait and one of the best pleas for charity I've ever read."

I had no chance to read it then, but stuffed it in my pocket with the books I had bought myself. By the time we reached Birmingham—where our aircraft first landed—it was merely part of a miscellaneous collection I declared to the Customs inspector—a half-bottle of cognac, a hundred cigarettes, a model of the Eiffel Tower, a scarf, a pipe, and a small library spread out through my suitcase and my pockets.

The inspector had a look at the cognac in its cardboard carrier and then dismissed me, but as I was walking away he said accusingly: " You have something in your inside pocket." I looked of course as lumpy as an old mattress and had already drawn his attention to the books with a cover-all gesture that included me as well as the suitcase. He glanced at their titles as I brought them out and then said I could go. But while I was in the adjoining lounge, trying to rearrange my clothes to

79

make more room in the suitcase, the inspector suddenly loomed over me.

He asked to see my books again, and so I got them all out of my pockets and the suitcase, and piled them in front of him. I'm afraid, Marie, that it was your book that seemed to interest him most. He took that away and with it *Naked Lunch,* by William Burroughs, which a colleague had asked me to bring back because it had been recommended as an American avant-garde novel. The inspector checked my other books with a printed list he had—Pasternak's *Safe Conduct* and *An Essay in Autobiography,* Graham Greene's *In Search of a Character,* Harry Golden's *For Two Cents Plain,* Schwarz-Bart's *The Last of the Just,* Salinger's *Franny and Zooey,* O'Hara's *Ourselves to Know,* Paton's *Too Late the Phalarope,* Dostoevski's *The Brothers Karamazov,* and Hemingway's *In Our Time.* He seemed surprised none was on his list, but he left them alone.

I then asked for the return of your book, Marie, but the inspector said that it and *Naked Lunch* would have to be confiscated as they were not allowed in Britain. Reddening with irritation—no doubt he took it for guilt—I asked him for an official receipt, but he said they did not give receipts, and so I requested an address to which I might complain. He gave me the address of the Customs and Excise headquarters in London. After his early accusing air, he was as polite and helpful as a man can be who is merely carrying out a list of rules.

Before you jump to any conclusions, Marie, let me say at once that this incident shocked me as much as it will no doubt amuse you. After the " Lady Chatterley " case, I had assumed we were ready at least for a subtler—and maturer—distinction between literature and pornography, and the recognition that it is not truth that corrupts but half-truths. But you, Marie, coming from an artistic nation, know this better than I and will merely be wanting to know what happened to your book. Well, I did try to get it back. . . .

A Customs and Excise spokesman at the London headquarters explained that about all I could do if I wanted to pursue your book was to appeal within a month and then the case could go to the Courts. I said I could appeal against the principle of this kind of censorship, but how could I appeal for a book I had not read? Might I first read it and check that I fully endorsed the critics' view—not to mention yours, Marie—that Genet's book is a serious literary work? No, I might not; once a book was taken, that was the end of it unless the Courts released it. I asked to see the list to discover which other books were on it, but this also was not allowed. How then could we know which books not to buy when returning to Britain? We couldn't.

The basis of this censorship, Marie, is the Customs Consolidation Act, 1876, which gives a list of prohibited articles—" indecent or obscene prints, paintings, photographs, books, cards, lithographic or other engravings, or any other indecent or obscene articles. . . ." But how is " indecent " or " obscene " defined? The Act is no help there. The interpretation is supposed to depend a little on " the climate of public opinion," but how do you decide what that is? I could not discover precisely who draws up the list and does the interpreting. The Customs and Excise is an autonomous body with the Chancellor of the Exchequer as its political head. The commissioners are responsible for the list and about all a spokesman would admit was that they sometimes seek " expert advice."

The spokesman said that the commissioners co-operated with the Home Office (which is interested in stopping the sale of " indecent " and " obscene " books inside the country) and the Post Office, which is equally keen not to be a carrier of them. The " great majority " of the books on the list were " downright pornographic " and were obvious candidates—but then, Marie, your gift is doubtless one of the minority, those books which tell the truth we apparently cannot be trusted with. Examples of the " downright pornographic " are already available in back-street shops in any British city.

Although the spokesman was cagey about how it is drawn up, the list is obviously kept up to date—the inclusion of *Naked*

Lunch shows this—and presumably the commissioners must have a team of far-ranging scouts on the lookout for any new examples of the "indecent" and the "obscene." The spokesman said that if an inspector found a likely looking book not yet on the list he might send it to headquarters for consideration. But from my experience in passing through the British Customs about twenty times, Marie, little attention is paid to one's books. There is presumably not a big enough staff to examine every item in one's travelling library unless an inspector has some reason for being suspicious—as the one in Birmingham probably thought he had in my case when he checked the contents of my lumpy pockets.

What more can I say, Marie? If I want to read your book, I shall have to buy another copy in Paris and read it there. Should I appeal now without reading it—or would it be better to wait until I have read it, then, if I agree with your view of it, bring it back, no doubt have it confiscated, and appeal then? You will probably think this case a perfect example of British hypocrisy. I can hear you pointing out that "downright pornography" is already available here and that we accept the corrupting half-truths of politics and commerce without blinking. To you this would make nonsense of our kind of censorship. But perhaps it is the price we have to pay for not being an artistic country, for not taking writers seriously enough to be able to distinguish between the truth tellers and the commercial liars. Dear Marie, please do not think too badly of us —particularly when you remember your own political censorship.

Yours in embarrassment,

W. J. W.

Jeremy Brooks

A RESOUNDING STRIGGLE

Musing, in the pages of *The Spectator,* on the men who have
given their names to the English language (Banting, Boycott,
Shrapnel, Hiram S. Maxim and all), the essayist Strix came up
with his own bid for linguistic immortality:

STRIGGLE, v.t.   To deal in trivialities at regular intervals; to
be tiresomely facetious; (*mus.*) to drone or pipe in a monotonous manner.

[Jane: Oh, do stop striggling about class-warfare. Sir J.
Osborne: *The Wren Goes To It,* 1981. From *Strix,* a minor
literary hack, *circa* A.D.C20.]

It is not at all a bad word, and might well be made to stick
if we could agree to use it also as a noun, and a noun's deriva-
tives. Strigglers are a dying breed, and it is time, before they
are squeezed out of journalism altogether, for them to be
distinguished by a title all their own. *Good-bye to the Bombay
Bowler* (Hart-Davis, 15s.) by Peter Fleming, is Strix's final
collection of striggles, and for those who like this kind of thing
the occasion is as sad as the book is entertaining. The only
top-rank strigglers left to us now are Paul Jennings, Michael
Frayn, and Patrick Campbell, and one doesn't have to be
Professor Francis Williams to estimate that when the sun sets
on these amiable lunatics there is not going to be any space
available for the embryo artists (or artistes?) now striggling
hopefully away in their school magazines.

For what a striggler needs, above all, is space. Strix was
lucky. Not many national journals would give up 1500 words
of their precious space to a genial burbler who wishes to spread
himself on his uselessness as a committee member, the schizo-

phrenia induced by being self-employed, or a whimsical letter to a decayed tooth. No doubt there are many—those tight-faced people who always know exactly what they think about H-bombs, or how to cook *scampi*—who would question the values which allow the channels of public communication to be used up in such a way. I'm sure they would be wrong. Strigglers need space—regular, and if necessary *wasted* space—precisely because what they have to say about the world is not direct, organised, preordained. As well as being described and criticised, the world needs to be found; and in journalism it is the strigglers who set out to find it.

Michael Frayn

BINGO BONGO

God knows, Mike (*said Rollo Swavely, the well-known public relations consultant*), I'm only Christopher Smoothe's personal P.R. adviser, but, by God, I can't help admiring the way he's managed since they gave him the Ministry of Chance and Spec.

Take the debate this week on supplying British bingo equipment as comforts to the U.N. forces in the Congo. Poor Christopher was harried mercilessly on all sides—but in spite of it all he remained absolutely unwavering. By that, of course, I mean unwavering in allegiance to the fundamental Conservative principles of flexibility and healthy opportunism.

He had a damned tricky job to do. The debate had been called, you may remember, as a result of the statement which the Lord Privy Purposes had made the day before declaring that Britain would fulfil her solemn obligations under the United Nations Charter by supplying the U.N. forces in the

Congo with fourteen sets of bingo equipment, on condition (*a*) that they would be used for entertainment only, and (*b*) that they would not be used in such a way as to distract from their work any employees or potential employees of mineral undertakings in which British shareholders had an interest.

What Christopher had to do was to explain that overnight Nigel Sharpe-Groomsman—that immensely colourful Conservative backbencher whose company has done such splendid work bringing bingo halls to darkest Africa—had kindly brought to his attention an item in the *Screwe Advertiser* which changed the situation entirely. Christopher read it out to a stunned House. " According to a U.N. spokesman," it said, " Britain will supply U.N. troops in the Congo with equipment for playing bongo."

Christopher rose to the occasion superbly. " When this country supported the Security Council resolution of 4th November," he said, his voice charged with immensely convincing emotion, " we made it absolutely clear that we were voting for bingo. Now we learn that this resolution is being used to justify a policy not of bingo but of bongo. Bingo and bongo are entirely different matters, and until we have obtained a full clarification of this statement from the U.N., not a single bingo set shall pass."

It was at this point that Mr. George Snugg (Labour, Isle of Dogs) rose and asked if the Minister was aware that the *Screwe Advertiser* had explained since that the word " bongo " was a misprint.

Christopher didn't bat an eyelid. With ineffable aplomb he replied that he was well aware of this, and that if Mr. Snugg had been patient he would have heard that the Government had remodified its reconsidered policy. " I am fully conscious of this country's solemn obligations to the United Nations," he said.

Well, this brought Harold Debenture (Conservative, Epsom Downs) to his feet. In his edition of the *Screwe Advertiser*, he said, the word was not " bingo " or " bongo," but " bungo."

Did the Minister propose to introduce the unknown hazards of bungo into what, prior to its invasion by Irish revanchists and Swedish imperialists, had been a remarkably bungo-free province?

I tell you, Mike, Christopher had reversed his policy even before Debenture had sat down. With the sort of passionate sincerity that brings tears to a public relations man's eyes, he declared: " The Government will never let its solemn obligations under the United Nations Charter stand in the way of its conscientious refusal to aid and abet the degeneration of bingo into bungo, nor its unswerving adherence to a policy of flexibly reviewing the remodifications of its reconsidered decisions in the light of the latest information available from interested shareholders."

Oh, he was magnificent (*said Mr. Swavely*). His policy was vibrating like a well-tuned G-string. When Simon Sheermurder (Conservative, Rottingdean) rose to ask why on earth the U.N. wanted bingo sets in the first place, when they were supposed to have no money to play with, Christopher took the House into his confidence and said that frankly he had been deeply suspicious of the whole idea from the beginning, and had always personally favoured the idea of bongo as being more suitable for the Congo. Frankly, Mike, he made his critics look like bongling fools.

Michael Frayn

BEST FROM THE WEST

Mike, old boy (*said Rollo Swavely, the well-known public relations consultant*), you gave us quite a nice little spread over that bingo debate, and frankly I should like to do something for you in return. Have you ordered, by the way? They do an awfully good *tournedos* here, you know.

The point is, Mike, I've got a story that's rather up your street. I'll be putting it out to everyone to-morrow, but I thought you might like to have it to-day—for old times' sake, and strictly off the record, of course. You remember I have the personal account for Christopher Smoothe, the Minister of Chance and Spec? Well, he's going over to Berlin next Friday to visit the Wall.

Oh no, old boy, he's not the last—I don't think the Minister of Ag and Fish has gone yet. Anyway, here's his programme:

12.0 noon: Arrive Tempelhof Airport. Met by Federal Minister of Bluff and Counterbluff. Exchange speeches about West's faith and ideals.

1.0 p.m.: Lunch with leading West German armaments manufacturers. Gives speech about necessity of remaining strong in face of the Communist threat.

2.30 p.m.–2.45 p.m.: Applause.

3.0 p.m.: Drives in state procession to the Official Wall Viewing-point.

Now here's where we're going to need a bit of very delicate timing. The Official Viewing-point has a fantastically busy schedule, of course, and it's booked up for months ahead. They only managed to get Christopher in at all by cancelling Cynthia Stocking, the former prospective Deb of the Year. Even so, he's timed to arrive at 3.35—only a minute and a half after the departure of the last visitor—Rock Richmond, the famous rock 'n' roll singer. (Incidentally, I hope this burgundy's not too jejune for your taste.)

3.37 p.m.: Official Guide explains history and architecture of Wall, pointing out in particular any features of chance or speculative interest.

3.40 p.m.–3.43 p.m.: Mr. Smoothe looks at Wall.

3.44 p.m.: Mr. Smoothe mounts to viewing platform and looks over Wall into East Berlin. Uses panoramic direction indicator marking principal political prisons, etc. Official Guide directs his attention to any secret police arrests, forced labour, mass starvation, or other signs of repression which are to be seen, depending on visibility.

3.47 p.m.–3.50 p.m.: Mr. Smoothe lost in silent contemplation.

3.51 p.m.: Mr. Smoothe is photographed looking into distance with compassionate expression.

3.52 p.m.: Mr. Smoothe is photographed turning back towards West with look of determination to preserve the solidarity of the Western alliance.

88

3.53 p.m.: Overcoming his evident emotion, Mr. Smoothe speaks.

"When I came here to-day," he will say, "I little guessed how deeply—how very deeply—I should be moved by what I saw. But now, thanks to those brave and selfless West Berlin carpenters who erected this viewing platform, I have seen the Communist world at first hand. I have seen, with my own eyes, what look for all the world like the streets, the houses, and the people we know so well and love so dearly in the West. But what a terrible difference there is! I think I need only say that whereas we are on this side of the Wall which you have shown me with such heartfelt hospitality, they are on the other side."

It's a rather short speech, but at four o'clock precisely the next V.I.P., Walter Wagstaff, the Free World Showbiz columnist of the *New York Herald-Angel*, is due at the Official Viewing-point. But later on in the day we hope Christopher will return to the Wall and switch on a chain of giant loudspeakers to inaugurate the Free World Bingo Game. The calls should be audible all over East Berlin, and we hope resistance workers will smuggle the cards in and out.

Well, that's the programme, Mike. (Shall I order another bottle, by the way?) It should nail those absurd stories that Christopher's not deeply and passionately interested in human affairs. There's only one tiny worry I have—and this of course really is off the record—and that's exactly what we'd do if the East Berliners built a viewing platform on *their* side of the Wall, and started running V.I.P. trips to stare at Christopher and the rest. I know it would seem absolutely unbelievable cynicism to us, but I wouldn't put it past the Communists to use a situation like this for the purposes of propaganda.

Hella Pick

RETURN TO REASON IN LEOPOLDVILLE

The time: a Sunday afternoon; the place: the huge King Baudouin Stadium in Leopoldville; the occasion: a cup final football match. The stadium is crowded to overflowing. Suddenly all is still and at attention—a black limousine purrs in, preceded by outriders; and there emerges the short thickening figure of President Kasavubu, the Head of State; a tidy military band plays the "Chant de Libération" and the president takes his seat to the cheers of the crowd. A few minutes later Prime Minister Adoula arrives to a new wave of cheers. The match begins, the crowd remains ordered, the teams obey the referee. Then it is over, and, in the best of traditions, the president hands over a cup, shakes hands, and drives off.

How commonplace it all sounds—except to those who knew the Leopoldville of only a few months ago. The mere fact that the two teams were playing instead of arguing says something for the new atmosphere here. The growing respect for the Head of State is another sign of return to the normal. That nobody has yet thought of changing the stadium's name from King Baudouin—or indeed that no Belgian statues have been removed or streets renamed—shows a surprising absence of rancour.

Undoubtedly tension still exists in Leopoldville—the existence of 100,000 refugees from Angola would alone account for it—but the Army and police are now well behaved and even a house-to-house search in the residential quarter, where an American diplomatist was recently murdered in an apparent *crime passionnel,* was carried out in a perfectly orderly manner. Some of the European population, which is substantial, with a constantly increasing return of Belgians, almost proudly display a war-time fortitude in the face of shortages, and the local hairdresser, for example, will offer potatoes under the counter.

But in fact the shortages are often more imagined than real. The black market is a genteel institution, and Leopoldville's many excellent restaurants serve good meals at prices that compare favourably with other African cities. It is perfectly possible to lead a comfortable, peaceful existence in Leopoldville —even to the point of attending Scottish dancing. So far, the city seems to have avoided any feeling of decay and indeed is in excellent upkeep. Even the beflowered traffic roundabouts are being kept in trim and the African quarter is spick and span. White United Nations jeeps drive through the town unmolested, Nigerian police regulate traffic points, and U.N. technical advisers working in Ministries side by side with Congolese are now fully accepted. The U.N. officials are no longer regarded as arch-enemies of the Central Government.

The return to reason in Leopoldville, and also in many other parts of the country where law and order really are being effectively restored, roughly dates from July and August when the Congo's unexperienced parliamentarians were shut up behind electric-wire fences at Lovanium University and told by the U.N. that they would not be let out until they had voted themselves a government. It took them two weeks of wrangling to pick Cyrille Adoula.

M. Adoula, forty years old and a former trade union leader, who refused to serve under either Lumumba or Kasavubu when those two men were first battling for power at the time of independence, had somehow managed to keep a clean record during the Congo's post-independence agony, and it says something for the basic sanity of the Congo that this moderate, intelligent, and thoroughly realistic man should have emerged and won the support—often, admittedly, the somewhat grudging

91

support—of the overwhelming number of the Congo's factious politicians.

He has known how to establish a working relationship with Kasavubu and sees the importance of having a respected Head of State. He understands the Congo's problems in all their glaring reality and seeks practical solutions. He sets an example of much-needed personal honesty and moderation. But what constitutes his outstanding virtue is also his great drawback: he stands head and shoulders above the vast majority of his Ministers and has great difficulty even in finding himself collaborators who will relieve him from routine work and allow him to get on with the major political problems.

At the time of Lovanium, and in order to keep the hounds at bay and give himself breathing-space, Adoula picked himself a Cabinet from all shades of interest and political rumps (political parties worthy of the name are few and far between), except from M. Tshombe's Conakat, which did not attend Lovanium. He landed himself with three Deputy Prime Ministers and enough Ministers and Secretaries of State to make up a Cabinet of forty-two. Few of these, alas, have any great conception of what it means to run a Ministry, and in any case such a vast Cabinet can scarcely be considered a working proposition. But M. Adoula has to proceed tenderly to prevent the old factions from breaking out into battle.

Already he has won one major victory—the virtual elimination from the scene of M. Antoine Gizenga who considered himself Lumumba's spiritual heir and proceeded with certain external assistance to use his vice-premiership in the Central Government as a means to bring about the secession of Orientale Province. The Central Government claims that in the process, Gizenga indulged in a number of murderous activities—for which he is now under detention awaiting possible trial.

Next, M. Adoula is trying to win himself both an effective Minister of the Interior and remove Gizenga's closest supporter from a seat particularly suitable for mischief-making: he has appointed M. Cléophas Kamitatu, certainly one of the Congo's ablest leaders, to succeed M. Christophe Gbenye at this key Ministry. M. Gbenye's departure has been more than reluctant. It is not yet clear whether he will accept the honorific but less important vice-premiership he has been offered, but this incident only underlines the extreme difficulty which would face M. Adoula if he were yet to attempt a major Cabinet reshuffle and cut it down to rational proportions and working Ministers.

In any case this is perhaps the lesser of the Central Government's problems now. The key questions that faced M. Adoula when he was elected six months ago and which in spite of remarkable progress are still far from final solution, are the restoration of law and order throughout the country and the establishment of the writ of the Central Government in Katanga, Kasai, and all the other wayward areas of the Congo. Coupled to this is the urgent need to restore external confidence in the Congo and obtain sufficient external aid to prevent the economic collapse of an economy which so far has shown remarkable resilience.

Clare Hollingworth

MORTAR SHELLS NEAR CASBAH

A brutal act was staged this afternoon against the Moslem population of the Casbah by the O.A.S. of ex-General Salan. Five three-inch mortar shells were lobbed on to a Moslem crowd in the Place du Gouvernement, within 100 yards of the main entrance to the Casbah.

In the confusion afterwards it was impossible to be certain of the number of casualties but it is believed that four people were killed and sixty-seven wounded.

A lawyer who was having his shoes cleaned at the time by one of the many shoeshine boys of the area, described the scene to me:

" After the shells fell the wounded and everyone else ran from the spot in panic. This rush of bleeding and wounded people set up a second panic. Some firing took place. I don't quite know how it started but a crowd of Moslems who had rushed into a street, the exit of which was blocked, was certainly fired on by a soldier and two Moslems in the crowd were killed.

"In a crowded street nearby a harka (Moslem soldier in French service) began threatening to shoot when a French major who is in charge of the defences of the Casbah and well known and liked by the population there, walked among the crowd, snatched the revolver from the harka, smacked his face, and ordered him back to barracks. He then shouted to the Moslems saying, ' Obey your own orders and not mine—go home.' The major then chose two likely looking youths from the crowd and said, ' Get cracking, get your people off the streets and into their houses.' "

When I arrived on the scene the Moslems in charge were still at work ordering all the Moslems back into the Casbah and those who did not obey were given a brisk cuff on the ears.

Four taxis, one private car, and several food stalls were destroyed by the mortars. Pools of blood amid the wrecked taxis and the stained bread-basket which had been left behind were no less moving sights because they have become common in this city during the past few months.

A French officer told me that the three-inch mortars were captured from the French army. He guessed they had been used at a range of about a thousand yards, obviously from a site in Bab-el-Oued, but he added that he was certain no one in the area would offer any information.

After visiting the scene, I moved towards Bab-el-Oued to buy the brandy I badly needed. News of the outrage had already become known and a group in a public bar began to drink to the health of ex-General Salan. A man said: " We have shown them we are there and they never know (" they," of course, refers to the Moslems) when we shall strike by day or night."

There seems little doubt that one reason for staging this abominable act was to revive the spirit of the O.A.S. supporters in Bab-el-Oued. Until this incident occurred Algiers city had been quiet throughout the day. Helicopters had been busy dropping leaflets. Most of them dwelt in simple terms on the benefits of peace.

This morning in the European quarters I saw people who picked up the leaflets beaten over the head by men who tore them up on sight. Many Europeans expressed open disappointment that the leaflets were issued by the French authorities and did not contain some message of explanation or encouragement from the O.A.S.

Outside the police headquarters this sentiment was openly expressed and the guard on duty at the building of the prefect, the senior civil servant in Algiers, also boasted of his own intimate ties with the O.A.S. and made excuses to me, as a foreign journalist, for the fact that ex-General Salan had not yet undertaken the sensational action which had been expected of him after the declaration of the cease-fire.

Indeed this guard suggested that in view of the extraordinary military precautions which had been taken in Algiers, Salan had been wise to continue the war of nerves and delay the sensational action expected of him.

Many of the Europeans of Bab-el-Oued who have inherited some of the political violence of their Spanish Communist fathers were openly dismayed this morning because, as one woman said to me, " The O.A.S. have not yet lit a gigantic fire round the Casbah with all the Moslems inside."

Perhaps to counteract this anger and before staging this evening's incident the O.A.S. have issued several new posters to-day. One is a parody on the authorities' press bill of a European and an Algerian walking hand in hand looking to the

95

future. In this one the sand dunes of the Sahara are covered with crosses and pillars marking Moslem and Christian graves. One grave is labelled M. Dupont and another Mohammed. The slogan beneath the poster says, " They died for nothing."

There was some confusion among Europeans about the continuation of the general strike this morning. Banks and large offices did not open. Public transport did not function but about one in five shops lifted their shutters. The ships were still waiting outside the harbour to come in but the electricity and gas supplies have been restored with unwilling requisitioned labour.

All is not calm in the bled (countryside). Since the cease-fire the O.A.S. appears to have used its " paid " Moslem hands who claim to be members of the M.N.A. (the Algerian Nationalist Organisation of Messalihadj). The M.N.A. is an extremely nationalist group which has very little support in Algeria though some in Metropolitan France among the workers there.

At Rouiha, near Algiers, the Moslems are said to have disobeyed the F.L.N. orders and staged a victory parade with the F.L.N. flag flying. The French troops arrived to intervene and in an exchange of fire four Moslems were killed, two of whom were women. However, in spite of these tragic happenings, the O.A.S. supporters still expect what they now call " a big bang."

An example of the power they hold over civil servants was well illustrated to-day. A party of French journalists who wished to leave Algiers went to the Air France office to buy their tickets. The clerks there informed them that their tickets could not be sold until they had produced an O.A.S. exit visa. A journalist protested loudly saying that under no circumstances would he have dealings with this outlawed gang of civil servants. Others managed to obtain the address of the O.A.S. bureau in Algiers where they could go to obtain the visa.

The authorities, however, appeared to realise that the Frenchman who had made the protest was in some danger and they sent two armoured cars and two jeeps to escort his taxi to the airport. The manager of Air France has been called in for questioning. So have the clerks.

Michael Adams

THE TRUCIAL STATES

Here at the foot of the Persian Gulf on what the geographers of the early nineteenth century knew as the Pirate Coast, and which is still a favourite jumping off place for smugglers running gold to India, you are at the eastern extremity of that loosely constituted entity, the Arab world.

You are very far removed from the modernism of Cairo or Baghdad to say nothing of the night-clubs and the water-skiers of Beirut, in a corner of Arabia still moving to older rhythms—tribal, patriarchal, feudal—still sustained (or should one say constrained?) by a delicate nerve system of traditions and custom which in most parts of the Arab world are to-day mere empty echoes of a pattern of social organisation which has lost its meaning.

This is Arabia before the deluge or at least with the deluge not yet fully under way (though there is oil to the south-west in Abu Dhabi and even a few television aerials here in Dubai whose proud owners can enjoy the cowboy films and the Hollywood extravaganzas put out from the American oil base at Dhahran—and what they make of them is anybody's guess); a territory in roughly the same state of development as England at the time of the Wars of the Roses.

Essentially it is an extension of Lawrence's Arabia where the potentialities of modern civilisation are making their first faint impacts on a tribal society, and where the Land-Rover has challenged but not yet routed the camel in a country without roads; whose lines of communication follow dry wadis and bedouin tracks across the open desert.

The telephone is a novelty, electricity was installed a few short months ago, and the sheikh when he travels beyond his own gateway rides out with an escort of a dozen fully armed men. Even the humblest of his dependants jogging to the market on his donkey feels as ill at ease without his rifle as would a city clerk at Ludgate Circus without his bowler hat and brief-case.

" The Sheikh " is the ruler—or a relative of the ruler—of one of the seven Trucial States which you might compare to seven English counties, the largest a match for Yorkshire, the smallest no bigger than Rutland, but each as jealous as the other of sheikhly dignity and prerogative. Together they occupy an area the size of Ireland, though with a population smaller than that of the Isle of Wight, straddling the Musandam Penin-sula, between Muscat and the unidentified borders of Qatar and Saudi Arabia.

Six of the seven Trucial States—so called because of the " perpetual maritime truce " established between their rulers and Queen Victoria a century ago—line the Arabian shore of the Persian Gulf while the seventh looks on to the Indian Ocean; and in either case with desert or mountains behind them their access to the rest of the world is by sea.

They have strong links with Persia and India, with Muscat, and even distant Aden, but their knowledge of the affairs of their Arab cousins far to the north-west in Syria and Egypt and Iraq is vague and their interest in them lukewarm (Cairo after all is twice as far away from them as Karachi, and the great Arabian Desert a much more formidable obstacle to travel than the Indian ocean.

This fact and their physical remoteness and the lack until very recently of education and of any means of rapid communication have kept them from involvement in the mainstream of Arab nationalism and preserved intact the fabric of a primitive and paternalistic society which elsewhere in the Arab world is yielding fast to the pressures of the modern world.

Whether this isolation has been to their advantage or not is open to debate, but certainly they seem content with their present condition, which on paper and to the apostles of progress in Cairo must look suspiciously like one of enslavement to colonialism. Is there not in Dubai a British political agent responsible to the political resident to Bahrain and doubtless charged by him to extort from the Trucial sheikhs their complete submission to the will of Whitehall? And is not this state of affairs by definition (and never mind the wishes of the people concerned) contrary to something vaguely conceived by political theorists as the Spirit of the Age?

Maybe—but on the ground and in practice it all looks very different. There is indeed a British political agent in Dubai, the scope of whose authority seems to be defined with a genial lack of precision and whose resonant title ill-suits the personality of the scholarly young administrator who must wear it. He can advise but his advice is not necessarily followed; he cannot as far as I can make out order—or perhaps he is merely too prudent to do so lest his orders should not be carried out; and when he moves from one sheikhdom to another he is careful to ask permission in advance from the ruler whose " frontier " he must cross and to pay his respects on arrival with all the proper ceremonial so dear to sheikhly hearts.

This is of course imperialism, and there is no getting away from it, but neither, happily, does there seem to be any desire on the part of the inhabitants of the Trucial Coast to sever the British connection whose benefits are too new and too obvious to be overlooked.

The British Government spends a modest £100,000 a year on development schemes in the Trucial States particularly on public health, agriculture, and education (for which Kuwait, Bahrain, and Egypt have also provided teachers and school equipment), but easily the most important contribution Britain has made to the progress of the Trucial States is the establishment of law and order in an area which ten years ago knew neither.

Until 1951 to travel the few miles from Dubai to neighbouring Sharjah, where there is an R.A.F. station, was to court the attention of brigands; venture farther afield and you were liable to end your journey in the slave market at Buraimi on sale to the highest bidder.

But all that, and the tribal raiding, and the local wars like that which smouldered between Dubai and Abu Dhabi from 1947 to 1949, came to an end with the formation just ten years ago of the Trucial Oman Scouts, originally a detachment from Glubb Pasha's Arab Legion but now recruited locally in the territories along the Persian Gulf and as far afield as Dhofar, Aden, and Baluchistan. The scouts, with thirty or forty British officers, number slightly more than a thousand men, and if the general tranquillity of the Trucial Coast is evidence that their main task of establishing order has already been accomplished they contribute in many other ways to the welfare and the advancement of the Trucial States, offering employment, setting an example of discipline, maintaining an embryonic system of communications, and providing basic education and training for their recruits—besides the chance to earn the 2000 rupees (£150) a man needs to buy his own rifle.

If Britain were in a position to dictate to the sheikhs of the Trucial Coast she would probably ordain that they unite their tiny principalities in a Trucial Federation which would permit more constructive use of their modest resources and provide greater security against such shadows of aggression as have fallen across Kuwait farther north. But if there was even much hope that the sheikhs would agree to federate it has faded now with the discovery of what promises to be very extensive oil reserves in the westernmost sheikhdom of Abu Dhabi.

Apart from Dubai, which with its flourishing entrepôt trade and its even more profitable smuggling connections with India is well able to stand on its own feet, federation with its other neighbours would only mean for Abu Dhabi the chance of sharing its wealth with a number of poor relations.

Oil production from the off-shore concession granted by the Sheikh of Abu Dhabi is due to start in the summer at Das Island and so the uncomfortable prospect looms ahead of oil money pouring into one more tiny sheikhdom with a population at present estimated at about 20,000 bringing with it the benefits and the headaches of which Kuwait and Qatar have had warning experience, while in the surrounding desert and across often disputed frontiers the neighbouring Arabs look on with envious hostility.

Michael Wall

TRISTAN ISLANDERS ARRIVE

The islanders of Tristan da Cunha reached these shores yesterday and quickly endeared themselves to all who met them. From six a.m., when politicians, dignitaries, organisers, reporters, and cameramen invaded the liner *Stirling Castle* in Southampton dock, until late in the afternoon in the old army camp at Merstham, Surrey, they suffered the speeches, the questions, the flashlights, and the stares which are part of a world of which they know nothing, with patience, dignity, and gentle good manners.

A few of the islanders were leaning over the rail as the liner slid to its berth in the early morning darkness and inside many of the women were already sitting holding their children, waiting without emotion or expression for whatever was to befall them.

Gathered together in the tourist lounge they looked what they are—a hardy island people who have lived for generations with almost no contact with the outside world—a people who

have now lost their homes, their livestock, and their possessions
—a people whose future is uncertain and even perilous.

The 264 islanders range in age from Jane Laverello, who is
eighty-five and the widow of one of the two Italians who were
shipwrecked on the island seventy years ago and whose families
are among the seven of which the community is made up, to
Margaret Green, born five days before the islanders took to
their boats and fled.

At first they seemed a sad and solemn people, speaking in
low voices with an accent that has a strong tang of Australian,
and answering questions as they probably deserved to be
answered. " What is the weather like in Tristan? " " Some days
are hot and some days are cold." " What do you think of the
English countryside? " " It's all right." " What are you going
to do? " " We must wait and see."

But later, after driving through the English countryside with
the sun streaming on to the green, russet, and gold of field and
wood—a sight to lift the heaviest heart—the men's faces were
quick to wrinkle with smiles; and they thought that Pendell
Camp, prepared for them by a swarm of W.V.S. workers, was
" very nice indeed."

Mr. Hugh Fraser, Under-Secretary of State at the Colonial
Office, made a speech in the ship, telling the islanders that the
Government willingly accepted responsibility for looking after
them in this country and that plans for their future should not
be rushed. They listened in silence and gave him a generous
clap. Their chaplain, the Rev. Charles Jewell, read a message
from the Archbishop of Canterbury, and their Administrator,
Mr. Peter Wheeler, told them to go and get their breakfasts and
be back by eight, because the Mayoress of Southampton wanted
to meet them.

Mr. Fraser and Willie Repetto, the island's Chiefman, sat
down again together before yet another set of microphones and
cameras and Martha Repetto, the Head woman (she is Willie's
sister), welcomed Alderman Mrs. Gladys Barker.

" It's a long wait," Adam Swain said. He was not one of

those who thought the community should stay together at all costs. " I think the young men will want to go out and see the world a bit and make some money. I can build and fish and farm."

Eventually the welcomes were over and the population of Tristan da Cunha came down the gang-plank on to English soil. Their immediate greeting was warm, emotional, and unrestrained. The daughter of William Rogers, who had left the island to marry a sailor twenty years ago, was waiting for her parents, and three other younger girls from the island were also there, as were many English people who had lived on Tristan at one time or the other. There were hugs and kisses and many tears—but few words.

With Glass, Rogers, Green, Swain, Hagan, Laverello, and Repetto as the only family names, the islanders use only the Christian name. If there are two of the same they become Big or Little Gordon, Willie, or whatever it may be. Whatever their family, there is a remarkable facial resemblance in each member of the community, although some are fair-skinned and light-haired and others are quite dark.

Basil Laverello was greeted warmly in one of Merstham's inns. When he spoke the landlady asked: " Where on earth did you learn your good English? " " English is the only language we speak," he replied. She was visibly relieved. " If they are all as good-looking as you, you will be very popular."

Basil, the only male who has been off the island before (he joined the survey ship *Shackleton* for a voyage to Montevideo and the Falkland Isles), said he was worried about the old people. " It is they who have become children again. They know nothing of the world and it will be hard for them to learn. They will have to be told that a red traffic light means stop and a green, go."

On the island, he said, they lived as one people. " Some families had more stock than others, but they shared what they had. It will be hard for us to be the same here." He thought the young people would move away and find work, but he knew that if they did it would be harder for the older people to survive.

On the island they had rules but no laws; there was occasional misbehaviour for which the offenders were sometimes fined, but no crime. He said the stories that had been printed in England about the Chiefman forbidding the girls to speak to strange men were nonsense. "If we cannot speak to you how can we ever settle down in your community?"

For the time being the islanders will stay at Pendell in the wooden spider huts, which are heated with coke stoves and made as friendly as possible with coloured quilts on the beds and flowers on the table. Their future presents an immense problem. If the community is settled on a Scottish island to farm and fish it will make little headway if its young men leave to seek their fortune. Yet simple farming, fishing, and some carpentry is about all the men have ever done, and for the older ones it will be very hard to learn another trade.

The women, too, in their hand-knitted white stockings and coloured headscarves, used to rough and simple living, would find urban living beyond them for a long time. The mother of one of the women who has lived here refused to travel in a car with her daughter. "She says she will not leave the others even for an hour. She is very stubborn."

Their health will be a problem for some time to come. The liner's tourists' lounge echoed with coughs and sneezes, and the Red Cross and St. John's Ambulance nurses who met the boat and staff the camp's sick quarters expect that they will be busy. On the island there were no germs unless they were carried in and the islanders accordingly have little natural immunity to any illness.

J. R. L. Anderson

THE ROYAL CHARTER GALE

On the night of 25th-26th October, 1859, one of the worst
storms in history struck the west coasts of Britain. Wind
forces of 104 knots were recorded, 133 ships were destroyed,
and about 800 lives lost. The storm is known to this day as
" The Royal Charter Gale," because of the loss on the Anglesey
coast of the crack passenger clipper *Royal Charter,* with nearly
500 lives. Mr. Alexander McKee has pieced together the
evidence from inquests on the victims and at the Board of
Trade inquiry, and from contemporary newspaper accounts
(including some of Charles Dickens's finest reporting) to retell
the story of the loss of the *Royal Charter* in *The Golden Wreck*
(Souvenir Press, 21s.).

The wreck was " golden " because the *Royal Charter* carried
a large consignment of bullion from Australia, and many of
her passengers were bringing home gold from the Australian
goldfields—gold which in some cases helped to destroy them
because money-belts weighed them down as they tried to
struggle ashore. The wreck aroused peculiar horror, partly
because all the women and children on board perished, partly
because of stories of Anglesey villagers robbing corpses for gold,
but mainly because the ship broke up only about twenty-five
yards from shore, and the ship's company were battered to
destruction in full view of onlookers powerless to help them.

The master and all the officers were lost with the ship, and
the evidence of the few survivors about what actually happened
at different stages of the tragedy was often conflicting. Mr.
McKee has done a masterly job in reconstructing as much of
the story as can be reconstructed with reasonable credibility.
There was outstanding heroism, notably by a Maltese seaman,

Joseph Rodgers, who volunteered to swim through the appalling breakers to get a line ashore, and by a clergyman on board, the Rev. Charles Vere Hodge, who comforted those about to die and died fearlessly himself. The villagers of Moelfre, on whose rocks the ship was wrecked, also acted with great heroism in rescuing whom they could from seas that battered rescuers and shipwrecked alike.

Rodgers got his line ashore, and many people might have been saved by it had not the ship broken in two, cutting them off from the line. In spite of some wild accusations by half-crazed survivors, there is no evidence of the breakdown of discipline among the crew, and the passengers, although there was inevitably panic, for the most part acted gallantly. The villagers of Moelfre came in for bitter denunciation as corpse-robbers, but this was grossly unjust. They were not articulate, few of them could even speak English, and their heroic rescue work was largely ignored in the public hysteria that the wreck aroused. Mr. McKee has done historical justice here. Certainly there was beachcombing afterwards, but extremely poor fisherfolk who make their living from the sea have some excuse for regarding as theirs what the sea brings and the dead have no further use for. In fact, most of the bullion was recovered by divers for the underwriters, and substantial amounts in gold coin, whose ownership could not be identified, went to the Crown. If some odd sovereigns went into the cottages of Moelfre, few would grudge them.

The gale itself was a fearsome visitation. A modern liner would probably have meteorological warning of it, but a modern liner, caught on a lee shore as the *Royal Charter* was, would be in little less danger. The great power of modern engines would help, but the enormous force of a 100-knot gale and sea raised by it could overpower the strongest of engines. In such a storm a ship's hope of survival is in sea room, and on a lee shore there is no sea room. The hymn " Eternal Father, strong to save " means as much to seafarers as ever it did.

Glyn Dixon

THE SECOND MATE'S IDEA

It was the second mate's idea that we should go sailing when we docked at Durban. Whether he felt morally obliged to sail in the true sense, or whether he really liked sailing, is a moot point; anyway, he was obsessed with the idea of getting one of the lifeboats down and demonstrating his prowess as a helmsman.

His fellow-officers were rather sceptical about the whole affair, but after much canvassing he mustered a crew: one of the cadets, the second carpenter (chippy's mate), and myself. None of us, excluding the second mate, had much experience in sail. A ship's boat has notoriously poor sailing qualities, her lack of lateral resistance and her unweatherly rig tend to make her sail like a crab, but inspired by the second mate's enthusiasm we put our heads together and hit upon what we thought were one or two rather clever ways of overcoming some of the more obvious snags.

First, we decided to use the eighteen-foot boat, our smallest, and rig her with a mast and sails from a twenty-six-foot boat. We reckoned that by fastening a stout oar over her bow as a bowsprit and using an extra foresail we would have a gaff cutter. Next we wanted some sort of false keel, or lee boards. Lee boards were definitely out because the "old man" had given strict orders that under no circumstances were we to make any permanent fastenings or drill any holes. In the end we decided to sling a hefty piece of timber under the boat's keel, held in position by cheek plates and a couple of double wire strops which completely circled the hull. These were tightened by the crude though effective Spanish windlass method. We rigged her in the davits, and waited impatiently for Durban.

The eventful day dawned, and the keen, fearless crew assembled on the boat deck. We put her over the side without a hitch, and tumbled in. Durban harbour is quite an extensive area of water, frequented by divers craft of many nationalities. Add to these general harbour craft, a few whalers and factory ships, season with the odd yacht or two, and you have the perfect recipe for a day's sailing—that is if you like sailing a bath tub in a crowded anchorage.

We pulled away from the ship's side for a couple of hundred yards before attempting to hoist any sail. The second mate took the tiller, and the cadet the mainsheet (the main was loose footed, of course). Chippy's mate and I handled the head sails.

The wind was light and she was filling nicely on a port tack, when two snags made themselves apparent. Not only was she making an astonishing amount of leeway but she also carried a dangerous amount of lee helm. The second mate decided to reduce the press of canvas on her head to try to lessen lee helm. There was practically nothing to be done about the leeway she was making and caution seemed the only answer.

We held our rather oblique course as best we could, then tried to bring her about. Helm hard down, haul on the mainsheet, back the foresail—she fell away miserably. We tried again and again, and got ourselves in irons. She paid off with the hard use of an oar. There was only one thing for it, wear her round —and it was either that or keep on rowing. We managed after what seemed an eternity of hectic ducking and diving to wear ship, and after about half an hour's sailing in ever increasing circles we more or less had the feel of things. Then the wind fell away to practically nothing. Our sails, which were the colour and texture of leather, hung lifeless. Swallowing our pride, we manned the oars.

While we were in this unbecoming situation, all pulling merrily together, a beautifully proportioned Bermudan sloop ghosted across our bows. The dashing sailor at the helm nodded in a friendly though somewhat condescending manner. The set of his sails was atrocious, but compared with us he was flying along. The second mate grunted testily, and the cadet stuck his knife in the mast and whistled viciously through his teeth for a wind.

It came as quickly as it had left, but it came back changed in character. It had left us as a balmy breeze, but it came back like a young cyclone, hitting us with the impact of about a ton of wet cement. Our boat, poor old soul, tried to lie down to it as best she could, decided she couldn't, and went surging forward with every timber and fastening in her complaining in agonised harmony. She seemed to gather her skirts about her and dash madly forward like some old dear running for a bus.

We were thoroughly enjoying ourselves, for this was the first time that the boat had approached anything like sailing since hitting the water. She was fairly hammering her way forward. The wind was whistling through the rigging in short staccato gusts. The second mate was looking pleased with the world, and the cadet was hanging on to the mainsheet for dear life.

Suddenly there was an immense crash, and in a flurry of canvas and cordage the mast went over the side. All that was left inboard was a jagged stump sheared off just above the mast band. The " old lady " had collapsed through sheer exhaustion. Dejectedly we hauled the sodden sails and splintered mast inboard and stowed them as best we could.

Our ship seemed miles away. For we had to row against the tide. It was surprising just how much distance the boat had managed to put in between herself and the ship. We pulled in silence, not having the breath to spare for speech. I wondered what the " old man " would have to say about this lot, but, anyway, that was the second mate's pigeon.

When we finally reached the ship's side there was a reception committee lining the rail. The boys had enjoyed the whole spectacle immensely. Cheers greeted us:

" *Well done, lads.* "

" *Home is the sailor.* " . . .

" *The best wreckers in the line.* " . .

" *I tell you mate—you couldn't trust 'em with a pram!* "

I have never really understood why that mast carried away. Too much canvas, perhaps, or rotten timber badly supported. Those may have been some of the causes, I suppose. Could that knife that the cadet played fast and loose with have had anything to do with it?

Francis Chichester

SAILING THE ATLANTIC ALONE

The drawbacks of racing alone across the Atlantic for forty days may be obvious, but what are the advantages, which must be great to make one wish to do it again? Loneliness, which you would think a disadvantage, only lasts for a short period of time while breaking contact with the land and for a few hours after that. From then on it seems to me one is only in a long race. I mean that if you were in a cross-country race you wouldn't worry about being alone, and a trip across the Atlantic is only a longer race. There is the obvious thrill of surging through the Atlantic swell and seas with all sail set, and lovely bow waves combing each side. There is the adventure of 3000 miles of the Atlantic ahead of you. A voyage is like a classical drama: it starts slowly and works up with many adventurous incidents to the finish.

When I am alone on an adventure I become more efficient. I seem to be twice as efficient, and I become vitalised. I don't know why—perhaps it is because when I am with someone else I am concerned with their comfort or safety rather than getting on with the job. I have always been keen on doing things alone. When I was a boy I used to wander all day through the woods of North Devon by myself. I used to go bird-nesting, but only to get a single egg from some particularly difficult buzzard's nest, or crow's nest.

One day, when I was about eleven, I caught a viper. I thought it might be hungry, and I showed it a beetle which I thought would make it a good meal. It hissed, and bit me instead. For twenty hours or so, I was told, it was touch and go whether I would survive. Perhaps I made things worse by the fact that I travelled seven miles as fast as I could running, and on a bicycle, hampered for the first part of the journey by the snake that I was still carrying. Perhaps this adventure with the snake ought to have taught me a lesson in sticking to the job; if I'd killed the snake instead of trying to please it, none of this trouble would have arisen. But I did try to please the snake, and got bitten for it. When you are quite alone you don't have to think about pleasing anybody, or anything else. You can give your whole being to the job in hand, and there is immense pleasure in using manual dexterity.

When on a solo adventure, it seems to me that all one's sensations are magnified: the sensation of excitement, the feeling of accomplishment of fear perhaps, or of pleasure. All one's senses are more acute. One sees and perceives more the beauty and details of the sky and the water, their colour or shape. One's touch is more sensitive, and the feeling of water and wind and things becomes more real and more acute. One tastes things more sharply: everything tastes better, or worse, than usual. One's hearing is more acute. One becomes so tuned up that the slightest change of conditions, of weather, of noise, or movement will be perceived and, in fact, will wake one up after being alone for a while. Another curious thing about prolonged solitude is that time seems to change its rate. Some- times there seems a long interval between two words you are thinking, as if you dropped them separately into a pool; sometimes when you are in some difficult situation time goes incredibly fast, sometimes incredibly slowly. Time's values change.

Apart from boyhood adventures in North Devon, my first big adventures alone were with mechanical power in the air, when I flew Gipsy Moth I solo from England to Australia in 1929, and made the first east-west solo flight from New Zealand to Australia across the Tasman Sea. A voyage in sail has advantages over a flight because you are using natural forces, the wind and water, for your power. Secondly, you are using more physical effort, and this always results in more pleasure than a nervous effort. Thirdly, because a voyage in sail takes longer, the experience is more protracted.

In the 1960 solo Atlantic race my own ambition was to cross from Plymouth to New York in thirty days. It is 3000 miles as the crow flies, if he could fly it (which he couldn't), but I came badly unstuck; it took forty days and a half. Among the reasons for this was, first of all, fog. This didn't slow me down directly, but I couldn't get to sleep sometimes for two or three hours when charging into fog, especially on a dark night. This made me more tired and, therefore, less ready to make the sail changes necessary. Then the seas were much greater than I had expected, and I found that the yacht simply would not go fast in big seas. Sometimes she would have gone much faster than I could stand, with the boat jumping off the top of the waves, and landing in the trough; I felt that she would break up under the strain. She got some terrific cracks.

Then there were headwinds. I had expected westerly headwinds, but as things turned out I was on the wind for twenty-six and a half days, and I sailed 4000 miles in order to cover the 3000-mile distance. Then there was the inconstancy of the wind: in the Atlantic I had expected it to keep steady in direction or force for at least a number of hours at a time, but I found that it was just as fickle as in the Channel or the Solent. This meant frequent changes of sail and this in turn meant a lot of fatigue, and fatigue is the great enemy of ocean racing.

The last thing I misjudged was the storm I had. I had expected to get one good gale as a ration going across, but I had a number of gales, and I ran into one big storm which meant almost a total loss of four days' sailing. The really heavy part of the storm, when the wind rose to 100 miles an hour, only lasted a short while, but I lost a day in repairing damage, chiefly to my self-steering wind vane. I spent fourteen and a half hours on end repairing the damage. And then on the fourth day I was so exhausted that I sailed very badly.

This year my ambition again is to make the Plymouth-New York course in thirty days, starting on June 1 at 11 a.m. I realise that this is a very tough project. In the 1960 race I averaged seventy-five miles a day. This may not seem very fast, but you must remember that it becomes eighty-four and a half miles a day from Great Britain to Newfoundland because of the Atlantic current, which you have to buck the whole way across, and which averages 9.6 miles against you daily. This means that every day I was sailing for two hours forty-four and a half minutes simply to regain the loss from the continuation of the Gulf Stream. Because of that, and because of the head-winds, I actually sailed an average of 100 miles a day to make good the seventy-five miles a day. To do the course in thirty days means putting up the average distance made good to 100 miles a day, an increase of one third, or an extra knot throughout the whole trip.

What chance have I got of achieving this? In 1960 my yacht Gipsy Moth III was almost new; I had her only the previous autumn. I had never had a chance, for example, of trying her out downwind with the self-steering gear, or in rough weather. I had had to rush the design and construction of my self-steering vane, and I got no chance to find out before the race what changes to rig or to the wind vane should be made to increase efficiency. I learned as I sailed, and I learned a tremendous lot.

As a result I have remasted Gipsy Moth III, completely rerigged her, redesigned the self-steering vane, and I have had that rebuilt. With my increased experience, and the hope that this time I can dodge a four-day storm, I am hopeful. I can hardly wait to find out if all my little ideas and devices to get me across the Atlantic ten days faster are good and true or not. That is what drives one on in an enterprise of this sort.

You may say that all this sounds rather selfish, but there is a co-operativeness behind solo adventures. I could not have undertaken the 1960 adventure without my wife's help, for instance; I could not undertake this forthcoming adventure without her help again, and the help of many other people. This help means everything.

Alison Adburgham

THE FASHION WRITER'S PREDICAMENT

Some years ago now I was watching a fashion show in Rome. It was my first visit to Rome, and everything enchanted. It was all of a piece, the old and the new, the colour and the form, brilliance and shadow. The clothes and the way they were worn were part of the pattern and the atmosphere of fashion was quite different from that of Paris. It was a wholly Roman empire, and it needed a wholly Italian word to convey its especial ambiance. Turning to an Italian journalist beside me, I asked:

" What is your word for elegant? "

"We say *elegante*."

" Isn't there another word? "

" We also say chic."

" Is there nothing else I could use? "

She thought for a little while and then replied, " You could use smart."

So much for foreign aid . . . in Rome, Paris, London, or New York the same words torment you. The fashion writer's predicament is a love-hate relationship: longing to have done with them for ever, you find you cannot do without them. And the vocabulary of fashion is further limited by there being long periods when some words are out of use:

> For last year's words belong to last year's language
> And next year's words await another voice.

The Italian was wrong when she said, " You could use smart." That year you could not, because smart was totally unsmart. A few years later it would have been possible, or many years earlier. In the 1880's a columnist noted: *Smart was formerly employed only by servant girls in reference to their finery. But now the mistress and all her surroundings are smart. A lunch, dinner, or ball must be a smart function, and must be attended by smart people.* The 1960's may be less snobbish, but who will deny that last year's words are as dated as last year's hats? The fashion writer must know when to drop a catchword.

When first she launches upon the smooth seas of high fashion she may think she will have a fine disregard for the ephemeral fancies of vogue language; but soon her nerve ends become responsive to the language in the air, soon her fingertips refuse to type phrases that are out of date. Something sufficiently out of date to rank as " period " is another matter. A Restoration word can be effectively placed in a colloquial modern sentence just as an interior decorator places a piece of Victoriana in a contemporary setting . . . calling it, according to the current phrase, a witty accent, a rewarding motif, madly amusing or delicious, *but* delicious.

Words are a powerful influence in the capricious world of fashion. Until the end of the 1920's the name Jaeger was associated with a German doctor and men's underwear of a peculiarly unattractive colour. I seem to remember, perhaps wrongly, that it was also associated with Bernard Shaw; and, surely, there was something about the Bishop's Jaegers? Then suddenly the Jaeger Company went in for young feminine fashion, and advertisements appeared of which this is a sample:

" My lovelies. With Paris and Berlin doing the most angular things with concrete, glass, and metal—so stimulating—one does heave the old bosom just once to find mahoganised, diluvian London shedding the mildew at last! I mean, on the new floor at Jaeger's positively all the fungus has died in the night. My dears, they've gone completely chromium! Tuby chairs, vulcanite tables, glass walls, plus-ultra pictures, and wholly immediate carpets. A simply gladdening spot, darlings. Utterly 1930 and corpse-reviving! The cerebral background, of course, for the stupefying smartness of the new Jaeger clothes. Tweeds —the most contagious tweeds! Tailored to a slenderising centi-metre. Too plastic! And woollies—millennial patterns, cut with lethal precision but touched with coyest inconsequence. There never were such caressing, emotion-causing clothes!"

And there never was such wholly immediate language, utterly 1930. Jaeger's shot straight away from fuddy-duddydom (not then the word) to become the most avant-garde shop in London—although avant-garde was not, at that time, the term. What was? If we could remember, it might make a useful substitute for that abominably overworked import.

To avoid using foreign words and phrases is not the least part of the fashion writer's problem; for they are adored by modish exponents of the decorative arts, and much of the language of dressmaking is French. Often there is no English equivalent, particularly in the technicalities. In some cases a French word has been adopted, through coy genteelness, that is not, in fact, used in France. The garment which was called up towards the end of the First World War to reinforce the camisole was at first named bust-bodice. Soon it was renamed brassière —an odd choice, since in France it is known as *soutien-gorge*. Brassière, awkward as well as irrational, is now usually shortened

116

to bra. This, with its suggestion of being a pet-name, has a dreadful contemporary coyness; yet it is becoming impossible not to use it, since brassière now sounds pedantic.

And all the time, around and about, the banalities of publicity infect and the euphemisms of the dress-trade distract. Fat women are not so slim; they have fuller figures. Wives are budget conscious; they shop on slender purses. Bad complexions are called sensitive skins, girls are teenagers, and clever young marrieds dress on a shoe string. No woman is ever old; she is not so young or more mature. Everything is revolutionary and brilliant new ideas are, paradoxically, what every woman has been dreaming of for years. To your desk, by every post, come announcements wrapped up in hyperbole, some written, it is only kind to suppose, by people out of their minds . . . as an instance, this announcement which came some months ago:

Reaching this country close on the heels of the new President of the United States, and gaining about as much popularity, is the Muu-Muu.

It would have been understandable if the Muu-Muu were destined for the zoo, since the British are known to prefer animals to people; but it was, in fact, a kind of short nightdress.

Absent thee from publicity awhile! Seek decontamination in some far place inhabited by a peasantry! This I did last month. It was a Ligurian village to which no cars go because there is no road, where neither English nor French is spoken, and where there are no clothes shops. Occasionally, among the fruit and fish in the market, there were a few stalls with fabrics, blouses, and scarves. One day I paused by one of these, and a swarthy trader flung a stole around my shoulders. " *Molto chic, Signora!* " he cried. " *Molto elegante!* "

Alison Adburgham

MONKEY ON A STITCH

The salon of Norman Hartnell, Royal Dressmaker, is not like any other *couture salon* in London. It combines the respectability of the monarch with the shamelessness of the aristocracy; one imagines that the parsimony of the privy purse is balanced by the profligacy of the all-conquering coquette. That is how it seems; but these things are all in the imagination, which needs must feed where it can, to fend off ennui, during the week of the London Collections.

Here then, at Hartnell's, for those who have a nose for it, can be savoured a delicious *goût de scandale*. Imaginings are stimulated by the mirror-lined walls, the French *vendeuse* dressed in Parma violet with violet rinse and turquoise necklace, by the chandeliers and the satin, the sequins, the sables and, above all, by the monkey fur. Yes, monkey fur, naughtiest of all the furs and, truth to tell, the nastiest.

Yet how welcome was that model called " Monkey Tricks," with its underskirt deeply fringed with this provocative pelt, its fling-on coat dripping with dreadful hairiness, its complimentary hat by Claude St. Cyr whirled all round with monkey fronds quivering like ospreys. Seeing it, one knew that Hartnell was on form. Long live Hartnell, and God Save the Queen.

Alison Adburgham

NOTHING TO LOSE BUT YOUR HEAD

Millinery, it may be remembered, was the one and only extravagance of the ladies of " Cranford." In matters of dress, they practised perforce, as in everything else, an " elegant economy," persuading themselves that all money-spending was vulgar and ostentatious. Their frivolous feminine yearnings, instinctive to all women, were allowed expression only in their choice of new caps for special occasions. Miss Matty commissioned Mary Smith to bring her a sea-green turban from her milliner in Drumble (Mrs. Gaskell's name for Manchester), and it was a dreadful disappointment when Mary brought her instead " a pretty, neat, middle-aged cap " which she considered more suitable to Miss Matty's " small, gentle, mousy face."

We all of us have our dreams of sea-green turbans; and most of us have a Mary Smith around to bring us to our senses . . . hinting that such dreams are dangerous, such hats unsuitable. Yet if anything is more ageing than an unsuitable hat, it is a " suitable " hat; and suitable hats, alas, are England's speciality. Colourless, shapeless, meaningless, safe, they are the stand-by stock of a thousand shops, and the laughing-stock of Europe.

In Rome there lives an intensely elegant lady named Irene Brin, who is the Rome editor of *Harper's Bazaar*. Not long ago, she contributed to a feature in which writers of different countries gave their views of the English. Hers was a mockingly affectionate little bit of writing, in which she said that the Italians were delighted with Queen Elizabeth when she visited Italy: " We did not find her elegant in a sophisticated way, but in a rich one. She had lovely gloves, not to mention her jewels, and her handbags are definitely improving." The article ended with the simple statement: " We do not understand British hats."

Had the urbanely beautiful Irene Brin lived in Cranford (unimaginable hypothesis!), she would undoubtedly have been on the side of the sea-green turban. Faint heart never made fair lady, and if you are going to wear a hat at all, be decisive and go the whole hat. In making a courageous choice of millinery, you have nothing to lose but your head . . . and in any case, a safe choice in hats is always fatal. Fortunately this autumn there are all kinds and conditions of hats in fashion, to go with all kinds and conditions of faces. No single style dominates the scene, and it is possible to make a choice that is becoming to the individual as well as immediate to the mode.

Becoming to everyone are the fur-abouts which frame and flatter the face, in mink of all mutations, in fox, squirrel, or any of the inexpensive but pretty pelts which are hardly less engaging in their softness. There are also miracles of simulation to be found in man-made furs. More demanding about the kind of faces they go with than these close hugging fur hats are the pillboxes which are first favourites with many milliners—and, incidentally, with all hairdressers. The 1961 pillbox is worn well to the back of the head and demands features that are perfect, or at least provocatively impertinent, and a coiffure in which not a hair is out of place. It must be worn with a sense of assurance, and a dandy total turnout is essential: the pillbox does not go with casual dressing.

Less demanding are the big, baggy berets which appeared so frequently during the Dior collection in Paris. They, also, are worn well back, but their bagginess provides a softening surround to the face. Moreover, the complete coverage they give to the back of the hair is convenient. When hats stop short of the hairline, there is all too often an untidy depressed fringe at the back, disastrous to the effect. This applies very much to the tall, brimless, dome-like superstructures, so splendid for adding height and sophistication, *providing* the hair is well groomed.

Velvet, as a millinery material, has come back in full force.

A big-brimmed black velvet hat is a dramatic accessory for a tall and handsome woman. No brim is permissible this year unless it be very wide and up-turning. So the shorter woman should be content for her drama with a black velvet Venetian beret or, alternately, a small, round, coloured beret in a richly glowing velvet.

At cocktail time, a velvet or brocade turban is something new at present—more notable than the ineffectual bits of fluff and veiling which have been around so long. These turbans are not so very different from the kind worn in Cranford at the same time of day, but not for the same kind of refreshment. The Honourable Mrs. Jamieson dispensed tea with wafer bread and butter and sponge biscuits " and she was sister-in-law to the late Earl of Glenmire, although she did practise such elegant economy." Gracing just such an evening party had poor Miss Matty imagined the sea-green turban which never was to be. She never recovered from her disappointment, to the very end of the book. All women, surely however mousy, should be allowed to fulfil their sea-green dreams.

Phyllis Heathcote

THE HE AND SHE APPROACH

I have received recently a charming brochure of autumn fashions from one of the well-known French knitwear firms. It tells the story of a very good-looking young person who, for the purposes of publicity, lives in a château in the Sologne—" *nimbè de brume aux frontières d'une forêt pleine de légendes.*"

Our heroine seems to live an enviable existence and to be possessed of a vast (knitwear) wardrobe; for, needless to say, she changes on every page and for every occasion: coming in from the garden with her gardener who carries baskets overflowing with luscious fruit and vegetables while she poses with a bunch of autumn flowers in a three-quarter coat in brushed mohair against a pink brick wall; in the kitchen in a shirtwaister having a cosy chat with the cook; out in the larch woods with the spaniels (green pleated skirt, pale blue turtle-neck jumper, harlequin wool stockings, a wide Alice band in her hair); sitting on a pile of logs in a tweed jersey suit and pull-on hat discussing a ferret with her gamekeeper; sitting, relaxed, in the long gallery doing charmingly nothing in a scabious blue two-piece with thick-knit collar and cuffs; sitting in a Louis XIII chair toying with an embroidery frame; up in the lookout tower watching for friends who are coming in for drinks; cocktails in a "fully fashioned" pure silk ensemble with an attractive looking man ("*châtelain voisin, qu'elle ne connaissait pas*") watching her from a vantage point by the roaring log fire; she changed again for coffee and is now in a Fabulosa and Lurex ensemble, the boat-necked cardigan jacket closing with jewelled buttons, while her admirer, who is evidently by this time in a fair way to falling in love ("*conquis par sa grâce et son charme discret*"), sits against a tapestry in a Louis XV chair.

He is evidently a fast worker, for on the next page he is round at the château again. It is the next morning and she is wearing a most appropriate little Courtelle and wool polo two-piece while he just looks tousled and interesting and the dog bored. On the back cover he is making his declaration in the woods, she in a blue thick-knit cardigan suit demurely plucking at a broom flower picked from the bushes that surround them. Dressed in a suitable knitwear, they will, you feel, certainly live happily ever after.

This eruption into our fashion world of the male element is not new. We are already inured to men models and their pseudo-nonchalance on the catwalk. The Prêt-à-Porter and Knitwear people have been making a feature of these mixed showings for some years now while the *Haute Couture*, so far, reserves the " him " element to its *boutiques*. The Cardin one on the Faubourg is neatly divided into the men's *boutique* on the right—stitched velvet trilbys, stocks, embroidered braces, crocodile coats, ties, jewelled cuff-links, leather jerkins—the women's on the left. The farther end of the vast Dior *boutique* on the Avenue Montaigne is given over to similar enticements to which I see, have now been added, comfortable camel-hair bedroom slippers with hand-worked initials on the vamp. But it was a walk down the Avenue Franklin Roosevelt (ex-Victor Emmanuel—" Oh, France, *guéris-toi des individus!* " as someone once said) brought home to me how the " he " and " she " approach is gaining in the beauty business. Two of Millot's three main windows are dedicated to Madame, the one in between to Monsieur. The " her " windows are draped with pale yellow crêpe-de-Chine—in honour of their " Crêpe-de-chine " scent—on a bottle-green ribbed silk ground tricked up with brown silk roses; " his " is made of sterner stuff—red gros-grain and white trelliswork, the bottles of " Partner " (" *Eau de Toilette*," " Aftershave Lotion," etc.) and the " Partner " soap and " Partner " shaving cream wrapped in Glenurquhart check worsted. . . . (I am told by those who know that the sale of men's beauty products is going up in leaps and bounds. " You see," my informant told me, " men buy for themselves—not like women who as often as not—especially in the case of scents —wait till someone gives them as presents.")

Of course, care is taken to give a befittingly manly name and wrap to these usually pretty expensive items—in order, I imagine, that no misunderstandings or misinterpretations occur. Hence " Partner " and the Glenurquhart check. " Calèche," and a leathery smelling wrap *chez Hermès*, Rochas's " Moustache " scent, Schiaparelli's " Si " *Eau de Toilette* for men bottled in a container fashioned like a pipe, and *Dessès ters* " *Celui* " scent for men.

I should say at a guess that it was the Knize toilet water that set the whole thing going; that—one must admit—very fresh, out-of-door product packed in a stout miniature packing-case with Knize stencilled in black on the sides.

On the same wicket [if our men take to scent—perhaps they have?—what a jolly range of cricket terms they will have to pick from for the names: " Bails," " Wicket " (why not " Good Wicket "?), " Long Off," " First Eleven "—it is simply asking for it . . .] one household linen firm at least over here has brought out " he " and " she " towels with " *Lui* " and " *Elle* " woven or printed across one corner. But the he/she distinction that beats them all by its niceness is the wording on a neat little triangular leather book-marker that slips over the corner of a page; it reads: " *C'est ici que je me suis endormi* "; or " *C'est ici que je me suis endormie.* "

Letters

COEDUCATION

Sir,—You report Mr. Fred Peart, M.P., as saying at Blackpool, " I believe that every boy and girl should go to the same school." How comprehensive can you get? And where will it be situated?—Yours, etc.

JOHN W. KENNEDY

Alice Bragg

THE POLICE OF MY AUNT

Police were my aunt's hobby, or, to put it accurately, her life's work. It would not have been so remarkable to-day, but a hundred years ago it was a curious form of welfare work for a young woman to adopt. However, my aunt, Mary Hopkinson, was a strong and even masculine character, and in her early twenties she started her activities by holding a Sunday school for young policemen in Manchester, where her family had made a name for itself in public service. She then organised a police orphanage, a benevolent society for police, and embarked on an endless round of visiting members of the force either in hospital or wherever her help was needed.

Her conversation had to be interpreted in terms of police. Reference to a station, a superintendent, a sergeant, head-quarters, when made by my aunt could only mean police. All her relatives knew of this obsession. My aunt, it was often said, was " wedded to the police "; in fact she never married. We were proud of her and I remember as a child, my father telling us at breakfast one day that my aunt had been co-opted on to the Watch Committee, and that she was the only woman to serve on it. Everyone seemed so impressed that we children did not like to ask what my aunt would watch, but we felt sure that it could only be the police. From then on, it was fun to go about with her occasionally and be saluted by policemen, and handed across the road, my aunt holding up her long braided skirt.

Towards Christmas time she would start on one of her major tasks for the police, the sending out of about three thousand personal cards. I can see her now, settled in her sitting-room, which was all sage green and dark red, the table with its velvet cloth fringed with bobbles, covered with these cards, the texts, and her own specially printed Christmas " message." All three items had to go into each envelope. She was assisted by her cook, who in cap and apron, sat sorting and folding, but forbidden to address the envelopes. This cook was with my aunt for over fifty years, and was allowed certain liberties such as an occasional joke about police, which my aunt would not have tolerated from any other quarter. When my aunt went off to the railway station to carry out her various missions the cook would hold her bicycle while she mounted, and with a gentle push-off send her on her way.

A short time after my marriage I most mistakenly decided to take advantage of my aunt's unique position with the police. One Sunday morning when we were away the wall of our front garden was breached, apparently by some heavy vehicle. I wrote to the Chief Constable (casually mentioning whose niece I was) and asked his help in the matter. Within twenty-four hours the act had been pinned to the driver of an ice-cream van. Armed with his address, we confronted him in his shop, with the result that he and his mate came over and mended the wall. Delighted, I made a good story of this to my aunt, but she was not amused, and indeed very angry. I was only restored to favour by giving a tea-party in our garden to a selected group of sergeants and wives who arrived, headed by my aunt, in two bus loads. Smoking was not permitted in her presence, but I think she knew quite well that my husband escorted some of the guests to the bottom of the garden for a quiet smoke behind the bushes.

There was no question that the police respected, admired, and, I think, loved my aunt. In later years she became rather deaf, and once when crossing the road, was knocked down by a tram. It was difficult to persuade the police that this accident was in no way the fault of the driver. The force was shocked. I was driving my father to the hospital to visit her one day when I was stopped by the policeman on point duty. I had that instant feeling of guilt that grips one on these occasions, and waited. Slowly the man walked to the car window, his face grave, " How's your auntie? " he asked anxiously.

After fifty years of devoted service the police decided to mark the occasion by giving my aunt a party and presentation. This, it was generally understood would be the moment for her retirement. A watch bracelet and a radio, suitably inscribed, were given to her, and there was an air of farewell about the occasion. But for once the police had reckoned without my aunt. She rose, and in thanking them all heartily, said that this tribute had put new life into her and she now felt ready for another ten years' work with them.

Time passed, and my aunt was rising ninety when she confessed to us that she wished that she might witness her own funeral. There would undoubtedly be a police band, police singing her favourite hymns, the Chief Constable reading the lesson. Since her active participation in the event was out of the question, she went over the ceremony in detail with the Chief Constable, and derived great pleasure from discussing arrangements which were, in due course, carried out according to plan.

Letters

WANTED, A 'CELLO HOLDER

Fitting a 'cello into a car is tricky, as a musical aunt of mine has found to her cost. For this reason when she decided to buy a new car suitable for driving to rehearsals, she asked me to help. The outcome was a trip round the motor showrooms that revealed not only the shortcomings of many cars as 'cello

THE HORSE LED TO THE WATER

holders but also the resentment of their salesmen to criticisms or suggestions.

My aunt's present car is a 1957 Singer Gazelle and she can just tuck the 'cello between its back and front seats, provided that she slides the driving seat right forward. Unfortunately, inserting the 'cello is rather like threading a needle, and when in place it disqualifies one of the back seats from use. Furthermore the 'cello case has been chewing slowly into the back of the front seat, and also abrading the roof lining. Armed, therefore, with an empty 'cello case, and glad we were not shopping in Chicago where it would immediately have been recognised as concealment for a machine-gun, we set off to find a new car into which it would fit comfortably.

In the first showroom we met a salesman so solid and superior that he should have been selling Rolls-Royces instead of mid-dling cars for suburbanites. He managed to get the 'cello case into one model by turning it (the 'cello) upside down and blocking both back seats. This provoked me to suggest there was more room in a Mini-Minor, and to ask why the motor makers did not design a medium-sized car with the same rigorous attention to space planning. " People wouldn't buy it, sir," he replied self-confidently. " If you put the back seats of a medium-sized car over the rear wheels, as in the Mini-Minor, you would get a poor ride."

The next showroom offered an amiable young man and a Wolseley 15/60, into both the boot and the back-seat foot-well of which the 'cello case fitted satisfactorily. Only the increased size of the new Wolseley over the old Singer was unfavourable.

At the last showroom we encountered a powerful built, blue-suited junior tycoon. He had several models of the same car to offer, and made much of the glories of two-tone styling. I asked if there were any difference among the engines of the various models. " Oh no, sir," he said proudly, " they're all the same." My suggestion that a bigger oil cleaner or disc brakes would be better value than multi-coloured paint earned me such a glance as a Communist might get at a Tory tea-party.

Salesmen ought not to get cross about customer demands for such reasonable items as better space planning. They should channel such information back to the makers. Think what a splendid car B.M.C. could make with their B-range engine and a scaled up Issigonis body. They could make a utility model, and one with Wolseley class finishes. Certainly if they did, my 'cello-playing aunt would buy one.

T. M. P. BENDIXSON

A 'CELLO IN THE CAR

Sir,—Many years ago a small group of musicians who met at my house on Sunday mornings expressed a wish to play Schubert's "Trout" Quintet. This required the enlistment of a double bass player and an appeal was put out for volunteers. A gentleman telephoned offering his services for the following Sunday morning. The news that we had obtained the services of a double bass player caused some excitement among my musical friends, and there was much speculation as to how he would arrive. We conjured up a picture of a man trudging up the drive carrying the huge instrument on his back somewhat reminiscent of Atlas. How wrong we were! He arrived on a motor-cycle combination with the double bass resting where the sidecar should have been, and it wasn't even fastened in any way. Possibly this is a solution to the problem for Mr. Bendixson's 'cello-playing aunt.—Yours truly,

JOHN HOYLE

THREE DOUBLE BASSES

Sir,—Some twelve years ago I used to carry a double bass on a motor-cycle sidecar chassis. Later I bought an old Lanchester 10 saloon. In this car I have carried three double basses, and on longer journeys two double basses and a passenger. Once, after a performance of the Sadler's Wells Theatre Ballet, when a harpist could not get a taxi, I conveyed her to the station, with harp and luggage.—Yours truly, RONALD SMITH

Sir,—A friend who owns a Berkeley three-wheeler has perfected a method by which her 'cello and a passenger may be transported simultaneously, it being understood that the latter acts as 'cello rack or holder.

The passenger takes her place in the front seat and stretches out horizontally, head hanging back limply and to the right. The 'cello is eased into the car until it projects over her left shoulder, then lowered gently to rest on the passenger's toes. It is held firmly in this position by an almost involuntary embrace.—Yours sincerely,   MARGARET TURNER

A 'CELLO IN THE CAR

Sir,—I, like Mr. Bendixson's aunt, am a 'cellist. And I know the answer to his problem: it is an estate car. My 'cello has been transported in a Bedford Dormobile and now in an Austin A55 Countryman. These are both fairly large, but I have seen on occasion two 'cellos and four people in a Standard Ten Companion.—Yours sincerely,   ROBERT B. L. OWEN

Sir,—I appreciate the difficulty of Mr. Bendixson's aunt in finding a car large enough to take her 'cello. Not so long ago, however, I saw a local enthusiast transporting his 'cello with great ease in an old hearse.—Yours sincerely, ERIC JONES

Sir,—Mr. Bendixson's aunt can be thankful she did not play a double bass. Ownership of this instrument involves the musician in endless transport difficulties, to say nothing of the ridicule of being found often stuck fast half-way through an ordinary door. I have, however, found a car capable of holding a full-sized instrument with little difficulty and still leaving room for three people. The new Hillman Minx saloon has to be entered by the instrument head first through the offside rear door, the nearside front door being previously opened. With the head thus thrust over the back of the front seat (a final twist to the bulging rear end will see it out through the diagonally

opposite door) there is room to swing the bottom in and up on to the rear window ledge. One then has to double round to the front door and adjust the head so that it fits snugly into the front passenger's shelf under the dashboard. Both doors are then ready to be closed. One passenger can still sit in the middle of the front seat with the driver, the remaining passenger shares the back seat with the bulky part of the instrument, which lies across the backs of the two seats. All praise to Rootes.—Yours sincerely,
K. W. CORDEN

Sir,—As Mr. Bendixson's 'cello-playing aunt I feel it is time I came to life if only to express my admiration for the ingenuity of double-bass players in solving their transport problems. However, I have now happily solved mine by buying the Wolseley 15/60, into the boot of which my 'cello fits easily in its Paxman " Carrilite " case complete with large Dunlopillo cushion to rest on. This enables me to take three passengers with their violins or violas.—Yours sincerely,
(Mrs.) BARBARA M. BENDIXSON

Edward Greenfield

BEECHAM IN REHEARSAL

" I'm all against rehearsal—a most tedious and unnecessary affair." That is the *obiter dictum* of Sir Thomas Beecham on a fascinating rehearsal disc that has just appeared (H.M.V. ALP 1874), and needless to say most of what one overhears in the rehearsals on the disc completely belies that ironic remark. But in a way it is double irony. What will astound most listeners, particularly in the rehearsals of Haydn symphonies, is the almost

complete absence of detailed rehearsing. Beecham creates the
mood with exhortations and jokes beforehand (the Cup Final
a favourite topic in these particular sessions) and then just lets
his players enjoy themselves, interrupting them only rarely.

It would be very easy from this to take Beecham's irony
seriously, to conclude that he relied on love rather than technical
accomplishment, that he was really an amateur—a view that
his detractors often tried to voice. But Beecham himself
provides the answer—tongue still in cheek but only just. "After
a very long experience I have discovered that the only way to
have a really living and vital performance is not to rehearse.
Then everyone will be struggling hard in the music and that
makes a great tension, you see. I assure you it affects the public
that way: they don't know what's going on, but they feel
there's something unusual." In Haydn symphonies at least,
works which the Royal Philharmonic players could perform
standing on their heads, technical analysis is largely superfluous.
Beforehand, as the record shows, Beecham is very ready to
clarify the text in detail, even to accept suggestions from his
players, but he realised that overanalysis, overpreparation only
sucks the life out of a performance, particularly in the recording
studio where there is no audience tension to help the players.

On the second side the rehearsal is of Mozart's *Entführung*,
and there Beecham's detailed methods become clearer. He
roars like a mad thing during Osmin's fierce aria " O, wie will
Ich triumphieren," rampaging at the poor flautist and generally
jumping around to get everyone in the proper mood before
they give the performance of their lives. Every last joke (many
of them rather flat when repeated cold) has its purpose. " At
the very end there's a hell of a row—is that clear?" he shouts,
and a hell of a row there is to the greater glory of Mozart. It
is all enormous fun, a great personal performance by the maestro,
the rehearsing method plainly intuitive rather than analytic.
But if anyone thinks that on that account Beecham was an
amateur he misses the whole point. Bruno Walter's recorded
rehearsal " Birth of a Great Performance " was fascinating in

its detail, but this much more is a human document, less helpful to musicians perhaps but immensely important if one is to understand Beecham's genius.

David Holden

SAVOYARDS UNDISMAYED

"House Full." For eighty-six years, from end to end of Britain and from coast to coast of the United States, this most coveted piece of theatrical décor has been displayed by the D'Oyly Carte Opera Company in sublime disregard of the ordinary laws of change. Two world wars and the decay of the British Empire, Freud and Marx and Rutherford and Einstein, the welfare state, and the affluent society have erased the world in which it all began. But Gilbert and Sullivan and the D'Oyly Carte are with us still, three in one and one in three, a theatrical Holy Trinity of the English-speaking world.

Three generations of D'Oyly Cartes have grown rich on the profits of this remarkable collaboration. Four generations of singers have won affection, fame, and a rather modest fortune in its service. Hotels and theatres have sprouted from its generous loins. And for millions of people it signifies the quintessential joy of the theatre, something between Shakespeare and Peter Pan and—as any Savoyard will tell you—sweeter, fruitier, and more lovable by far than either.

For all these years the traditional blend of sentiment, wit and satire established by William Schwenck Gilbert and Arthur Seymour Sullivan has been preserved in spirit, if not in every detail, through the exclusive right of Richard D'Oyly Carte and his descendants to the production of the Gilbert and Sullivan operettas. But change cannot for ever be denied; and last night in spite of petitions to Parliament by half a million Savoyards, who fought to preserve the trinity intact to eternity much as Rome once battled for its exclusive rights to Christianity, the last protecting copyright ended and the doors of the church were opened to the Protestants. Fifty years after Gilbert's death in 1911, his words are now free for anyone to kick around.

Sullivan's music has been free from copyright for eleven years, so to-night the reformation begins, with the Sadler's Wells presentation of *Iolanthe* at the Stratford Memorial Theatre, under Mr. Frank Hauser—the first professional Gilbert and Sullivan production in Britain that has not been undertaken by the D'Oyly Carte. Others are to come—Sir Tyrone Guthrie is bringing to London in February his Canadian productions of *H.M.S. Pinafore* and *The Pirates of Penzance,* and the Bristol opera school is even cobbling up a new opera called *Engaged* from an old play by Gilbert and some tunes of Sullivan's, to show us that the D'Oyly Carte have not squeezed the repertoire dry.

The Savoyards, however, show no dismay at these intrusions. They were present in force last week at the Savoy Theatre, their attendances at *Princess Ida*—never one of the most popular works in the canon—broke all records. On Saturday night, with the "House Full" notice at the door and half a D'Oyly Carte company's administrative staff on-stage with the singers to take a series of rapturously insistent curtain calls, they joined hands throughout the theatre, strangers and friends alike, laughing, tearful and utterly loyal, and raised their hesitant British voices in " Auld Lang Syne."

In the stalls were seventeen present and former members of the company, breathlessly recognised by the devotees around them, and themselves the guests of one of the greatest devotees of all —Mr. John Stell, art master at Chester City Grammar School, who was born on 31st December, 1911, and whose fiftieth birthday therefore coincided with the expiration of the Gilbert copyright. For Mr. Stell, this was one of the great moments of his life. Ever since his father took him to see *Iolanthe* at the Manchester Opera House in 1926—the year that Malcolm Sargent first conducted a London season for the company—he has devoted part of his life to the D'Oyly Carte. He has entertained their singers in his home, followed their tours to half the towns of England and decorated with Gilbert and Sullivan motifs the birthday, wedding and christening cakes for dozens of company celebrations. On Saturday night, with his friends in the stalls, and forty guests at a party afterwards in the Pinafore room of the Savoy Hotel, he was plainly as near to his seventh heaven as any mortal ever could be. "Look at them," he murmured, "these are the golden years, the vintage people."

There was little Nellie Briarcliffe, who sang as soubrette with the legendary Henry Lytton and last appeared in 1929 at the opening of the new Savoy Theatre. There were Marjorie Eyre, soubrette of a later era, who stayed with D'Oyly Carte for twenty-two years, and her husband Leslie Rands, principal baritone for just as long, and John Dean who was singing Cyril in *Princess Ida* thirty years ago, and half a dozen others who each served the company for at least a score of years. And there were Isidore Godfrey, still conducting after thirty-six years on the D'Oyly Carte rostrum and Mrs. "Cis" Blain, wardrobe mistress since 1922 and still going gay and strong.

There were the youngsters too, from the present company, for this was a family reunion, and much more of a birthday party than a wake. Nobody was shedding any tears, except of sentiment and affection and everybody thought the competition that will face the company from to-day should do it nothing but good. "This isn't the beginning of the end," said Mr. Frederic Lloyd, the general manager, bravely, "it's only the beginning."

Among them all Mr. Stell moved in a quiet haze of happiness, like a man alternately amazed by his own temerity and bemused

by his success. In response to the cry of " Happy birthday ! "
at midnight, he revealed at last the measure of his devotion to
the Savoyard legend. A lifelong collector of antique silver
spoons, he had, he told us, sold his spoons to pay for the party.
" This is my present to myself for a lifetime. I can buy more
spoons—but I can never buy this again."

And so to the future. Can the Holy Trinity survive? There
is no sign yet of their demise, or even of their decay. Sir
Malcolm Sargent is back on the Savoy rostrum this season, as
happy with Gilbert and Sullivan now as he was thirty and forty
years ago and impressed anew with the high spirit of a company
that seems to him now absurdly young, but still manages to
retain the old tradition. Amateurs up and down the country
average nearly 1000 productions a year of Gilbert and Sullivan
in the established manner. The D'Oyly Carte has 3000 applica-
tions on its books for places in the company. And when you
look at the audiences that stream out of the Savoy Theatre you
know it is going to take more than a few new productions elsewhere to shake their loyalty, at least for the next generation.

They are not a fashionable audience. They are predominantly
middle class and decidedly suburban with plum-coloured
waistcoats and club ties and sensible tweed coats and plastic
overshoes. They are bent and elderly parties, nursing their
memories, and youngsters just discovering what music and the
theatre are about. They do not hear great singing, or see fine
acting or exquisite productions; but what they want, and
what to their delight they seem to get, is good, clean and skilful
fun, with a hearty dash of sentiment and a bit of vulgarity
thrown in. It is a superbly English mixture that the trinity
provide, for a supremely English crowd. After " Auld Lang
Syne " on Saturday night, the house sang—as few other theatre
audiences ever do—" God Save the Queen " as if they meant it.
As long as people go on doing that, Gilbert and Sullivan and
the D'Oyly Carte will probably be all right. No " seats at all
prices " for the trinity, I fancy—just " House Full " in the
established tradition.

Neville Cardus

A COMPLIMENT TO DEBUSSY

In Debussy's centenary year the Vienna State Opera has paid the first tribute to the unique genius of *Pelléas and Mélisande* by means of a truly beautiful presentation—an evocation rather—in French, conducted by Herbert von Karajan. Before the event you might think of Karajan as the last conductor to enter the habitation of silences which is the world of this music-drama. For isn't Karajan a man of our modern world, a musical apotheosis of it, with a flair for glamour, closed eyed in his personal appeal, master of the spectacular, and a sort of Svengali brought up to date, an exhibitionist *au fond*? What is Karajan to *Pelléas* or *Pelléas* to Karajan?

This Vienna performance gives the astonishing answer. Karajan goes to the heart of the work and plays on the superb orchestra—yes, superb—yet with penetration and subtlety of nuance. Debussy does not allow the conductor of *Pelléas* an extensive dynamic range. But Karajan, within the prescribed gamut, obtains a wide variety and reach of tone—a pianissimo which is warm and eloquent, not merely a matter of diminished sound. Also the climaxes were beautifully proportionate, the texture fine, and intense at the right moments. Karajan conducted Debussy with obvious devotion. Moreover, he knows the difficult score—difficult to memorise—apparently by heart. More important, he responds to the inner drama and does not meander in a loosely controlled wash of modulating harmony. He kept the thematic connections and relevances clear and pertinent. Such an interpretation made nonsense of two fallacies about *Pelléas* (but they will persist, all the same!).

First it is still taken much for granted that *Pelléas* is not a

" dramatic " opera, that though the music ravishes the senses, the characters and action are unreal, without flesh and blood, shadows in a passing dream. To my own way of thinking, it is the average opera that is " unreal," undramatic, a convention of pasteboard characters non-existent outside the theatre. *Pelléas and Mélisande* is a drama of the inner, the really " real " world, a drama of implications, of psychological conflicts too secret to concentrate into the obvious attitudes of life, exhibitory and active. Here is the drama of things that cannot be spoken, passions, fleeting happinesses, and eternal sorrows, not of the transient day, but of enveloping night. Sometimes the suspenses are quite unbearable, the music holds breath. Mélisande is so much " alive," fragilely " alive "—that I often think that a poor performance of the part might do it a physical hurt. In fact a poor performance of *Pelléas* seems to me to inflict a pain on the score which, surely, it feels. " Atmospheric? " " Vague? " —why, the score is a marvel of fineness of touch, of imaginative aptness and relevance.

The most isolated tone in the woodwind is a cry in the night. A string tremolo is fateful. The night is omnipresent. A gleam of instrumental colour is a dramatic visitation—not a mere piece of orchestration. " Abstractions "—it is Titurel, not Arkel, who is " symbolic " and not " dramatic." Arkel is old-age poignantly particularised. The music by which Debussy gives him grief and wisdom is bowed in its sombre slow-moving phrases and harmonies, so pathetically in contrast to the golden-throated lyricism of Pelléas; the innocent youngness—but older in herself than she knows—of Mélisande; and the simple manliness of Golaud, that unfortunate horseman.

All these people are pulsatingly themselves. But we see them from a distance: they move in a permanent timeless dimension. It is ourselves, watching and overhearing from *our* clock-measured, active, merely phenomenal world, that are unreal. Debussy doesn't describe, he evokes. His orchestra, unlike Wagner's, does not *point*. It covers everything, a veiled un-heard, yet heard, presence—omnipresent. A score entirely original which came from nowhere and has—greatest sign of its genius—had no "progressive influences." It is a prosaic view of a work of art that it serves a purpose in a "development" or evolving series logical and sequential as science.

I can make no better compliment to Karajan, the Vienna State Opera Orchestra, and the singers than to say that all these intrinsic qualities of the work, not generally understood, were brought home. I confess that more than once I came near to tears, eyes as misted as the beautiful stage settings of Gunther Schneider Siemssen. The opening forest scene was an endless world of high trees, alluring and mysterious. The fountain in the park was an enchantment, with the orchestra at the beginning spray irridescent in the bright light, all seen and heard in a reflection from afar. What magic of tone-chemistry is here! Different but in perfect harmony was the grotto scene, dark and the darkness more and more revealed when a glow of the outer night entered. The settings mingled with Maeterlinck and Debussy indivisibly; the whisperings of wind, echoes and shadows, all the invisible shaping powers in a love tragedy that comes to a cruel climax because of the chattering of an innocent child, Golaud's son, Yniold.

To give the right stage gestures and movements to this opera sets an almost insoluble problem. Operatic attitudes and any rhetorical action of body or arm would be blasphemous. On the other hand a stilted rigidity should be avoided at all costs. In this performance a more or less happy balance was found, though Eberhard Waechter's admirable Golaud became over-emphatic and even a little spasmodic and melodramatic in his scene with Yniold. But his singing and acting on the whole were eloquent and natural. The voice of Henri Gui was Pelléas's own, and I shall not soon forget the impulse and ecstasy of his rapturous "*Je les nous*" outburst. No melody in *Pelléas and Mélisande* ? The scene is full of melody, but it is melody refined to an essence of the French language and its own intonations.

As Mélisande, Hilde Gueden was extremely engaging to ear

and eye alike, her song-speech nuanced sensitively, her voice in the proper tonal scale. Perhaps a Mélisande too immediately lovable. But this was highly intelligent singing by an artist of extraordinary versatility. Elisabeth Hoengen, as Genevieve, made the magnificent most of her one great opportunity when she intoned the heartbreaking recitative of the letter: "*Un soir, je l'ai trouvée tout en pleurs.*" Here is another artist of fine musical and poetic susceptibilities. The Arkel of Nicola Zaccaria had patriarchal gravity and a voice maybe a little too assured and firm. We of course don't want an Arkel babbling, but even without whiskers we should know him at sight as a man well past the age of, say, Pogner.

The orchestra, though, provided the long-to-be-remembered experience. It was a pretty irony to hear this moving presentation of a music drama in which Mélisande never closes her eyes, or seldom, directed by a conductor who doesn't often open them. A triumph of Karajan, the Vienna, all concerned, in a worthy tribute to the most sensitively poetic of all composers of the last century and a half.

Mary Crozier

MRS. DALE'S DEPARTURE

I guess there will be a lot of up hill and down dale before the doctor and his wife move from Virginia Lodge to the four-bedroom house in that gloomy industrial town. Yesterday, the first day of *The Dales* was mildly jazzed up at the start with a replacement for that old-worlde harp, but we got little further than breaking the news to Mother-in-law and getting her over the shock. Mrs. Freeman took it in a predictably hoity-toity way, with many a plaintive cry about Gwen and the boys. The doctor's prospects in the new partnership seemed less vital than whether Mrs. F. would agree to go with them. Already the hint has been gently dropped that they could get her a nice little flat in a block nearby—not for *old* people, you know, but for people living alone. But Mrs. Freeman may not go. She might want to stay. After all she's got the shop and Gwen and the boys.

Dr. Dale has also broken the news to his young partners, Ivor and Lionel. Ivor is envious, but must think of Joanna settled at Parkwood Hill with the baby and her friends. He longs to follow Dr. Dale to an industrial practice. I have a suspicion that the gods who decree the changing course of mortal life in radio serials are seized by a burning desire to make practice in industrial districts seem more attractive. Are not the Archers dear to the eye of the Min of Ag? Could it be that a solicitous Min of Health broods over the fortunes of Dr. Dale?

Meanwhile the change is not without its placebo. Mrs. Dale will be near a shopping centre without cars. Town planning, you see. Up to date. There will have to be a higher fence between the gardens so that the dog can't jump over. (Glad they are keeping the dog.) Their new neighbour will be one of the works managers. Different social stratum? I can't foresee whether this will make everyone more like us or more like them. At present the Dales are just the same old sleepy old Dales, the perfect lullaby, getting me faintly worried about the fuss Mrs. Freeman will make when they sell the larger furniture. I don't think I'll listen that day. *Plus ça* threatens to change *plus c'est* the *même dose.*

Mary Crozier

WAITING FOR PILKOT

Italian peasants slowly, laboriously learning to write, utterly absorbed, from television lessons; poor families, wide-eyed, watching the communal set as the crackle of Western gunfire echoes in the tropical night; luxurious little American children lolling in the bath as they watch the Western in the bathroom —these were some of the pictures that remained in the memory from *Television and the World,* Richard Cawston's brilliant documentary film reviewing television in nine countries, which was repeated by the B.B.C. last night.

Over eighty countries now have television and one or two more start every day. Though this film did not survey them all, it gave a striking impression of the two extremes at which television operates, and which come into dramatic contrast whenever one considers television as an influence in people's lives. One thing it cannot be, and that is neutral. It is not just simply a means of giving entertainment or news. On the one hand it can be, as in the Italian lessons for the illiterate, an unmatched means of teaching. On the other hand it can purvey the packaged culture which, as one saw the faces of people all round the world reacting in fascinated awe to the American gunplay, made the film seem a sad and disturbing document. In the middle, and very important, but always for a minority so far, even in the most developed countries with the most television, are the sensible, serious uses of television for drama, current affairs, the arts, and education generally rather than specifically.

Control of television varies from the direct State authority through the public corporation to the free-for-all of commercialism. Correspondingly television will be used largely for propaganda, much of it implicit as in the U.S.S.R., at one extreme, and at the other for advertising, which can have admirable by-products in the form of programmes. In the end the shape and quality of what people see will always depend on the ultimate authority behind the screen. And at the receiving end, the effect it has depends very much on the single individual who sees it. Who is to say what picture of far away places or what serial of a book may awaken a new interest? And who is to say that, on the contrary, a constant diet of the silly, the superficial, the ephemeral, and the sickly (which describes much of television) does not make the mind dwell in a false shadow world?

Then there is the question of violence. Surveys and statistics in Great Britain and the United States have never shown so far that children and young people are influenced by the amount of crime, shooting and fighting, slogging and sudden death, that they see, but this is a thing that statistics cannot show. Common sense would suggest that the unprecedented amount of this kind of thing brought every night of the year into the home must affect the climate in which the mind grows up. In this country the B.B.C. has applied a definite code to eliminate violence at certain times, the I.T.V. has improved on its earlier standards. But there is something inherent in television's demand for action which makes wrong more interesting than right, and you cannot fill the hundreds of hours of television with the uneventful annals of the good.

In Britain "Waiting for Pilkington" has become an occupational disease. We are all in some sense waiting for Pilkot. Deluged with evidence and pressed upon by pressure groups, Pilkington will emerge this year with The Report. Are we to get one more television channel, two more channels, no more channels, another commercial channel, another B.B.C. channel, a new educational channel? Some of the talk about a complete educational service has been rather disingenuous. Certainly television has enormous potentialities for education, pioneered by the B.B.C.'s pilot scheme for schools lessons which grew naturally from their excellent sound broadcasts, and then followed by I.T.V. The idea is of course recognised also in the B.B.C.'s many general programmes (and some of I.T.V.'s) which are educational in the widest sense.

But there is a limit on hours, enforced by the Postmaster-General, which makes the expansion of educational television impossible, and this will first have to be relaxed. Even then we should have to ask seriously how far a complete educational television service in this country would be feasible, and at what levels it could usefully operate. Our idea of what the undergraduate wants is rather different from that in the United States, for instance. At the other end of the scale we do not need the elementary lessons that are useful in an illiterate country. And our huge, solid, comfortable, working middle class has not so far shown itself dead keen on the more serious television features, and might prefer, no doubt for its own good reasons, *Bootsie and Snudge* to biology and *Coronation Street* to the classics.

The autumn of the year saw the jubilee of B.B.C. television, twenty-five years of a service which deserved acclaim, since it is certainly the best in the world, and has never lost sight of its threefold charge to entertain, to educate, and to inform. These words have a priggish sound, perhaps, but they serve to describe a system on which one can see, for example, Shaw's *Candida* or all the chronicle plays of Shakespeare; *Monitor, Panorama,* and *To-night*; the Maigret stories; *The Black and White Minstrel Show, Look,* and the Grand National, besides constant comment on Parliament and politics. The end of the year also saw I.T.V. being slowly denuded of many popular features by the dispute with its artists. *Emergency—Ward* 10 was an early casualty; the cosiness and tragedy of Oxbridge is now but a memory. Old films fill more and more of the gaps in the ranks. The B.B.C. creeps more often, like a temporarily neglected but staunch uncle, into the Top Twenty.

No television is perfect and we could all make a choice of what we would like to see less of. I should like to see less interviewing that tries to harry the subject over the sidelines and prevent him from sticking to the object of the exercise. And since Ministers are always expected to appear on television, but everybody knows they cannot say anything more than everybody knows already, I should like to see them allowed to voice their diplomatic platitudes without being pressed to say what everybody knows they can't. I should also like to see very much less of the latest irritating technique (specially bad in *To-night*) of giving a long biography of someone we're going to see before telling us who it is.

I should like to see more arts programmes; more about pictures, to which the moving camera can lend a new enchantment; more about sculpture, more about old buildings, and much more about architecture, for which television seems to me the heaven sent and largely neglected medium. I should like to see more definite series of world drama; plays on television at present seem to me rather a muddle. And I should like to see more science but not so much tarted up as in the past.

For purely personal viewing I could fix this sort of list. Afternoon: steeplechasing, best of all winter television sports. Pause for quiet till 6.0. Might even read a book. Then news, followed by *To-night*, *Roving Report*, and something funny. Pause for a meal to be eaten *without* television. Then a play (perhaps one of the *Age of Kings*); a hard-hitting documentary on politics, *not* on drink, disease or divorce—I've seen so many; then a spot of nature with *Look* or *Survival*; then an interview with somebody like Dame Edith Sitwell (I don't insist on it being called *Face to Face* because Mr. Freeman, as an archetypal TV personality, rather frightens me). Then a Maigret programme, followed by a talk by Sir Kenneth Clarke about a picture. A tiny bit more news? Well, anyway, the R.A.C. report on road works with its little maps to show a bridge being rebuilt in Devon or an obstruction in Midlothian. These take me far afield. A long evening? Not so long as most, for in this

146

evening that will never happen, there has been no writing, and there was a meal without pictures winking at me across the plate.

John Rosselli

AN ENCOUNTER WITH NARCISSUS

When a British intellectual monthly sells close on thirty thousand copies something is happening which we thought had gone out with the decline of the great Victorian reviews. *Encounter*, which publishes next week its one hundredth number, has trebled its circulation in the eight years since it was launched and doubled it in the past four. Although it sells at 3s. 6d. it is not far behind a ninepenny weekly like the *Spectator*. Some of its articles on class, sex, or royalty have had a lot of free publicity, but they are for the most part several thousand words long, unrelieved by illustrations, and addressed to highly educated readers. What kind of a magazine is it that enjoys such unlooked for success?

Before discussing what *Encounter* is like one had better say what it is not. Since the first issue came out in October 1953 with a ruthless, penetrating article by Leslie Fiedler on the Rosenbergs, the reputation of the magazine among many British intellectuals has been that of an ice-making battery in the cold war, run with American money in the anti-Communist cause. Its real failings are, I think, other; they have to do with British not with American-inspired attitudes. But there is just enough truth in the image to make it worth a look.

Encounter is an offshoot of the Congress for Cultural Freedom,

147

itself founded during the most rigid period of the cold war, between the Berlin blockade and the death of Stalin. The congress is "an independent world-wide organisation of scholars, writers, scientists, and artists" ranging—the words are those of Melvin J. Lasky, *Encounter*'s co-editor—"from the non-Fascist Right to the non-Communist Left." Its honorary presidents include Reinhold Niebuhr, Salvador de Madariaga, and Jayaprakash Narayan. Its office in Paris, under its secretary-general, Nicolas Nabokov, organises congresses, seminars, and other international palavers; it helps to rouse support for imprisoned Hungarian intellectuals and the like; and it administers a few "para-academic" fellowships for writers. Finally, the congress sponsors or has ties with sixteen periodicals in twelve countries.

All this is paid for by American foundations, chiefly the Ford Foundation. Recent attempts to enlist European support now that Europe is prosperous have come to nothing outside Switzerland; the trouble is said to be chiefly that in much of Europe "culture" is hopelessly entangled with the Church and State conflict. *Encounter* too depends on the foundations to make up its loss. Unlike some other quality periodicals, it cannot translate rising circulation into profitable advertising revenue, no doubt because a lot of its readers have more intellect than money.

For the rest, *Encounter*'s editors, Mr. Lasky and Mr. Stephen Spender, have personal ties with other congress luminaries abroad. The editors of the "loose federation" of congress magazines sometimes take articles from each other; they may club together, for instance, to send Arthur Koestler to the Far East, but because national tastes differ they do it only desultorily.

When *Encounter* first came out, announcing that Stalin's death and the East German revolt between them signified "the death of the Marxist-Leninist creed," it did show a marked anti-Communist temper. But this never swamped the magazine; it is still less noticeable now that communism, both internally and internationally, is in a less desperate stage. *Encounter*'s feature "From the Other Shore"—giving news of Eastern Europe—does suggest a certain obsession with the Communist world; yet the last instalment, on Ilya Ehrenburg, showed exemplary balance.

In that first number Mr. Spender and his then co-editor, Mr. Irving Kristol, said that the paper would be international in content and Anglo-American in editorship; it would discuss such problems of our time as nationalism, hunger, and the reconciliation of equality with liberty; finally, it would regard "literature and the arts as being values in themselves, in need of no ulterior justification." A rough judgment might be that *Encounter* has been only stutteringly international but fully and usefully Anglo-American; that it has discussed ideas and current affairs with great vigour; but that literature and the arts have come off second best.

Encounter has one-seventh of its circulation in America; it also circulates in India and Japan and takes a good deal of notice of both countries (Mr. Nehru is said to have sanctioned publication of *Lolita* on the strength of Lionel Trilling's *Encounter* article). Yet it is the work of people like Dwight Macdonald, David Riesman, Edward Shils, Mary McCarthy, Marcus Cunliffe—Americans or concerned with America—that has given the magazine a sense of international exchange, rather than the odd piece on "the literary situation in Japan," the isolated story or poem by a Mexican or Italian, or the report on some international congress by a peripatetic French "*cher Maître*." In all this *Encounter* probably does no more than reflect the spirit of the time.

Mr. Spender and Mr. Lasky might say the same thing of the balance the paper has held between ideas and the arts, between comment and creation, between dissection and representation. It has leaned heavily towards ideas, comment, and dissection, so much so that fiction has of late years almost vanished. Mr. Spender says that good creative work is hard to come by and people in England are anyhow most interested in "their own condition." True, but it seems characteristic of *Encounter* that although it has taken up new writers who have arrived with a bang it has printed not a scene from a John Osborne play but Osborne's muddled attack on the Establishment, not part of Kingsley Amis's work in progress but a story with a dog-eared look about it, only a swatch of Colin MacInnes's poetic evocations of teenagers to a yard of his documentary raw material. "We've had to hold out Herbert Read's poem again to make room for Jo Grimond on the monarchy," Mr. Spender said recently. Poetry is not urgent.

Against this the paper has had the merit of keeping to a "central" path without falling into the hands of a coterie. But as a review of ideas it has been central in a livelier sense. Articles like those of Anthony Crosland on the future of the Labour movement, Nancy Mitford on U and non-U, Michael Young on meritocracy, Wayland Young on prostitution, are what has set people talking and thinking and incidentally raised circulation (though Isaiah Berlin on Russian thought and Trevor-Roper blasting Toynbee may keep better). Whether the things that really stirred the intellectual British public in the 1950s will look well in future is another question. There seems about them a strong tinge of narcissism—of a society's minute self-absorption. *Encounter* can say that it has shrewdly held up the mirror to Narcissus. To try to tear the mirror away would no doubt require another sort of publication.

Francis Iles

CRIMINAL RECORDS

Mrs. Agatha Christie is our nearest approach to perpetual motion. And not only does she never stop, but she drops the ball into the cup nearly every time; and if one is sometimes reminded of those automatic machines where one pulls a handle and out pops the finished product, that is a compliment to the automatic machine and not by any means a reflection on Mrs. Christie. For the latest tug on the Christie handle produces a product which is not only up to standard but even above it. *The Pale Horse* is in fact the best sample from this particular factory for some time, and that is saying plenty (Collins, 15s.). The black magic theme is handled in a masterly and sinister fashion, and to give away what lay behind it would be unforgivable. This is a book which nobody (repeat, nobody) should miss.

I always enjoy the work of Mrs. E. H. Clements, who can construct a complicated plot to rival anyone's and outdistance most (though I do wish at times that Alister Woodhead would not be *quite* so ungracious, especially in his dealings with young and distressed females). In *A Note of Enchantment* (Hodder, 15s.) we get some very solid and rewarding reading, with a scene that ranges from the Ministry of Scientific Research in London to St. Jean-de-Luz, and plenty of excitement thrown in: in fact a really top-class thriller, only let down, as usual in this kind of story, by the machine-made and computer-like ending. Just the same remarks about the dénouement can be applied to *My Brother's Killer,* by D. M. Devine (Crime Club, 12s. 6d.). Here is a genuine detective story, proceeding by the successive revelations of concealed actions by various interested parties. Perhaps the police procedure is not all that it might be, but with these reservations this is a most promising and competent first novel.

Besides Mrs. Christie there are three Old Hands still writing real detective stories more or less on the classical pattern; and by a coincidence all three of them publish a new book for this list. The three are George Bellairs, with *The Body in the Dumb River* (Gifford, 10s. 6d.), pleasant as usual, not too far-fetched, and with plenty of this author's own very individual quirks; *Corpse in the Congo,* by Belton Cobb (Allen, 13s. 6d.), also a pleasant work, though it would be a pity to make Detective-Constable Bryan Armitage such an ass that he would never have been taken into the detective branch at all; and *The Case of the Dead Man Gone,* by Christopher Bush (Macdonald, 12s. 6d.), containing an almost too manufactured plot, with everyone double-crossing everyone else—and why should it be left to a reviewer to spot that a line is missing on page 105 and others are all out of place?

Finally *Requiem for a Schoolgirl*, by American Ivan T. Ross (Heinemann, 15s.), and any schoolteacher in this country who ever contemplates going on strike should be given this book to read for his homework. He will then see that he has never had it so bad as did Mr. Ross's Ben Gordon (who incidentally has to punch a time-clock just like a factory hand). This latest instalment of the American Way of Life suggests that any pupil in a mixed American high school is likely to be a call-girl, a dope addict, a gangster's moll, a thug, or a teen-age prostitute. Well, well, well. Three Cheers for the Red, White and Blue, in spite of everything

Philip Hope-Wallace

MOLLYWOLLY DOODLINGS

More about Shaw's Mollywolly-tompkins, alias Mollikins, alias Mrs. Lawrence (or Laurence) Tompkins deceased of Atlanta, Georgia (*Shaw and Molly Tompkins:* Blond, 25s.). More than enough? I don't want to sound sour. She seems to have been one of those voracious lifewomen and it is rather touching the way she bulldozed herself into Shaw's paternal affection and friendship, and into Charlotte's forbearance (though Mrs. Shaw did tell her at a picnic, which seems to have been a more than usual terrible example of that uncomfortable style of refreshment, that her behaviour was unladylike). The blurb expresses amazement that Mollywolly did not feature in the " official " lives of the great man. But is it so surprising? She really seems to have been an extraordinarily tiresome person in some ways and under the courtesy of Shaw's many cards and letters, and interwoven with the advice which the old childless celebrity naturally found it flattering to impart, there is a perceptibly defensive tone.

Shaw's cards and letters to Molly Tompkins were carefully kept, and recently we had them in facsimile in a large, handsome, and, one had rather hoped, exhaustive album, collected and edited by Peter Tompkins, son of the lady (actress, paintress, Italophile expatriate). But if Shaw kept her letters they have never been found. Does that deter the son? Not a jot. With the aid of remembered talks, " tape recordings," recollections from his own childhood, he has worked up a book which purports to tell Molly's side of the story in detail, and which I fear me will one day be turned into a two-act theatrical ding dong like *Dear Liar* from the Mrs. Campbell letters.

So here it all is, the thoughts which possessed her, the cold in the head which afflicted her at the very moment when rat-tat-tat came that kindest of cards from Shaw saying—I paraphrase—"I am so interested that you are doing this and that. Don't make a fool of yourself and of course if you *are* coming into this part of the world by all means look us up." Some people will think every letter that Shaw wrote worth glancing at. Mr. Tompkins has been clever at eking out the material and naturally the lady being his mother, he writes with vivid affection of all her ups and downs and vicissitudes in Italy in the late thirties, whence she only got away betimes. Shaw wrote to her after her return to the States, bemoaning his existence and saying he has outstayed his welcome in the world and that he is much poorer than people think.

It was a book just worth doing. But enough is enough.

Edward Shils

A MOURNER FOR EMPIRE

In the nineteenth century, England was the wonder of the world. Its workshops were the models of diligence and inventiveness; their products and representations were of the highest reliability. Above its proud and sober bourgeoisie, stood its universally admired rulers. In Church and State, in law court, in the armed forces and in country houses, they embodied an art of life involving, in its best instances, modesty, gravity, dignity, a sense of obligation, and a disregard for personal convenience or comfort. Christian humility, coupled with cheerless willingness to accept the responsibilities of power, and a bearing which impressed the subjects of that power, evoked the admiration of all Europe. It appeared to be a Utopia to Europe's conservatives shaken by 1789 and the rumbles which, following it, were signs of worse to come. To Europe's liberals it was an ideal amalgam of stability and freedom, of order and progress. It even got the better of the revolutionaries and caused them to believe that British policy never nodded and that the appearance of doing so was only a snare for the unwary.

These so greatly admired virtues were precipitated in a type of man. That type was the " gentleman."

The English gentleman of that period which is now nostal-gically referred to by radical young scholars as the "long Indian summer of the Empire," was gentle, he was measured in expression and deed, he avoided flamboyancy, he respected the past and gracefully assimilated it into the inevitable present. He was a Christian Knight, a Platonic ruler. He was of the pro-consular breed. He did his job quietly, smoothly, and without throwing his weight about. He possessed an ascendancy which was basically moral in every sphere of life from the family estate to the vast Empire.

The glories of Empire have dissolved, leaving a sad grey tone in the spirits of all. Its dissolution has depressed both those who took pleasure in contemplating the Empire in its majesty and those who gained their pleasure from the discom-fiture of its protagonists and exemplars.

Now Simon Raven, in a lively, regrettably sloppy, and most miscellaneously composed book, *The English Gentleman: An Essay in Attitudes* (Anthony Blond, 21s.), tells us the gentleman is being extinguished. He is unviable. Contemporary society will not have him. The gentleman, according to Mr. Raven, is constituted by this personal excellence in bearing, in moral quality and in achievement. Contemporary society rushing, like the Gadarene swine, towards Welfare and Equality will not tolerate such excellence. Mr. Waugh allowed Guy Crouch-back to find ultimately a safe haven in the remnant of his estate. Mr. Raven thinks that gentleman could still be safe in the army

—as long as the vulgar equalitarianism which prevails in England cannot reach it. He also gives good marks to King's College, Cambridge. Indeed, "the authority, unquestioned and un-resented which obtained in King's College presents the one alternative of gentlemanliness" which might "replace the vanished gentleman's authority in the guidance and government of the nation." "Authority between equals," such as he collided with in his happy misadventures at King's, would save our souls and our society. "Any authority must in the last resort of all depend upon respect. But alas, in the world at large there is no respect."

Is Mr. Raven justified in the sardonic and smiling crocodile tears which he sheds on behalf of the gentleman? Is the gentle-man really as out of date and out of place as Mr. Raven makes him out to be?

His image of himself as a fallen angel, making the amends of acknowledging his fall, is a tribute which vice pays to virtue. Does not Mr. Raven really confuse the external institutions of gentlemanliness, masculine institutions, professional military careers, landownership, support of the Church, and a reasonable conservatism with the essential virtues of seriousness, solicitude, compassion, and uprightness of character? Is Mr. Raven not giving expression to the sense of bereavement following on the loss of Empire and mistaking this for the disappearance of genuine virtues of character?

It is possible that Mr. Raven is right. The unique conjuncture of gentleness and puritanism, of uprightness without self-righteousness, of achievement without arrogance might have been a passing thing. It might have been a product of a moment when moral self-confidence was sustained by apparently un-challengeable power and obedience, when Christian belief was still strong enough to give a tone to conduct, when there was security of social position and confidence in the future. I myself doubt it. Seducers, cold-hearts, defamers, moral cony-catchers, peculators, bullies have never been in short supply, just as at present. Gentlemen have probably never been so plentiful as to have been a drug on the market (although they could and can often be quite boring). Nor is there any good reason to think that the ordinary English adult is any less appreciative of genuine achievement or of moral integrity than his ancestors of seventy or sixty years ago. Mr. Raven's arguments, consisting as they do of oddly assorted tales of Bohemian silliness and the cranky anxiety of the parents of National Service men, certainly prove nothing about these problems. Nor is his insight into contemporary Britain commended to our confidence by his ostensible belief that the present-day pressure for equality is a creation of the beastliness of the popular Press.

There is some truth in Mr. Raven's assertion that equalitarianism has challenged the legitimacy of the idea of the gentleman. The image of the gentleman contains the image of authority, a benign, forbearing authority, strong enough to hurt but too gentle, too kind, too sympathetic to do so. It is no accident that Mr. Raven has found his gentlemen among army officers and Cambridge dons, each of whom exercised such authority over him. But such gentlemanly authority might also slip easily into a version of itself to which pride and condescension have been added.

This version of gentlemanly authority too often can be wounding and it can stir revolt in its subjects. The great gentlemen who ruled the Empire in Asia and Africa were not, in spite of their gentlemanliness, entirely free of traces of this injurious solicitude and not everyone wished to go on with it indefinitely.

The moral ascendancy of the civil servant in bush or jungle, dressing for dinner nightly, never letting standards down and impressing equally the guileless and the wily natives, was essential, not to the gentleman as such but to the image of the gentleman so much praised by jingoes, stuffed shirts, and, I fear, Mr. Raven too. Now there are no more natives. There are only undeveloped countries whose representatives compete in denouncing us all in the United Nations. So Mr. Raven mourns implicitly the passing of Empire through mourning the passing of the gentlemen who ran it as civilians or as soldiers.

If Mr. Raven, in spite of his refined and self-conscious wickedness, were not such an old-fashioned patriot, he would appreciate that the virtues of the gentleman can well survive the passing of imperial institutions. As long as there is authority which can be misused, there will be some persons who will forbear to misuse it. As long as there are real or apparent achievements which can be boasted about, there will be some who will not boast. As long as there exist opportunities for one individual to discomfit other individuals, there will be some who will restrain themselves. As long as there are possibilities of taking advantage of the weak, there will be some who will not do so. Indifference to these temptations is the virtue of the Philistine; yielding to them is the vice of the brute. Resistance to them is the virtue of the gentleman. There will always be a few and there were never many more.

Michael Frayn

SARDINIAN SHERRY

One of the principal benefits that matrimony confers on the young professional class (which is where my hideout is located) is that it enables us to give up that tiresome pretence of being interested in spiritual and cultural matters—forced on us by our education and our courtship rituals—and lets us settle down to a frank and total absorption in our financial and material circumstances.

When, for instance, you call on the newly married Crumbles

—formerly socially-conscious Christopher Crumble and sensitive, musical Lavinia Knudge—do you talk about the problems of secondary education, or English choral music of the sixteenth century, as you would have done back in the good old days of Crumble and Knudge? You do not. Because Lavinia says . . .

LAVINIA: Before you do anything else, you must come and look over the flat!

CHRISTOPHER: . . . that's right, just take your coat off—I'll hang it on this automatic coat-rack . . .

LAVINIA: . . . which Christopher made himself, didn't you, darling?

CHRISTOPHER: Got a kit from Rackkitz of Wembley—costs about half the price of an ordinary automatic coat-rack . . .

LAVINIA: . . . and it's fire-resistant, too . . .

CHRISTOPHER: . . . now this is the hall, of course . . .

LAVINIA: . . . which we made ourselves by partitioning off part of the bedroom . . .

CHRISTOPHER: . . . with half-inch Doncaster boarding, at a shilling a foot, if you know the right place . . .

LAVINIA: . . . Christopher got it from the brother of an old school-friend of his, didn't you, darling? Now—mind your head on that steel brace—this is the bedroom . . .

CHRISTOPHER: . . . we picked up the bed for a song in a little shop I know in Edmonton . . .

LAVINIA: . . . and fitted it out with a Dormofoam mattress. They're so much the best, of course. In fact there's a waiting list for Dormofoams, but we had tremendous luck and got one ordered for someone who died . . .

CHRISTOPHER: . . . and this is the kitchen opening off in the corner here. It was really the handiness of having the kitchen opening directly into the bedroom that made us take the flat . . .

LAVINIA: . . . you should have seen it when we first moved in. But Christopher had the brilliant idea of covering up the holes in the floor with some special asbestos his uncle makes . . .

CHRISTOPHER: . . . so we got a discount on it. We're

frightfully proud of that stainless steel boot-rack, by the way. I don't know whether you saw it recommended in *Which ?* last month . . .?

LAVINIA: . . . it's so much more practical than all those silver-plated ones you see in the shops. According to *Which ?* they pounded it with 140 average boot-impacts an hour for seventeen days before it collapsed . . .

CHRISTOPHER: . . . I'd take you out to show you the lavatory, but it is raining rather hard. Remind us you haven't seen it next time you come, won't you, and we'll make a point of it . . .

LAVINIA: . . . and here we are in the living-room . . .

CHRISTOPHER: . . . have you seen this Plushco plastic carpeting before? We think it's awfully good, don't we, darling? Half the price of ordinary carpet, and terrifically hard-wearing. We've had it down, what, two weeks now? Not a sign of wear on it . . .

LAVINIA: . . . I see you're looking at all those old books on music and education. You won't believe it, but we had those shelves built for five pounds—timber and all . . .

CHRISTOPHER: . . . by a marvellous little man we found by sheerest chance in Muswell Hill. Remind me to give you his address . . .

LAVINIA: . . . though I think he did it specially cheaply for us just because he happened to take to us . . .

CHRISTOPHER: . . . by the way, would you like a glass of Sardinian sherry?

LAVINIA: . . . we've developed rather a thing about Sardinian sherry, haven't we, darling?

CHRISTOPHER: . . . we get it by the gallon from a little shop in Sydenham. Found the place by sheer chance . . .

LAVINIA: . . . Tremendously practical, and it works out at six and four a bottle . . .

CHRISTOPHER: . . . incidentally, what do you think we pay for the flat? No, go on, have a guess . . . Well, I'll tell you—five pounds a week . . .

LAVINIA: ... it's an absolute bargain, of course. We only found it through a friend of my mother's, who just by sheerest chance happened to be ...

CHRISTOPHER: ... I say, you're looking rather groggy. Lavinia, darling, run and fetch him some Asprilux. I don't know whether you've tried Asprilux, but we think it's much better than any of the other brands of aspirin ... No, sit in this chair—it's got a rather ingenious reclining back—we just got the last one to be made. Comfortable, isn't it? What do you think of Lavinia, by the way? Such practical, easy-to-clean hands and feet. You won't believe it, but I picked her up by the sheerest chance at a little bookshop I know down in Wimbledon ...

Colin Watson

AHEAD OF THE JONESES

"God save us all!" hissed the Honourable Mrs. Ranula. "That man Revesby actually asked me if I 'wanted to spend a penny'!"

Her husband regarded her a trifle apprehensively. Business wise, he reflected, his Hon. better half (as the unspeakable Revesby doubtless would term her) was a more predictable asset on a company letterhead than in the flesh.

"I expect he just wanted to put you at your ease, my dear. After all, this is the first time we've been guests here."

She glared at him contemptuously. "He meant it literally. That's the whole point. Every blasted door has a slot."

High tea at Goodings, which had consisted of poached eggs on haddock, plates of bread and butter, two sorts of jam and individual pots of tea, was over. Their host's chaplain, the

Reverend Len Lavender, had said grace, into which he had surprisingly introduced the unliturgical word "scrumptious." And the guests were leaving the dining-room and filing across the east lawn.

Mrs. Ranula scuffed the turf peevishly and rejected her husband's arm. "And did you . . . no, I simply can't believe it." She tucked back her chin and mimicked: " 'Never mind folding your serviettes, ladies and gentlemen; this is Liberty Hall.' I tell you he's a sadist. It's the only possible explanation."

"He's a millionaire to the nth power—*that's* the explanation, Lil, and don't you forget it!" Mr. Ranula, flushing, spoke in a hoarse, imperative whisper, like that of a Vatican guide heading off a truculent Presbyterian. They both walked on in silence towards the main treat of the evening.

The Marketarium had been an observatory in the days when Goodings housed the astronomy-minded Earls of Fontanel. The last earl but one, tempted to seek solace for the declining vigour of his line in a somewhat extravagant form of voyeurism, had tried to train the great telescope downwards on the bedroom windows of girls in the village and wrecked the machinery. It was never repaired and, on buying the estate, Mr. Revesby had ordered his contractors to strip the building from dome to marble-flagged floor in readiness for optical entertainment and instruction of quite another kind. He and his guests sat now on round, leather-padded chairs that swivelled on steel stalks and tilted at the touch of a button to command comfortable range of the hemispherical ceiling. Hidden projectors transformed the dome into a twinkling, multicoloured firmament. The illusion was of limitless space, strewn with incandescent globules. Some glowed steadily. Others flared while they were being watched, then winked out. A third kind tended to draw into coalescence, first lightly adhering ("like lit-up caviare," said one guest who felt the need to reassert status after the Goodings haddock), then achieving symmetrical solidity and shining the more brightly.

Etched in the dome's ground glass skin were index lines, faintly illuminated so that the position of each star at any particular moment might immediately be read off.

"An improvement on the old ticker tape, eh?" remarked Mr. Revesby to the guest on his left, the Foreign Office's Sir Bernard Acropy. Then he called across to an equine featured woman of about fifty, who rode her slowly revolving chair with the air of an M.O.F. slumming on the dodgems. "You get the idea, do you, Lady Glanders? A sort of chart of fortune, as it were. Each light is a public company."

"But how heavenly!"

Mr. Revesby pointed. "There you are, you see—that's the Cotton-Clore galaxy . . . the red ones." (Somebody jested aptly about tooth and Clore.) "And there goes old Uncle Roy's comet—pretty little tail and all." ("Now why should that remind me of beri-beri," muttered Lady Glanders, inconsequentially.) "Oh, and that's Izzy Wolfson's bunch, of course—the blues."

A murmur of approbation arose, as from a Guy Fawkes party of the better sort.

"But what colour are yours, Mr. Revesby? Do tell us."

There was a pause. Then, "Er . . . yellow, as a matter of fact."

The modest, almost apologetic tone of the reply did not—could not—mitigate the obvious. Yellow orbs were as numerous and dominant in that money-made sky as kingcups in a June water meadow.

When the guests of Mr. Revesby, the richest man in all England, emerged from their remarkable entertainment in the Marketarium at Goodings, the prevailing mood was one of awe and unease.

They had seen demonstrated by means that were clearly of scientific impeccability (had not Mr. Revesby used the word "computerisation"?) their host's financial control of a whole milky way of commercial and industrial enterprises. Here, they reflected, was a man whose accumulation of wealth had outpaced human imaginings.

The thought was not welcome in minds normally preoccupied with making money or exercising in the invention and observance of rites demonstrative of success in that capacity. It was disconcerting, to say the least, to realise that Mr. Revesby was powered by such excess of millions as to have passed clean through their own social orbits and achieved the status of a fixed star, remote, invulnerable, yet menacingly magnetic.

The shrewder guests knew better than to sneer at the vulgarities of the great household at Goodings: the institution of high tea, the jocular notices in the bathrooms, the plastic gnomes installed on the terrace by the Garden Furniture Division of one of the most promising, cannibal-wise, of the Revesby groups of companies. These were not the gaffes of a parvenu, nor the smart inversions of a chronic party-thrower. They were, in one sense, a genuinely sympathetic memorial to the multitude of simple people who had been coerced by simian cries of "New!" and "Miracle!" and "Threepence Off!" into contributing to Mr. Revesby's success. At the same time they proclaimed his having reached that ultimate stage of amassing wealth when even the scale of values ordained by the money makers themselves may safely be derided.

All this, unfortunately for the Honourable Mrs. Lily Ranula, was beyond the scope of her reckoning. She came of a line whose recipe for prosperity specified such wholesome, old-fashioned ingredients as rack rents and coal royalties. Her grandfather had secured his title by honest dealing between gentlemen, and the family had been free thereafter to devote its talents to gracious living while professional retainers worked the money mill.

It was inevitable that this pleasant little world should be first cut off and then rapidly eroded by the tides of social change. Young Lily had jumped for survival at the last possible moment —into the arms of Bert Ranula, a personable young speculator who by sheer force of habit took up this option of a controlling interest and married her. But her experience had been a severe shock and she could never again contemplate a coal truck nor a row of tenements without a feeling of bitter resentment against fate. To help herself to forget she took up snobbery in her spare time and attained a degree of proficiency quite remarkable in one brought up without any kind of vocational training.

Mrs. Ranula towed her husband to take leave of the master of Goodings a full hour before any of the other guests. "So nice" —her smile was like an arthritic spasm—"to have met one of nature's gentlemen." Into the extended hand of Mr. Revesby's common law wife, Desiree Wilkinson, she slipped half a crown.

The moment epitomised the collision between privilege and democracy.

Democracy, of course, triumphed. Within two days a sizeable investment in Ranula Properties Limited was regretfully withdrawn, and by the end of the week the Fraud Squad was shaking a certain building society and listening to the lonely rattle of a St. Christopher's medal and a hair grip.

"Never mind, it could have happened to any of us, old boy," said Mr. Ranula's friends, loyally—and with absolute truth.

For Mr. Revesby's chaplain, the Reverend Len Lavender, the affair held a different but not less reassuring message, which he duly communicated to his wife. "It just goes to show," he said, "that Sir is only human after all. I'd consider that I'd failed in my job if money had made him insensitive."

Betty Thorne

A LOWER RUNG ON THE LADDER

We were going along pretty steadily. Debt collectors weren't unknown to us, but neither were they regular visitors. It seemed safe to suppose that as the children grew older we would be able to meet their increased demands, but now we have had the ground beneath our feet pulled away.

My husband works in a smelting shop. Fantastic sums of money are to be spent turning the furnaces over from the old method of firing to electricity. Increased output is anticipated, but fewer workers will be needed.

Thank goodness this is not the old days when men were sacked without warning. We live in an age of enlightenment, and my husband will have a job of sorts. He can never, however, expect to reach the same position as before. Down the ladder he must go and down must go the wages.

We have heard that compensation is to be paid for future loss of earnings, but of course this will not cover the gap in the next twenty-five years' wages. I cannot speak for my husband, but I would find it a bitter experience to have my job taken from me and be dropped down to a lower level.

We could have gone to another branch of the steel company in a different town. It would have meant selling our small heap of bricks called home which is our only bit of security and taking six noisy, fighting, lively children into a working-class suburb whose respectability they would just not know how to respect. Alternatively a large mortgage could have been incurred and stayed with for the best part of our lives, loaded with limitations. We decided that this was not for us and we would just wait and see.

So far everything had been pretty easy, but one morning a letter came informing my husband that unless he took a course of lectures terminating with an examination he could not be considered for the better jobs. I had thought there was no chance of a good job and that this letter was a hopeful sign. My husband said that the other men were taking the course but that he thought there wasn't much hope of a better job, course or not. This made me angry; knowing nothing about the job or means of selection, I took it upon myself to cause an argument with my husband over his own job.

Events seemed to have shown that my husband was correct in his approach, but now to me the more important thing is that I showed a complete lack of confidence in my husband. Not a solely economic factor!

Australia. . . . Have you heard of the marvellous life that old beachcomber has? What about those marvellous beaches? No more bronchitic children coughing away; sunshine and space; perhaps even a real horse instead of that tin toy in the backyard. What about unemployment, though, hopeless hostels, and doctors' fees? And why should we be forced to run away? Australia, as far as I am concerned, is strictly for Sidney Nolan and the kangaroos. To my husband it may be a chance of new horizons, but I say I won't go.

Then I feel guilty, with coughing children, niggling neighbours, and my husband's hatred of the stupid inconvenience caused by a burst pipe. I think I could be depriving them of a greatly enriched life.

It soon becomes obvious that the puerile status seeking which I foolishly try to take part in will have to stop. The compensation will tie up loose ends and then we must budget accordingly, just hoping that there will be no injury or illness. Anyway, nobody starves; there is always the National Assistance nowadays. The dividing line between managing and not managing seems a pretty nebulous sort of thing.

Will we go on the books of some welfare worker as a

problem family? No, we will not. We have always got along and we shall continue to do so. But now that fear has touched me.

David Bean

THE EMPTY CAGE

It is high noon in High Spen; a dog sits in the middle of the road lazily, safely, scratching itself. The sun is hot over the black pit heap which dominates the main street, tumbling down to the backyards of Collingdon Terrace. There is a suspicion of life behind the frosted windows of the Central Social Club (Affiliated), but no proof other than the half-open door. The Temperance Bar four doors up is shut, and its sign faded. Walk along a bit, and you begin to notice that the sturdy, honey-stone miners' cottages have no windows left. Someone has been round the Long Row and Cross Row and smashed them systematically. The back doors are open, as usual. You walk in and find no welcome—just a litter of torn wallpaper and glass. Nothing else. The great black stoves are cold, the whitewashed cupboards empty, and there are soot falls where the tin fireside tubs should be.

Through a pass in the gritty spoil mountains is the colliery. The great, dark-red headstock is still, and there is a notice outside the pit yard saying, " Property for Sale—Apply National Coal Board." Go to the shaft and you disturb a nation of birds; their wings beat among the dark beams like bats. The shaft is boarded up and padlocked, and you can hear black water rushing far below. Drop a stone and you get tired of waiting for it to splash.

In the little time office above the shaft you are nearly 1000 feet up, high above the moors of North-west Durham. The Tyne is not far away and all the horizons are sunny. But look immediately around you and you would think a bomb had dropped. The time sheets, old pit records, are littered about, meaningless.

Down in the yard there is a notice board lying among the nettles and it says: " National Coal Board, No. 6 Area—Durham Division. Accident Rate League II. Position this month: ——. Position last month: ——."

This month's position—last month's position—it is all the same now. High Spen Colliery, once a feeder pit for Consett Iron Co., five miles away over the moor, was one of the first casualties in the N.C.B. take-over. On Vesting Day, 1947, the lodge officials stood in the cold of the new year and watched the people's flag of nationalisation hoisted over their pit. It survived seven years. Now its 300-odd miners are scattered; travelling out at all hours to work in pits up to ten miles away. Or they have packed up altogether and followed the trail of so many of their ancestors—south to lighter industry, or even overseas.

Bob Woof, the local M.P. got up in the Commons recently and compared Spen to Goldsmith's Deserted Village. He was particularising, because Spen has no new building at all and wants it. But he could have generalised on the same theme with a lot of truth. North-west Durham is dying—as a coalfield at any rate. This was one of the earliest mining areas in Britain. The coal cropped out on the hill-side and you just followed it in.

These days it becomes harder and harder, dearer and dearer to win. So while the great, modern, mechanical coal-cutters go ravening through the eight-foot seams under the sea in the big, show-place collieries on the other side of the North-eastern coalfield, the west shrinks. The pits close, the weeds grow over them, the youngsters tumbling out of school are potential pit-fodder no longer, and their parents are forced to make another life-changing decision.

The old men, in their caps and their mufflers, still sit on the green public seats until the weather, or the routine of a younger generation, sends them home. They sit, and they do not talk a lot now.

If you sit with them and ask the usual questions, they will answer well enough—tell you how the Spen front street was as busy as Newcastle's Grainger Street when they were bairns, how if you wanted a first division footballer in those days you had only to holler down the nearest pit shaft and you would get a complete team, how they had sat down in the pit at twelve years of age and opened the traps until they were big enough to become putter lads, strong as young oxen, sweating for shillings. Their xenophobia crops up suddenly and they will get bitter about "them Eyetalians and foreigners" having the jobs, and how you cannot get one if you are a Britisher.

Then one will get a bit more expansive. "Looka, we've worked hard all our lives and now we're retired we just want to be left alone. But we never thought that when we got old the place would die with us. You're born in a place, hinny, and you like to think it's going to carry on when you've gone."

The veterans are not apathetic, sitting staring dreamily out over the farmland. Having struggled most of their lives, they feel they deserve a rest now. But nor are the younger people taking the slow death of their village easily.

This is an area with a history of protest. When the Chartists rose briefly in Newcastle, miners and ironworkers from Winlaton, Spen's next-door neighbour, headed the march into the city with home-made pikes. In the twenties, thousands of local miners and their families marched into Gateshead, singing "The Red Flag" behind their lodge banners, following their leaders, Henry Bolton and Sir (then Mr.) Will Lawther to court. There were baton charges by the police and High Spen lost its banner. Nearby Chopwell has been known as Little Moscow for years and its Marx-Lenin lodge banner is still a familiar sight at the Durham Miners' Gala.

Times are less spectacular now but still every eligible member of High Spen's 1400 population has signed a petition demanding new building and new industry in the area. For this, unfortunately for Spen, there is a considerable queue, and not only in the North-east.

The big estates of red-brick £3000 houses are steadily spreading out into North-west Durham to house those Tynesiders who can afford them. The views are splendid, but while the occupants are paying off their mortgages they will have little inclination to march round singing "The Red Flag." As Goldsmith put it:

> " A bold peasantry, their country's pride.
> When once destroyed, can never be supplied."

Richard Fry

LESSONS OF THE BIG BUSINESS BATTLE

The defeat of Imperial Chemical Industries' take-over bid for Courtaulds has left behind it a sense of failure that spread far beyond the boardroom at Millbank. Only the management and staff of Courtaulds itself can look back on the drawn-out struggle with any satisfaction; a skilful defence has at least secured the firm's continued independence. The City was distressed because the ruthless methods used in the fight have damaged the reputation of big business with the general public. The I.C.I. must be aware that much damage has been done to the " image " of a public-spirited, socially progressive organisation which has been so carefully built up over the years.

Once again the giant chemical combine has appeared to the onlooker to be out for expansion at any cost, pursuing naked power politics. Suddenly the idea of nationalisation to curb the growth of private power has been revived. It is now obvious that the judgment of Mr. Paul Chambers was at fault when he rejected Courtaulds' proposals for partial collaboration in the field of fibres and attempted to force through a complete merger against the opposition of the Courtaulds' board. The outcome is bound to affect faith in his judgment on other matters.

Nor does the Government come out of the affair with any credit. There can be two opinions on whether the take-over bid ought to have been stopped; but the Government's hesitations, changes of mind, and apparent lack of policy made a bad impression. Public opinion was uneasy about the matter from the start. The sheer bigness of big business always provokes suspicion, and it is a natural reaction of the individual to think that two industrial giants battling for more power can hardly be up to any good. Moreover, the thought that the destiny of thousands of workers and of a large team of managers, technicians, and specialists can be decided by a simple ballot of shareholders on the grounds that one side has offered better financial terms than the other is bound to arouse doubts about the state of the law.

In the Courtaulds camp the glow of victory after an exhausting battle may drown all questioning for a while. But the public argument has brought out serious weaknesses and the verdict can only have been justified by the fervent assurances of the board that things would be better from now on. The challenge forced Courtaulds to face the fact that it had for many years kept large resources invested in ways which produced little return and promised little improvement. A more dynamic attitude may have emerged from the struggle, and the mistakes of the past, which have been very frankly admitted, may be avoided in the future.

While there are evident political and economic dangers in creating a group of such overwhelming size with a virtual

*"—PITY YOU BOYS WEREN'T
AT ORPINGTON"*

monopoly in an important range of consumer goods, the argument in favour of the unsuccessful merger scheme should not be overlooked. Both sides needed strengthening. I.C.I. is strong on the chemical side but remote from the final consumer.

Courtaulds is probably the stronger in research and development as well as being traditionally close to the wearer of the cloth; but its heavy reliance on viscose and acetate fibres has become a drawback. There was much to be said for pooling the various fibre activities before foreign competition grows more intense

173

either on joining the Common Market or as a result of tariff cuts. Entry into the Common Market would have undermined any monopoly that might have resulted from the merger on the British market only. In any case it is always open to the Government to reduce or remove protective import duties in order to maintain competition.

In fact, it must not be taken for granted that a take-over bid is a bad thing in itself. In many cases these attacks have galvanised a stagnant business or put a whole industry into a more efficient condition, giving better service to the public. The real objection to this particular take-over bid must be based on the exceptional size of the two companies and the fact that both of them were already in a near-monopoly position in some important products.

Some lessons for public policy emerge. First, a gap in the present law for the control of monopoly and restrictive practices will have to be closed. We shall need something equivalent to the United States Clayton Act, which allows the Government to suspend a proposed merger until it has convinced itself that the public interest will not suffer. Next, the Government must clarify its own thinking on these matters. It set an awkward precedent when it disregarded the advice of the Monopolies Commission to demand that the Imperial Tobacco Company should dispose of a 40 per cent shareholding in Gallaher, its main competitor. Should I.C.I. now be permitted to keep its 38 per cent of Courtaulds?

Imperial Tobacco had to undertake not to interfere with the management of Gallaher. If a similar pledge were demanded from I.C.I. what would be the good of the shareholding, which cost some £30 million? On the grounds that the joint nylon enterprise of I.C.I. and Courtaulds has been a success, a wider industrial co-operation between the two might be industrially desirable. Where is the line to be drawn between such pooling and a conspiracy to reduce competition? Finally, these problems would not have become so acute if there was a more formal

174

obligation on company chairmen to observe certain rules of conduct in pursuing merger plans.

It is less than fifteen years since we revived legislation against monopolies and restrictive practices in this country. After a period of experiment, a fair advance was made with the Act now in force. The I.C.I.-Courtaulds case seems to provide an excellent opportunity for another step forward. One of the most powerful safeguards against abuses of industrial power is public awareness of the danger. So long as people are apt to welcome fixed prices printed on what they buy and to be annoyed by being charged different prices in different shops, they are in no mental condition to object to monopolies. It is not the law but public opinion that has given America such safeguards against business abuses as she has got. If the British Government is to take an active part in keeping industry competitive, it must have more public and political support for such a role than it has had in the past.

W. J. Weatherby

WHOLLY WRIT

Nottingham drizzled for opening night, a grey, lowering drizzle that made the city look like the Nottwich Graham Greene wrote about. The West Indians in the main streets were new since Greene's time here as an apprentice journalist, but what else looked new that night? The rain gave Nottingham a depressed, uniform, Industrial Revolution air. If the company were as nervous as actors usually are on opening night, even the weather would seem to be against them.

In the foyer of the Theatre Royal the local first-nighters wrung out their clothes like dirty washing. The West-Enders in the front stalls—they could be divided into the usual pro-and anti-Royal Court factions—sounded like foreign humming-birds among the local homing pigeons. It was " John " this, " Tony " that, and " Albert " the other, while the rest of the audience seemed to lie buried under its programmes.

John Osborne appeared from an exit near the stage. When last seen in the early days of *Look Back in Anger* he had been nervous and haggard: now he was plumper, tanned, more like a member of the Bow Group than a jumpy author on opening night. He must have looked reassuring to Albert Finney who was taking the lead and was said to be " as nervous as a thoroughbred."

Nottingham had a special feeling for Finney as he played a local factory worker in the film of *Saturday Night and Sunday Morning*. This personal connection, however, might not have been good for " Luther's " reception—or so the director, Tony Richardson, feared. He appeared behind Osborne looking equally tanned but more rangy and jumpy, and studied the audience like a Harley Street specialist listening to heartbeats. He was worried that many of the local first-nighters would be expecting Finney to give another *Saturday Night* performance and when they found Martin Luther instead, they might " turn ugly."

Probably like most of the West-Enders, he underestimated Nottingham's adaptability. After all it had already taken Sillitoe in its stride and D. H. Lawrence and Greene. Why not Osborne and Luther-Finney? The applause anyway lapped over Finney and the rest of the cast at the first and second intervals. The only aspect of the evening that seemed to try the local patience was the length of the show. In at 7.15 p.m., the first-night audience did not emerge until 10.50 p.m. Would every-one make his last bus? Many dashed for it while the company took several enthusiastic curtain calls.

Next morning the shadow of Nottwich faded with the rain,

and in the pale but persistent sunlight, Nottingham looked more varied and up to date—and also optimistic. It was a pleasant background for second thoughts, for the *Luther* inquest.

"There goes Mr. Albert," said a waiter watching Albert Finney walk past: in light trousers and an open-necked shirt, he looked more like the hero of *Saturday Night,* more the local boy going on the town than the Luther of the night before. He was soon in a hotel corner talking vigorously with John Osborne: had the inquest begun? Tony Richardson as director was the real "coroner" for the previous evening which was now past and therefore dead. Had any parts of the production died prematurely instead of ending through natural causes?

Tennessee Williams once remarked that if you had a flop on your hands you knew it by the mood of the inquest—"that special air of gentle gravity that hangs over the demise of a play." The atmosphere at this one was comparatively jaunty. Although he had a full list of points to correct, Richardson was obviously pleased. He had made mental or written notes of all his observations—from a church door on stage that refused to open until Luther put his shoulder to it, to the emphasis in individual performances. The heads of each of the sections of the production—lighting and design, for example—also had their own notes. The director compared his with theirs and made ready for another rehearsal.

The late finish was obviously one worry. With the memory of the heavy rewriting Tennessee Williams and some other dramatists do on the road, one asked if John Osborne thought it necessary to trim his script or refashion aspects of Luther's character, in the light of the audience's reaction and the criticisms in the local papers. Richardson replied that when Osborne completed a play he gave it to the production team as a finished work and therefore there would be no rewriting.

RICHARDSON: What I have been dealing with this morning is the physical things—the scenery, lighting, and so on. The shape of the theatre here is quite different from the one we shall be using in London. A lot of our effects there can't be achieved here—for example, having Luther preach in effect in the audience rather than at a distance from it as here. But the first thing is to make the play work in practical terms. The subtleties of performance and so on come later and the principals anyway will do much of that on their own. Technically certain scenes didn't come off. Why not? That is our job to find out to-day. We'll have certain things remade and that door rehung. I'll take up certain points about standing positions and such-like with Albert Finney—we'll discuss the value of certain scenes in the light of what we know now.

(*George Devine, who plays the Vicar General, John Staupitz, and looks like a Fabian philosopher, said that after opening night, an actor can generally " readjust " most of his performance for himself.*)

RICHARDSON: Yes, after a show opens, it settles down. At first you are just preoccupied with the technical points—making it work. In the ritual hysteria of taking a musical to Broadway, people want to fiddle with everything right from the beginning. But with a serious play like this—I feel very strongly the work is a sort of masterpiece—the problem is more one of how to stage it properly than to fiddle with the script in great story conferences. I don't think John is much influenced by the performance. I think he's always found it very difficult to rewrite, for after all he's done all his rewriting before it gets to us.

DEVINE: I think this is the way one starts with him—with the assumption this is the work and it's our job to make it work.

Q: What about the length of the show?

RICHARDSON: That is a problem because it is a long evening. I don't know what we are going to do yet, but perhaps the scenes will change more smoothly and thus take quite an amount of time off it. The play itself is composed in a series of movements like a musical composition. Perhaps one can alter the rhythm slightly so that some time is saved. You can't whip it along because it's not written that way. There's a Chekhovian close. Luther's life doesn't end with a bang, but it's theatrically satisfying in a definite way and it's our job to bring this out. It's a problem of architecture, most probably. Each scene has a different growth. And behind it all you have this psychotic personality of Luther—this extraordinary figure who almost literally stumbled into everything—without any real logical process.

Time then for another rehearsal—to put the findings of the inquest into effect. Playing in Nottingham at the same time was *Sanctuary,* the film based on two Faulkner novels that Richardson directed for Hollywood. Richardson seemed none too pleased at its presence and told a story of how he had wanted to use a passage out of one of the novels only to be told, " The only reason you want to use that is that Faulkner wrote it." Life on the road certainly has a logic that is often hard to find in Hollywood.

W. J. Weatherby

TEA AT FOUR

"Come to tea at four o'clock," said Miss Ivy Compton-Burnett, whose dialogue novels make English family life seem like Greek tragedies.

At five to four a maid in uniform opened the heavy front door of Miss Compton-Burnett's first-floor Kensington apartment. "This way, please," murmured the maid, closing the door again as soon as the visitors had entered, as if she were shutting out the world of contemporary London.

"Take a seat before the fire and we will have tea presently," said Miss Compton-Burnett, in a vast sitting-room that looked as though a Victorian family had only just left it, marooning her in the present.

"Someone said that you do not use—er—a typewriter for your work."

"That is correct. I write in longhand. My typist is very kind and reads my writing. I used at one time to destroy my manuscripts, but now you can sell the tiresome things. I have long bouts of not writing. That is why I take a fair time over a book. I do not write slowly or destroy much, but I have long spaces in which I do not write at all. After I finish a book I feel that all the virtue has gone out of me. People say, 'What do you do with yourself between books?' Well, I'm quite happy not to do anything."

"May I—er—take your picture?" asked Neil Libbert.

"You may if you show me what you take. Photographers nowadays never seem to take good likenesses," said Miss Compton-Burnett, her expression calm but watchful beneath her halo of grey hair.

"Are you writing a book at present?"

"Yes, but I am working very spasmodically. I do not know what is going to happen in it. It is better to start a book with the main line already prepared, but I cannot always do this. I have to start and hope for the best. I do not think I have ever regarded myself as a professional writer. Even when I was quite young I always thought I would write. I had a lot of family troubles in my youth and then there was the 1914-1918 war, and a very bad illness which prevented me doing anything much. One cannot say how much one is made up of environment and experience."

"Were you influenced by Greek tragedy?"

"When I was young I was classically educated, first by my brothers and then at college, where I read classics. I haven't been consciously influenced, but whether something crept in to stay, I cannot say. Critics claim I am a disciple of

Henry James, but I do not think I have read him enough for that."

"Do you—er—think family life has changed much since your youth, when you began to write?"

"Family life certainly seems to have changed, but I think it is more in the working class, the tradesmen's class, than in that of more educated people. Financially, it has certainly changed."

A bell rang loudly outside the sitting-room.

"Ah, tea is served," said Miss Compton-Burnett, leading the way out of the room, down the hall to another room, where afternoon tea for three had been laid out on a table.

"Help yourselves to bread and butter. I have my own on my plate," and she began to pour out three cups of tea. "Jam? Please do not take any photographs while I am eating. People might think I was greedy."

"Do you—er—find critics helpful?"

"If they like one's books, one is grateful. Sometimes one makes resolutions based on criticisms but one cannot generally keep them. I read a good review of somebody's new book and fly to the library with my heart high with hope, only to be disappointed quite often. I like a writer like L. P. Hartley, for example . . ."

"An American critic—he was oversimplifying for readers who do not know your books—said your books lay between the worlds of 'Grandma Moses and the Greek Furies'——"

"I do not know who Grandma Moses is."

"She was an old American woman who painted popular primitive paintings."

"Oh."

Miss Compton-Burnett emptied her tea-leaves into a bowl and refilled her tea cup.

"Well, if what he said persuaded people to buy my books, that will not be too bad. I have not a large sale in America."

"You once described your books as half-way between novels and plays."

"I find dialogue easy to write and I seem to think in conversations. I have never written a play, though I often go to the theatre. I saw that play *Look Back in Anger*. Can you tell me what that young man was so angry about? He seemed to be much more fortunate than most people. To-day there's such an effervescence of youth. It's like going back to the days of Henry the Eighth."

The conversation turned to a recent novel based on a murder case.

"I think in murder cases that not enough attention is paid to the victims. There is too much talk about people not being responsible for their actions," said Miss Compton-Burnett.

"Are your families entirely responsible for their darkest actions?"

"They are as responsible as people can be."

"Graham Greene once—er—suggested that a writer has certain obsessions——"

"I think of writing as the urge of a civilised human being who talks in language and wishes to produce something in language. So many people want to write but not everyone seems to be able to manage it. Will you have a piece of cake? So many people nowadays do not take afternoon tea. I think that is very bad. Do you?"

"Definitely."

"If your fingers are sticky after the jam, here is a finger bowl. Jam has a bad habit of getting out of bounds. More tea?" She refilled all the cups. "My maid witnessed a robbery. They pretended to look in a shop window and then when they came out they had a waiting car already wound up. I think many people do such things because they are bored. There are only a limited number of choices among honest jobs if you have not been educated. If you have finished, should we return to the sitting-room?"

"*Pastors and Masters* was my first novel," said Miss Compton-Burnett, back in front of the fire. "I sent it to an agent and they placed it somehow, but it didn't do anything much, though it's been reprinted since, you know. That was about . . . about

1924 after the First World War and my family troubles. After the First World War there was a large number of well-off single women. The men they would have married and their well-off brothers had all been killed. It was a manless generation. Many are still living though not so well-off now. People still had servants when I was a young woman, but life is now so different—at least superficially. People will give enormous rents for a flat and then do nearly all their own work. A relation of my mother's had £350 a year and she had a house, a cook, and a housekeeper. People tell me—though I do not know myself—that a great deal of money is still made in the North. Many people nowadays spend a lot but put it down to expenses. That is a new thing. And people now grow up younger. I am not sure that is a good thing either. If people are thrown into the adult world too young it may stop them maturing. A rather dull period in late childhood is a good thing, I think. Your brain and your character can grow up in peace. They always tell me—though I do not know myself—that the American people grow up very young, but do not alter much afterwards. I believe their standard is rather low. Here again I do not vouch for it, but they say when a person has got a degree at Harvard he is just about fit to go to Oxford or Cambridge. I do not know if it is true, but I have heard a great many people say so."

"Do the changes you notice—er—affect your books?"

"I put my time back in my books. I do not think people really know the time they are living in, particularly in this very mixed-up, changeable time, though in a way human life—the fundamental relationships—must always remain the same. But the moral standard is quite different. Things are condoned that once were not and are condemned that once were not."

"Have the new media affected your technique?"

"I hardly ever go to films and I have not got television," said Miss Compton-Burnett. "They say people do not watch television as much as they did. I do not see how they can grind out so much work and keep it all of high quality. Dr. Leavis in his attack on Sir Charles Snow referred to what he thought was the low quality of *The Observer* and the *Sunday Times*, and I think the *New Statesman*——"

"And the *Guardian*——"

"Oh, he didn't like anybody except the *Spectator*, in which his attack appeared. But to produce something very good day after day, week after week, is terribly hard. I find on a Sunday morning that those large papers are a little too much to face. I put that colour thing straight into the waste-paper basket."

Miss Compton-Burnett looked into the fire as if she suddenly felt tired.

"Well, thank you very much for—er—the tea . . ."

"Good-bye," said Miss Compton-Burnett, opening the front door herself.

Outside it was raining and the evening rush hour was just beginning. It was one of those days Miss Compton-Burnett summed up in the opening of *Darkness and Day*:

> *"Now, Sir Ransom, we shall have to have sunshine in ourselves to-day. There is none outside for us. But that should not be difficult for fortunate people like ourselves."*

The afternoon tea was already a part of the past.

John Mortimer

AUTHOR'S THEATRE

In his preface to the paperback edition of his plays (*Three Plays*: Mercury, 8s. 6d.), Mr. Graham Greene explains the pleasure of writing for the theatre after the lonely and unloved life of the novelist: the sense of belonging to a group of likeable people all passionately concerned with a joint enterprise, the surprise of finding that actors are not only able to understand what they say but can sometimes think of the play as a whole, the excuse to go out of a detested study to late-night cold meals in provincial hotels, and the joy of sitting in empty theatres listening to rehearsals of your own words, an activity which nicely combines narcissism, idleness, and the sense of being useful. It is in no way to grudge him all this to wonder what contribution he has made to the theatre. What stories, in fact, has he told there in a way which would not have been better managed between the hard covers of a boring old book?

Let it be said at once that Mr. Greene is no innovator. Three acts, one set and neatly arranged curtains, there is not much progress, in the shape of these plays, from the formula of Pinero. Directors have told him, he says, that he should write as he likes, and treat his play as loosely as a film. This advice Mr. Greene has conscientiously disregarded because, he says, he wants " an author's and not a director's play." But perhaps the surrender of Mr. Greene to the theatre, like the surrender of his characters to God, has not been sufficiently complete. The theatre is not the author's or the director's or the actor's, but the moment of performance, a kind of ritual fusion of common endeavour. In these terms how does Mr. Greene emerge as a dramatist?

The most theatrical of his plays is no doubt *The Living Room*. The room, the only one in the house kept open because it is the only one where no one has died, is a kind of mysterious setting which might be employed by Harold Pinter. The old speechless aunts, the brother in a wheel-chair, the strong and oppressive feeling of place, and one magnificent scene between the girl and the priest, all these things are written to be lived out in public. But once the girl is dead and the play resolves itself into an arid discussion between the psychiatrist and the priest about the nature of God the characters lose mystery and we are out of the living-room and into cold print.

The second play, *The Potting Shed*, is again deeply conventional in form, but expresses a view of life which I personally find so

185

ridiculous that it is tempting to think that only by its absurdity can it appeal to the author. It is possible, although hard, to believe in a God who drops atom bombs. It is not possible to believe in a God who plays unpleasant practical jokes and swaps souls like a schoolboy swapping stamps. However, Mr. Greene clearly likes this the least of his plays, and I am not here to quarrel with him about that.

The Complaisant Lover is a great pleasure to read. It appears really funny and savage as an account of contemporary middle-class adultery in which pleasure is constantly limited by fear. The characters are sad and pitiable and true to their natures, and the absence of God from the cast list is enormously helpful to the play. Reading it came as an especial surprise after the somnambulant West-End production, which revealed about as much experienced bitterness as Mrs. Dale's Diary. Perhaps the truth is that Mr. Greene's conventional way of writing plays invites their conventional production. We are less intelligent in the theatre than at home; we can't so easily recognise the contemporary heart under the old stuffed shirt.

Speaking of his conversion to the theatre, Mr. Greene says, " I had tried a new drink; I had liked the flavour; how I wished my glass were not empty and it were not time to go." Let's hope he has another, but this time a deeply intoxicating treble, so that the conventions are forgotten, the stuffed shirts burst open, and the bitterness and the despair burst out in a full flood of theatrical ideas.

Philip Hope-Wallace

THE CHERRY ORCHARD

The new production of Chekhov's wonderful play which is the
latest offering of the Royal Shakespeare Company at the Aldwych
is the work of Michel Saint-Denis whose production of *The
Three Sisters* seems in memory a poem of atmospheric and elegaic
sadness though last night I also recall its . containing some
wonderfully funny things.

Those who expect *The Cherry Orchard* to seem essentially a
touching tragi-comedy of a brother and sister who are not
quite brave enough to face realities and to break with the past,
all set in an almost tangible atmosphere of pauses, unspoken
thoughts and evocative noises, will be in, if not for a disappointment, at least a shock. We realise very early that Mr. Saint-
Denis has been closely influenced by the Moscow Art Theatre
performance which we saw here. It is a play with far more of
a comic thrust and tonic affirmation than the several others one
recalls from the last thirty years. It is not the end of Mme.
Ranevsky or Gaev which is to matter, not even old Firs's being
forgotten. We are to go away with the thought of Anya's
bright eyes looking towards " the new life," and the sound of
Trofimov's admittedly overweening aspirations for the future
of humanity, but aspirations to be respected in some way all
the same.

Meanwhile the servants have been enlarged clownishly: no
pathos in Dunyasha or Epihodov and only a little in Varya the
girl who does not get the proposal. And yet, to me inexplicably,
Lopahin though very sympathetically presented is not given
his head to exult when at length he returns, master of the estate
where he had grown up barefoot. Strangely, his pride is dis-

solved in maudlin tears: and somehow we have no tears for Mme. Ranevsky at this, her most painful experience. Dame Peggy Ashcroft plays the part with great art, but it is no longer the knub of the emotional pattern on its own. She is too appealing a person to appear in the least absurd which is as well, but there is scarcely a hint of the Mme. Ranevsky who finds life and its transience a tragic affliction. In her remembrance of the past in the second scene, however, she scores a wonderful piece of that Chekhovian acting which is poised on a razor edge between absurdity and pathos.

Otherwise I rather missed this, to me, characteristic division of our emotional reaction. Sir John Gielgud also acting brilliantly makes Gaev so feckless in his vanity that even at the end we cannot take his predicament as anything but comic. The news that he is going into a bank is greeted with loud laughter. Firs, played by Roy Dotrice with a plausible assumption of old age in everything but his young voice remains until the last minute, when it is too late, a purely comical figure.

Apart from his scene at the party which baffled me, I found George Murvell a convincing enough Lopahin and Ian Holm in a vigorous projection of the not wholly unadmirable Trofimov the "perpetual student" was fresh and interesting as indeed was his counterpart, Anya, played by Judi Dench. Dorothy Tutin kept right away from the stereotype of downcast Varya. Patience Collier playing the governess for the second time showed spirit.

Yet admiring much in ensemble and detail I felt cheated. Of what? Of a communion with these people and their unspoken thoughts, of being drawn into their world and living with them. Everyone seemed to be marching about in circles and shouting as though lifting a Shakespearian comedy off the floor of theatre in the round. Visually I was not persuaded by the sets of Abd'elkader Farrah nor the lighting of John Wyckham. The fresh approach is honourable. Don't miss it. Indeed for you it may be a revelation, though I must say for me it was no such thing.

Philip Hope-Wallace

PETER PAN

It was indeed the Never Never Land for about a third of the audience who never arrived. One touch of London fog and we are all Lost Boys. Still there were enough present at the Scala Theatre and advance booking has never been better. Little wonder: this play when it works, works powerfully. The children stop chattering: awed silence, followed by lusty cheering reward the players who continue doggedly through the yowling, the hasty exits of the unprepared or untrained, and the general hubbub of a young audience. These make little enough of the sentiment. It is the elderly critics who are tear-logged from the start. But the action (if well put together) the simple adventurous situations, the danger run by one of your own side whom with a shout, frozen in your mouth, you could still warn in time: these are the undying fires of theatre.

The present production looks well, as they go or have gone in the past. The producer is himself a fine ex-Hook, Richard Wordsworth, and I thought I noticed some considerable pulling-together which must be due to his command. There is little I'd take issue with: though it is certainly better in the ship scene if, when Hook knocks the barrel from under our hero, Peter merely remain suspended in the air where he was, and be not twitched suddenly aloft. But the lagoon and the underground house were pleasing to the eye; and many if not all the voices were pleasing to the ear; quite soon the music, which is a highly important element in the magic will cohere more surely under Donald Elliott's baton. Yes, clearly, the control is tighter.

The new Peter—didn't someone say it would be a boy in

very fact this year?—is Anne Heywood who has had stage as well as film experience. She has a nice figure, good legs and a pleasant direct manner: but there would be more to be had from the part with surer phrasing of the words and a more confident playing of the audience's emotions. Someone spoilt the Tinker Bell agony by shouting "Yes" too soon.

Little Wendy was ginger-haired Jane Asher who really had the nursery air—and what a nursery it is! What with Nana the canine nurse (the highly professional Tony Helm) Liza the nursery maid (Pauline Knight) and Mr. Darling (John Gregson, friendly enough here but a really dashing Captain Hook) the England of Edward the Seventh is still in every fold of the bedspreads. All the same when the windows fly open, there are lumps in the throat—the fog, no doubt.

Ian Low

"VICTORIAN VALHALLA"

MEMORIES OF THE CRYSTAL PALACE

For Londoners, at any rate, the blitz took the fun out of fire-watching. I mean, of course, that splendid old spectator sport for which no more is needed than a dark night, the air crisp but not too cold, a gleaming red fire-engine manned by a not too expert crew and a sawmill well alight.

For some connoisseurs, it must be a tenement building, complete with women tossing babies down into blankets but in my youth, in the dear, dead days before television, the blaze was the thing. Nobody was hurt and only the insurance company the sorrier.

From all accounts the night the Crystal Palace went up,

twenty-five years ago exactly, must have met the most exacting standards of such occasions. It started shortly after eight o'clock in the Egyptian Court, and within twenty minutes, helped by a gas leak and a brisk wind, had whipped through pitch pine partitions, and rooms filled with furniture to bring the central portion of the building down in a great cloud of sparks and flame.

By the time the Fleet Street reporters got there, the flames were being estimated at 300 feet and the crashing of glass could be heard miles away. The whole of South London had turned out and mounted police were beating a path for the fire-engines, ninety of them before the night was out.

At 8.55, according to one chronicler, the end wall of the South Transept fell. A reporter saw a spiral staircase inside become an incandescent pillar. By now someone had found and talked to the only people who had been inside when the fire started. They were members of the Crystal Palace orchestra who had been rehearsing with Mr. Holloway at the grand organ.

Not believing the first warning, they had carried on for a time. " We were playing 'A tale of Old Japan,'" Mr. Holloway added.

The aeroplanes were a fanciful touch. Like great moths attracted to the light, they circled above the crowds now numbered in hundreds of thousands: air liners were diverted from their routes to give the passengers a better view, and small planes specially chartered from as far away as Brighton, where the glow could be seen in the sky.

A cordon of police—which according to one report comprised 3000 men—had been drawn around the area. There was a danger that the South Tower, more than 200 feet high, would fall among the crowds. (It didn't and had to be blown up in 1941.)

Someone remembered the birds in the aviary and released them. They flew in hundreds to roost among the trees, but nothing could be done for the cats, which were there for a show.

The goldfish in the fountain survived, although they were stained blue.

The heat was terrific. Panes of glass, 30 inches by 40 inches and $1\frac{1}{4}$ inches thick and weighing as much as a man, buckled and melted to hang in great icicles when it was all over. (People still have buttons and other articles found embedded in glass like fossils.) The glare was visible over ten counties.

People were arriving from social functions. The Duke of Kent was there in evening dress. He got slightly splashed by a hose. The firemen could do little though they managed to save an ancient fire-engine among the exhibits.

At last it was all over. Twenty-five acres of glass and 9,640 tons of iron had become glowing rubble, and in the suddenly dark night the crowds made their way home.

The thoughtful authorities arranged special trains and late buses.

Next day, an obituary started: " Last night, we burned our Victorian Valhalla . . ."

The palace, erected in 1851 for the Great Exhibition in Hyde Park, and moved to Sydenham three years later, had fond memories for millions who had wandered among its preposterous statuary. ("Una and the Lion," " The Bather," or "The Dying Ishmael," "though a painful subject it . . . reflects great credit on M. Strazza.")

Many had sat in the great hall with the " Hallelujah Chorus " (chorus and orchestra of 3,400) exploding in their ears, or strayed half-scared among the massive prehistoric monsters dotted around the 300 acres of shrubbery.

It was one of those monsters which provided an after-dinner speaker with what must be the finest opening sentence on record. It seems that when the models were being put up, a group of savants held a dinner inside an iguanodon, and one of the guests, Professor Owen, seated appropriately in the skull, began his speech thus: " Gentlemen, the beast in which I am now speaking . . ."

His colleague, Professor Forbes, delighted the company with a poem which ended:

> The jolly old beast
> Is not deceased.
> There's life in him again.

The liveliness continues. Children when the keepers' backs are turned, still scramble into the monster's belly and light fires to see the smoke coming out of its mouth, or simply stick their heads out and pretend they are being eaten.

The monsters, of course, were there to instruct as well as amuse, according to the Prince Consort's formula, and when the palace moved from Hyde Park to its new home it exchanged its collection of contemporary wonders (like Croskill's Archimedean Root Washer, Brown's Patent Fumigator, Smith's Comic Electric Telegraph and the Sportsman's Knife with its eighty blades) for a series of courts in which every style of art and architecture was displayed.

The year of the exhibition was remembered by Hardy as "a precipice in time." It was "an era of great hope and activity among the nations and industries."

This zestful, earnest, cheerful pursuit of beauty and truth continued all through the nineties and the programmes at the palace reflect it. As the empire grew the spoils found their way to the hill. The programme note describing the visit of a troupe of Somalis in 1895 ends with these words:

Before they return to their own country they will probably arrive at the conclusion that Somaliland is not the most important country in the world, which is at present their fixed idea.

None of those who watched the "natives" in their prefabricated village can have had any doubts as to which was the most important country.

But the old palace, like many a monument, and remarkably for one so fragile, long outlived its day. By 1898 it was housing flower shows (dahlia, viola, rose, carnation and picotee societies in the one year) as well as Wulff's circus and Mr. Beerbohm Tree in *The Red Lamp*. And firework displays: you could see them free from all over London. The great triennial Handel orgies went on, but, by the thirties of this century, the place was shabby and given over to vaudeville, with dirt-track racing on the side.

To-day you may walk among the dead leaves and see only the B.B.C. television mast against the sky where "the great vitreous expanse" once stood. On the wind come the noises of the cranes working on the L.C.C.'s sports centre in the valley. The monsters stand self-consciously around the lake. The small artificial cliff from which the common man once learned geology is become a rockery.

Two hundred German bombs in the area completed what the fire began, leaving not a wrack behind.

Diana Rowntree

BUILDING IN CONCRETE

MI, the London-Birmingham Motorway, goes neither to London, nor to Birmingham. Last year, at the time the road was opened, this fact was taken as a symbol of the inadequacy of our planning methods. To-day it has a different look. After a long period of germination, planning theory in this country has started to put out shoots. Consider the newly thought-out town at Cumbernauld; the barbican scheme off the ice at last; a two-level arts centre actually to be built on the South Bank; and Newcastle upon Tyne in the running to be the most modern city in Europe.

The inadequacy of our planning machinery is beyond question, but our long delay in facing the problems of the motor age can now be turned to advantage. Just as countries like Sweden, which came late to industrialisation, could see the slums of Britain as an awful warning, we are able to use the lessons of the American scene. The Americans have built themselves some exemplary roads, but they failed to look ahead for the social consequences of so much mobility. The result has been a nation-wide move into shapeless suburbs that were designed only for private profit. If we had built comparable roads this whole island could by now have been covered with such a growth.

Our legislative deficiency in financing roads and reshaping our towns gave our planners an unwelcome theoretical spell, during which they were able to sift the problems of the motor-borne civilisation pretty fine. First they noted that the roads that solve traffic problems simultaneously create problems. Once people can move, they do move. Once the traffic block shifts, more cars come into town.

They found that our traffic estimates needed doubling, then trebling. Coventry had been splendidly planned after the war, with traffic segregation and pedestrian precincts, but not nearly enough space, as it turned out, for the parking needs of 1960. One car per family is going to be the minimum. At this level any picture of an American shopping centre shows a greater area of cars than of buildings. If we do not wish to look at a landscape consisting entirely of motor cars, we have got to build them in, or put them underground.

The motorist, too, has changed. Between the wars he was assumed to be a passer-by who could be syphoned off by means of ring roads. But it turns out that we are all motorists going about our daily lives. The long-drawn-out struggle over the Oxford by-passes has brought out the fact that the cars that clog such a town mostly have good reason for being there.

Even in Newcastle, with the Great North Road running slap through the middle, only 2 per cent of the load is found to be long-distance, through traffic. It is clear that the present volume of traffic cannot be cut down or diverted. It will increase in bulk, and it needs to penetrate to the city centre. Cities have to find a parking area as large as that centre. Now that a city as industrially minded as Newcastle proposes to organise itself on four or five levels, we can take it that multi-level planning is accepted at last as a practical proposition.

As the great cities adjust their sights to this revolution, a small town in Scotland is getting on with the job. The new town of Cumbernauld, near Glasgow, is being built on the two-level principle as regards traffic. Every house has motor access from a spur of the main street, and on its other side footpaths link up by underpass to the same town centre. Nor does this town sprawl over the countryside in the normal twentieth-century way; it is planned with the centralised urbanity of the eighteenth century.

We shall soon be saying good-bye to the concept of "ground level." Planners working on multi-level projects never speak of " the ground," but of " level 12 " or " 24." This is not a cause for lament. We have the job of creating a new environment shaped for a mobile life; it will be so different in scale and shape from anything that has ever been before that we have not even a name for it. The making of the great dual roads that will fly over the landscape, diving through the hills, and sending out tentacles to the communities they pass, could be called " landscaping," for it will certainly remake the landscape. Yet being built of concrete it will have some of the properties of architecture. And those cathedral-scale fly-overs had better be architecture, because they are very large, and very expensive, and permanent. They are also what future generations will judge us by.

Our landscape has been redrawn many times. The Roman contribution was mostly in hard materials, in brick, concrete, and tiles. But the bulk of what we tend to think of as the "natural landscape" consists of hedges, timber, and field crops, a landscape rooted in the earth. The contribution of the railway engineers was magnificent when seen in contrast to this natural landscape, but when it came to creating towns its designers grasped neither their responsibilities nor their power. The same cannot be said of us. We know that land is limited, that trees take a long time to mature and can be felled in minutes. We know that concrete is less easy to remove. This is why we must pause, and organise most carefully, before we start to pour the motor landscape in concrete.

The landowners who planted the hedges, the windbreaks, and the coverts, who occasionally laid out a vista to gladden the eye, had composite responsibilities. Farmers and building owners, they cared for the look of their property mainly because they had to spend their lives on it. The grander among them were competing in the fashion for landscaping. In this age of specialisation all the planning interests—layout, structure, economy, and appearance—can be represented only by a team. One would suppose that the team which would design a motorway should consist of traffic and structural engineer, landscape architect, architect, and quantity surveyor, under the chairmanship of a planner. Yet, at the recent joint meeting of the Institute of Civil Engineers and the Institute of Landscape Architects an engineer asserted that an engineer could perfectly well understand landscaping and could design fine roads unaided. This may sometimes be the case! Nevertheless by their very titles the two professions are shown to have different loyalties. Even an engineer with a strong feeling for landscape is unlikely to have as wide a grasp of the agricultural implications of planting as the landscape architect would. And the planner's part in relating the design of the road to the social context of the life of the region must be acknowledged. Only with a team led by a planner can we have any confidence that the roads are going where we want them, and will not take us to some unforeseen trouble in the way of unplanned suburbs or awkward shifts of population.

With speed as a new dimension to the shape of the earth, we can no longer design the roads and towns and "countryside" of a region as separate entities. The new motorways will eventually have to find some way of flowing smoothly in to the city centre. The junctions cannot be written off for much longer as odd bits of " engineering work " out on the by-pass. They will have to connect with the car parks and service roads of the new under-world to our towns. This underworld will be the supreme and awful test for architects. They have not yet produced an attractive subway—not one that you would walk through for the sheer joy of the scenery. It is time they started, for the subway and the multi-level intersection will be as basic to the coming age as the column and entablature were to the classical past.

If we are to make anything of this island during the next half-century the composite approach will be most necessary. We shall have to get out that British comic prop, " the team spirit," and dust it down. And if the multi-level age is to look its true size there is probably another profession that should be added to the team, alongside the tree expert and the quantity surveyor: this is the sculptor. The motorist's landscape will not much longer consist of villages strung together with frustra-tion; travelling on the motorway, the road itself takes control of the landscape. This idea of form seen at speed is new to us. The bridges on MI came in for severe architectural criticism. But consider the æsthetics of roads to the scale of the Californian project. Noel Moffett rightly described it as " sculpture in space." If some sculptors can tear themselves away from the design of commercial symbols and patio ornaments they may find an architectural set-up as expanded as the astronaut's. They will have to gear their minds to the scale of the Forth Bridge, to describe curves with a fast car rather than a pencil, and to learn to speak the language of the traffic engineer. If we are to get our money's worth for all this concrete, we have great need of sculptors of this order in the planning team.

John Dalton

STOP THE WORLD—I WANT TO GET ON

There is something supremely satisfying about an old pot. Especially when it's Sung. There it sits, 3-D like us, a body with a top and a bottom, without a stitch except for a slip, and as likely as not quite different inside.

The small exhibition of Chinese pottery and porcelain (mostly from the V. and A. Eumorfopoulos collection) at the Leicester Art Gallery contains a world apart. One which demands the long gaze that our day and age denies. Incidentally what gives a Rothko its impact is not only its hypnotic bands of sizzling colour but an ancient Stop, Look, and Listen simplicity confronting the Wall Street (I-want-to-get-on) scramble with Great Walls of real speculation, the possible paradise within. Take, for instance, this jar and wine vase from the Han dynasty: cool, silvery green, with warm red earth showing through. Or the small wine pot with tiny spout and one fat-finger handle with a reddish-brown glaze; the little vase with black glaze; the bellying stoneware jar, rust-brown on black—all Sung, made for jolly types and lovers. Or the early Sung vase and cover with incised floral decoration under celadon; the porcelain bowl, also incised, under light blue ying-ch'ing glaze; the Yüan lavender bowl.

Of the later Ming and Ching periods note the square brush-pot (tang pi-p'ing) porcelain with enamel colour of the *famille verte* with two landscapes and two birds (made while Christo-

MISSING MASTERPIECE

pher Wren was busy in the City), a blue pot with turquoise
rim as rich as Rothko, and a white figure of Kuan-Yin, the
Goddess of Mercy. What is frustrating is the overpacked nature
of the glazed exhibition stands. An extra stand, perhaps, with,
say, only four of the finest pots would do the trick, give them
the air and space they need and once possessed. More frustrating
still is not being able to touch them. Down with glass! How
lucky—if impecunious—museum assistants are: they can hold
them close, feel the pulsing shape, take off the lids and squint
inside, sniff.

Richard Seddon

A WALK IN THE PARK

"Margaret has gone for a tatta with Richard Seddon," wrote Paul Nash in a letter to Hartley Ramsden in April, 1946 (according to his biography by Anthony Bertram), "and I am alone again waiting for the alarm to go off twelve midday which reminds me I must take my digitalin pill. We have been talking art and philosophy since mid-breakfast and I have done my bread and butter watercolour for the day . . ."

The Nashes were staying in Parks Road in Oxford while their studio flat round the corner was being spring-cleaned; and I had gone over for the week-end, as I did from time to time. It was the year that Nash died; and, indeed, the last time I saw him. I remember that walk with Margaret Nash very well; and what we talked about as we walked sedately through the park in the pale sunlight.

I had recently been writing something about the Whistler and Ruskin quarrel:

"After the verdict went against him Ruskin relapsed into a tired, defeated old man," I said. "When he was no longer an oracle life held no meaning for him."

"It is not the only time a critic has come a cropper attacking an artist," said Margaret. "The same thing happened to Roger Fry; though not many people are alive to-day who know about it."

"What happened?" I asked.

"It was just after the First World War," she replied. "Paul had made a great name with his war pictures. There were four young men in their twenties who came suddenly into fame around that time—Noël Coward, Ivor Novello, Michael Arlen, and Paul. People made a lot of fuss of them . . . Some people, perhaps, were jealous. In those days Roger Fry's word was law in the art world . . . He wrote in that paper of his and went around the exhibitions of well-known artists praising and condemning. He used to walk into an artist's show, take a long slow look around him, shake his head ostentatiously, and say 'Oh, dear no! Dear me, no! . . .' in a sad sort of way but very loud; and then walk out again. . . . The artist would fail to sell a thing and if he was only recently well known he would be finished before he knew what hit him."

"Rothenstein said in his memoirs that Tonks regarded Fry as the counterpart of Hitler and Mussolini," I said, "and himself refers to 'Fry's dictatorship.' Did Fry ever try it on Paul?"

"He certainly did," answered Margaret. "He not only did the tut-tutting and head-shaking routine in Paul's exhibitions but he constantly wrote against him. He said that art history has shown that no great art ever came out of war; and things like that."

"I know that after the war nobody bought Fry's pictures," I commented. "He held a show in 1920 that was a complete flop. He blamed this partly on the wartime emotionalism which was driving the public and the artists what he called 'pall-mall' into romanticism under the guidance of the surrealists, and into what he derided as 'the new mysticism.'"

"Well, Paul was a mystical and romantic artist, of course," she stated, "and was wrongly called a surrealist."

We walked in silence for a while and then she gave her rich Irish chuckle and with characteristic inconsequence pointed to the distant spires of Oxford across the park.

"Paul once painted that," she declared. "He did it through binoculars to save himself the trouble of walking across the park. Muirhead Bone saw it and was very indignant. 'Oh, I say, my *dear* Nash,' he said, 'I hardly think that's *quite* fair, you know . . .'"

She laughed again as we continued our staid progress.

"About Fry . . ." I said.

"Well, after saying that no good artists were ever war artists, and things to that effect, and generally causing us distress, he went to Italy for a holiday. He left the paintings that he and Clive Bell were sending to the forthcoming New English show in the hall of his flat; and left the key with the people in an office in the basement. This office was concerned with a voluntary organisation doing welfare and war rehabilitation work and that sort of thing. The arrangement was that when the exhibition agent's van called for the pictures someone from this office would let the man into the flat to collect them . . ."

She broke off to admire the buds of early blossom on some small trees.

"Oh, look! Isn't that lovely? . . ."

"Very nice," I said. "About Fry . . ."

"Well, a young voluntary worker from the office—a sort of office girl—went up with the key when the agent's man called and let him into the flat. She showed him where the paintings were and locked up when he departed."

"So? . . ."

"So the pictures were duly shown to the New English selection committee, which at different times included really big names in British art, such as Sickert, Rothenstein, MacColl, Steer, and Augustus John . . . Clive Bell's pictures were all right and so, presumably, were Fry's, except for one. This one was, of all things, a ludicrous attempt at a war picture. It was quite absurd; outdated and jingoistic . . . something about three allied commanders all standing on top of the world and shaking hands in front of flags of all nations . . . Ridiculous from any artist of merit, and from Fry, after what he wrote about Paul, it was laughable. It was signed, too . . ."

"What happened after that?"

"A roar of laughter went round the very circles in which Fry had been cracking his whip. If Fry had been a decent, hard-working, and fairly modest artist he would perhaps have had his leg pulled a bit; after all, they all paint bad ones sometimes. Fry sent a frantic telegram to the office from Italy saying that

203

it was not one of the right pictures and should never have been included, and demanding to know how the mistake had happened. But it was too late by then.

"As it was, he had to stop pontificating and breaking careers. He seemed to deflate and sort of fade. He became shrunken and quiet and suffered ill health . . ."

"Just like Ruskin, after the Whistler verdict went against him," I said. "It is known that Fry certainly drifted apart from many of the artists concerned with the New English from as early as 1911."

"I have no doubt they were fed up with him as early as that," she replied. "But it was this final absurdity that finished him. No one paid any more attention to his criticisms of working artists. Not that he aired his views much after that . . . never in that way, at least. He was never the same man again."

"But how stupid of the girl from the basement," I said. "If she hadn't muddled things up the wrong picture would never have been included."

"It wasn't stupid at all," replied Margaret. "I did it on purpose."

Eric Newton

LOWRY IN LONDON

There was a time when each successive one-man show of paintings by L. S. Lowry was greeted with the not very bright remark that the more he changed the more he remained the same. The present exhibition that has just opened at the Lefevre Gallery (30 Bruton Street, London, w.1), is his ninth in London, and one is tempted to reverse the cliché. The more he remains the same wide-eyed student of human animals scurrying about among inhuman buildings (with an occasional perfunctory visit to the seaside or a melancholy range of hills) the more he changes. One of the paintings in this exhibition is entitled "Piccadilly Circus" and its subject is recognisably Piccadilly Circus, London, w.1. This is news on a "man bites dog" level.

A Press handout on the exhibition gravely notes that in order to paint this picture, Mr. Lowry "made several journeys" to that famous beauty spot. He "just stared and took in the scene" and then returned to his home near Manchester to translate what he had seen into another unmistakable Lowry. The journey was doubtless necessary, but it was not a journey of the spirit. Eros looks uncomfortably baroque after the harsh rectangles of the North of England—as though the God of Love had unaccountably strayed into the land of the Nibelungs. But Mr. Lowry pays no more than lip-service to Mount Olympus. His brush still moves in the same rhythms: the sky and the pavements are still off-white tempered with a delicate layer of dust and smoke and the buildings are still red and grey with punctuations of black. The inhabitants of London, it is true, are a little more agitated in their attempts to avoid the oncoming buses, but they belong to the same species of *homo industrialis* and they are accompanied by the same improbable little black dogs. Mr. Lowry's journey has not led him into a betrayal of his creed as an artist.

But a more subtle change than that of mere locality has gradually altered Lowry's tone of voice during the past few years. Once he was bewitched by his environment. An æsthetic love-potion had turned the grimness of the industrial revolution into a spectacle of sheer beauty. In the present exhibition more than a hint of the social commentator begins to creep in. "A Protest March" (we are now in the North again), is an index that the love-potion is losing its power and the picture is all the better for it. The same effect of human purposefulness can be seen in the grouping of "A Street Procession." The absurd dogs turn their backs on the advancing marchers, alarmed by these signs of human discontent. Another sign of the ardent lover giving way to the observant bystander is the intrusion of humour into some of his smaller paintings.

Lowry is nearing his seventy-fourth birthday and he begins to relax and giggle at what he sees. Four front views of children playing with ridiculous abandon, and three back views of children waiting for a bus with melancholy patience are social comments of an acute kind.

But these close-up extracts from Lowry's life are still not quite the essential Lowry even though they are a new departure for him. The largest painting in the show is a crowded panorama of the hill-side that rises behind Ebbw Vale. It is the most densely packed and the most highly organised picture he has ever attempted, and for once he has sacrificed detail to breadth. The inferno of cottages and streets that covers the landscape is seen with an all-embracing eye through an industrial haze and the mood becomes almost noble.

Stylistically there is little change between this and his last exhibition. The key of colour has become gradually paler and brighter. The whites are whiter, the blacks more patterned and insistent, the space more controlled and the skylines more articulated. The effect is of a man whose enthusiasms over the years have remained at the same pitch but who has slowly grown wiser and calmer and simpler.

Eric Newton

COVENTRY CATHEDRAL

If it is to remain affectionately in the memory, a good building must have a memorable personality. Beauty, in the conventional sense of the word, hardly matters; ingenuity—the kind of ingenuity that contributes to the building's function—is helpful but not necessary. A thoughtful ground plan and an effective elevation may be impressive on an architect's blueprint, but what matters most, as one enters an important building, is its sudden impact on the mind: a mood engendered in the architect's creative imagination must have been made tangible in terms of stone and glass, colour and light, height and breadth, simplicity and complexity.

A cathedral's function is both elementary and profound. It must be an enclosure designed specifically for worship. Like the plot of a play, it should contain nothing that interferes with that basic purpose, but, like the hero of a play, it must have a unique personality. If Hamlet were no more than a creature dedicated to justice and revenge he would be a bore. Shakespeare took care to make him complex, mysterious, inconsistent, and therefore startling. Sir Basil Spence has taken the same kind of care to make the personality of his new cathedral in Coventry definite and curious. Moreover, the building, like a Shakespearean character, develops and reveals its personality slowly as one comes to closer terms with it.

Not the least surprising ingredient in its personality is its initial modesty. Drama—the kind of drama in which almost any designer of a major architectural structure is tempted to indulge—is deliberately played down. The obvious drama of the approach to the new building, through the shattered and

207

slaughtered ruins of the old cathedral whose spire is still the outstanding feature of the city's skyline, is enough. The new cathedral is hardly visible until one descends the steps to the main west door, and even then the exterior is unimpressive. It is a building hardly meant to be looked at. Only when one enters it does its personality become apparent, and even then, in contrast with the spiky Gothic romanticism of the ruin outside, one's first impression is of puritanical austerity. No towering vaults, no umbrageous aisles, not even the classic architect's effect of mathematical perfection. Lightness and dignity certainly, but no colour, no sparkle. Plenty of plain surfaces, elegantly put together, nothing at first sight to arrest the eye except the big tapestry that fills the east wall, and even that looks less daring and less colourful than one had expected. From the west door its effect is delicate and its colour chalky. Only as one approaches do the angularity of its forms and the greens, reds, and whites of the surrounding imagery become insistent.

Yet even this double denial of Gothic mystery and classic clarity has its own impact. The starkness and modesty of the first view of the interior has the effect of drawing one towards the high altar and the tapestry behind it that fills the east wall from floor to ceiling. Where, one wonders, in so large an enclosed space in which no window is visible except the huge area of glass engraved with figures of angels over the entrance door, does the light come from? For the first impression is of an evenly spread, suffused, though not dazzling, light that pervades the interior.

One walks eastwards for no more than fifteen paces and turns to the right to meet the full impact of the baptistry window by John Piper, whose chromatic brilliance had been hidden by the deep projections of the rigidly squared-up tracery. There is no readable imagery in this crossword puzzle of colour with its subtle transitions from deep blue to a central area of luminous gold. The window is a carefully planned progress to a central radiant climax and is probably the most effective single unit contributed by an artist to the building, for although the baptistry is not screened off from the main body of the nave, it has its own architectural coherence and makes its own æsthetic contribution to the whole.

The baptistry makes a break—the only break—in one's progress eastwards. As one approaches the altar nothing changes except that, as one nears the tapestry details begin to emerge. The four Evangelists become more angular and colourful, the central Christ in glory more awe-inspiring, the minute (life-sized, to give scale to the whole) figure of a man more human, the Crucifixion below it more readable as a symbol of pathos and tragedy.

One ascends the steps of the chancel, passing between the solid, fenced-in blocks of the wooden choir stalls, to the second set of steps that lead to the altar, and one turns back towards the west door to discover oneself in a cathedral that has suddenly changed its personality. Simplicity and austerity have been replaced by rich and colourful detail.

The general plan of the side walls—five gigantic teeth from a large saw facing each other across the body of the building—is by this time well known. The side of each tooth facing west is an unbroken wall; the side facing east contains an elaborate stained-glass window, making ten windows in all, each with its own dominant colour and its own readable imagery. It is the light from these towering windows, hidden from the entrance, crowded together and in full view from the altar, that illuminates the west wall. And it is this sudden change of mood and of colour that turns the first impression of stark elegance into one of crowded preciousness.

It is this carefully calculated dramatic effect of puritanism transformed into exuberance that will make the cathedral unique as a stroke of architectural invention. Whether professional critics of architecture will approve of what might be thought of as an architectural *coup de théâtre* I cannot guess. Nor does the final verdict rest with the judgment of the professional critic of architecture. The device is deliberate and immensely effective, for it enables the full impact of what the team of artists and craftsmen have contributed to the cathedral to be taken in at a single and rather breathtaking glance. What the ten windows add up to, after a careful scrutiny of their colour-and-form symbolism, can be studied later and at leisure. What matters as a first impression is that here is a collection of undoubtedly successful single works of art concentrated, like paintings carefully spaced out and hung in a well-designed gallery, so that each of the ten units contributes to the effect of an artistic whole. Purple, orange, red, and gold follow each other processionally towards the predestined climax, which is, as it should be, both a visual and spiritual climax.

Separated from the main enclosed area of the cathedral are three detached buildings, each with its own religious function. Opposite the baptistry, leading off from the north wall, is the circular Chapel of Unity—a symbolical gesture to cut across denominational gaps within the Christian Church. Here the points of interest are the tent-like construction of the chapel, its elaborate marble mosaic floor by the Swedish artist Einar Forseth, who a generation ago filled the great hall of the town hall in Stockholm with golden mosaics, and slim windows of stained glass by Margaret Treherne let into the structure of the ten buttresses that support the roof.

At the east end of the cathedral, at the end of a slim corridor leading off the south wall, behind the main altar, is the circular chapter house and guild chapel from the roof of which will eventually be hung an enormous crown of thorns in metal.

Thirdly, wedged in unobtrusively between the corridor leading to the chapter house and the open space behind the high altar and leading to the base of Graham Sutherland's tapestry, is a tiny chapel—the Chapel of the Resurrection—fenced off from the rest of the cathedral by a wrought-iron grille, in the shape of a crown of thorns, designed by Sir Basil Spence himself, through which one sees a glittering low-relief figure of an angel holding a chalice. This is the only attempt in the cathedral to construct a small-scale gem of detailed ornamentation embedded into the larger concept of the building as a whole.

To examine such a building piecemeal, in the company of the architect who, one would guess, is never more pleased or more explosively eloquent than when he is bombarded with questions from an art critic, sheds a good deal of light on the kind of problem that has to be solved before a building can become a unifying environment for separate works of art. Some of those works of art are undeniably successful in their own right. And undoubtedly the cathedral succeeds in incorporating them into itself without disturbing the overriding mood of the building.

From the point of view of a creative mind envisaging such a building, the main problems to be solved are not those of symbolism or imagery but of scale and relative emphasis. In that sense, certain details have not quite succeeded. The glass screen crowded with engraved figures by John Hutton is a little diffuse. One searches for focal points and arresting intersections that would make for an intenser meaning and one fails to find them. The Piper window is a triumph and is, in fact, more impressive than one had thought a crossword puzzle could be. The complexity of triangular stars that hangs over the choir stalls and mounts to a pyramid over the bishop's throne, I find disturbing and restless, as though an army of migrating starlings had been released and got slightly out of control.

The tapestry is exactly right. It could have been overbold and overemphatic, and the solemn central figure could have dwarfed the building as the image of the Pantokrator dwarfs the semidome in the apse of Cefalu Cathedral. That overemphasis has been avoided and the surrounding panels of the evangelists on the tapestry hold it firmly in position without competing with its grandeur. In the long and sometimes radical series of afterthoughts and adjustments that have taken place on the architect's drawing board since the structure was first envisaged in his mind, the idea of a supernatural ikon filling the east wall has never changed. Whatever else was subject to readjustments, *that* was to contain the essence of the cathedral's meaning.

Christopher Driver

P.R. FOR THE PURPLE

Sydney Smith once confessed to having only one illusion left, and that was the Archbishop of Canterbury. The Bishop of Llandaff, introducing the essays in *Bishops* (What they are and what they do: Faith Press, 18s.), reports that at shopfloor level in Wales Dr. Ramsey's appointment to Canterbury was widely approved on the score of his venerable appearance. Dr. Simon is too shrewd a man to be much pleased about this reaction.

Yet it is perhaps surprising that the stock British reaction to gaiters is still so often affectionate, if ribald. From Whitgift to Wilberforce, the bishops courted (and received) an appalling press. Hence perhaps this attempt at rehabilitation—P.R. for the purple.

Dr. Simon, as editor, has at least picked up one principle of public relations: construct your image of the lively rather than the safe, the best rather than the typical. Himself an anti-nuclear bishop, his contributors include the Bevanite bishop, the Lady Chatterley bishop, two of the ecumenical bishops, and even (O Laud! Oh Montreal!) a Congregational bishop from the Church of South India. There is also a delightfully cool, frightfully learned piece by the late Dr. Sykes about that topic of current debate, the election of bishops. Between them they manage to avoid the suggestion that the episcopate is a static institution which is to be offered to Christians of other traditions on a take-it-or-leave-it basis. The Bishop of Woolwich is conspicuously non-static, and his sketch of a "New Model Episcopacy" is commended as "providentially opportune" by Dr. Hustable in a Dissenter's epilogue.

On the whole, Anglican bishops are no longer "proud,

prelatical, and pompous." But few—at any rate, in this country —can be regarded as capable of the "major social breakthrough" which Dr. Simon is brave enough to require of them—not so long as they are educated, accommodated, remunerated, and pensioned in a manner which, even if it is not by secular standards luxurious, effectively atrophies their sociological insight and their English prose style (cf. Lambeth conference reports, *passim*). Even some of the contributors to this book do little to dispel the feeling that there is something natural and inevitable about the association of gaiters with gas.

Philip Collins

THE LOWBROW GENIUS

Only lately has Dickens begun to receive the quality of attention he deserves. Dons have been shy of a writer so alien in outlook from themselves—the least bookish, the least educated, of the masters. And "his leading quality was Humour": Forster's truism has often been ignored in favour of more modish preoccupations. "Everybody can appreciate Mr. Micawber," writes Mr. A. O. J. Cockshut in *The Imagination of Charles Dickens* (Collins, 16s.), "but what can the critics say about him?" Mr. Cockshut throws in the sponge, and realises that his discussion of *David Copperfield* is accordingly unbalanced. But he rarely fails us thus, and the fineness of his chapter on Dickens's humour suggests that, had he persisted, he would have found many original and penetrating things to say.

Like his earlier books on Trollope and Victorian religious controversies, this is succinct, elegantly written, scholarly without fuss, and alive with thought. He aims to show how, by a continuous though slow and unself-conscious development, Dickens made assets out of the liabilities which accompanied his enormous visual and imaginative gifts. For, as Mr. Cockshut reminds us, his mind was coarse, untrained, and undisciplined. His reading was limited, he relished the cruder forms of melo-drama and sentiment, he lacked self-knowledge. His limitations and failures are so manifest that there seems every excuse for ignoring or patronising him: how could he yet be great? Mr. Cockshut, firm but never supercilious in registering the faults, gets beyond the usual answer, that we must swallow the dross for the sake of the gold. He takes a few recurrent, indeed obsessive, topics—prisons, crowds, justice, money, dirt, and violence—and shows that being a lowbrow has some advantages, for " it is very commonplace ideas like these that are inex-haustible." The items listed are familiar enough in recent Dickens-criticism, but Mr. Cockshut traces many new patterns and significances, and he beautifully analyses the " strangeness " of Dickens's achievement, " one foot in fairyland and one in the grimy realities of Victorian commerce."

Though accepting the current preference for the later novels (he is particularly acute on *Little Dorrit* and *Great Expectations*) he respectfully challenges Dr. Leavis's claims for *Hard Times* and rightly sees bluster and irresponsibility in much that has passed for political wisdom and penetration. In his criticism of society and institutions Dickens is, he says, closer to Kafka than Marx, " to the moral and personal anger of Samuel Johnson than to the reforming anger of J. S. Mill." But Mr. Cockshut exaggerates when he asserts that *most* of the social abuses Dickens castigated had ceased when he wrote about them, and there is more to be said about his dramatisation of social evils than that " He wrote as an artist, or a spectator, never as a citizen." In his journalism he is much more the citizen, with positive if not always very original or sensible notions about social policy; in his philanthropic work he displays an intelligent effectiveness lacking, as Mr. Cockshut complains, in his good characters. Such disparities between the novelist and the man raise fascinating questions about his imaginative processes, which Mr. Cockshut has had to pass by.

Moreover the journalist often invades the novels. Mr. Cockshut discusses the strange reappearance of David Copperfield's brutal teacher, Creakle, as a milk-and-water magistrate: he makes some interesting points, but the episode remains an artistic flaw —hilarious, but inexplicable in terms of the novel's internal logic or of Dickens's personal involvement with his hero. It belongs with the penological controversies of 1850, to which Dickens had already contributed; probably some other details are a private joke against a Middlesex magistrate with whom he had a personal feud. He was a great artist but never a pure one, as Mr. Cockshut remarks, and such topicalities and personal quirks account for so much that one is constantly driven to invoke historical and biographical explanations beyond the minimal use of them that Mr. Cockshut allows himself. One is tempted, indeed, to go too far, so that literary criticism disappears behind vast accumulations of fact (and myth) about Dickens's life and times. Mr. Cockshut errs in the right direction. His book—necessarily incomplete, as he recognises—is a timely, memorable, and delightful addition to the short list of useful Dickensiana.

Alistair Cooke

LIFE GETS COMPLICATED DOWN MEXICO WAY

Along the cottonwood banks of the Rio Grande, to the border town of Matamoros on the Gulf of Mexico and all the way west to Tijuana on the Pacific, the most important man in the

United States Government last week was John Dent, an obscure Congressman from Pennsylvania.

He is the chairman of an obscurer House sub-committee, that on the impact of Imports and Exports on American Employment, which has been holding hearings in Washington. It heard, among other complainants, a bankrupt tomato grower from Niland, California, and a labour leader from El Paso.

They all have grudges that involve, one way and another, the Mexicans or, as they say down here, the Mexican Nationals, to distinguish them from the Mexicans who are naturalised north of the border and are known as Latin Americans. The rest of us are Anglos.

For a century or more the travel books have played up the happy amiability of relations across the border. Most of the border towns, Brownsville especially, have annual fiestas before Lent. The Texans wear Mexican costumes and the Mexicans come as they are. Anything goes, except the mention of Pancho Villa.

For the rest of the year Tijuana on the California border and Juarez across the river from here maintain a pleasure "industry" which brings a nightly swarm of tourists to be victimised by a swarm of bead and spinach-jade pedlars, strip joints, doll shops blazing in magenta and green, dubious book stores, " native dance " halls: Hollywood's B-film version of a frontier town, mitigated only by the humble gentility of most of the Mexicans and by nightly bouts of the swiftest and most beautiful of all ball games, jai-alai.

By day relations are a little more complex. Juarez is the East Berlin to the Western sector of El Paso. Thousands of Mexicans cross the bridge to earn their daily bread. Lately it has been very good bread. The Latin Americans, who have always gone to school with the Anglos and intermarried at every social level, cannot any longer provide the work force for the great prosperity, for the valley building boom, the expansion of the natural gas, smelting, cement, and cinder block industries, to say nothing of the less skilled services required to

216

house and feed the 28,000 resident troops stationed at Fort Bliss and Briggs Air Base.

Consequently the demand for Mexican nationals is clamant, and their demand for equal wages is understandable, some people say outrageous. One bitter employer moaned: "You get better work across the border for a dollar a day than you get on this side for eight dollars." Anyway, the enterprising Mexicans leave their dumb brothers to bake tamales or run a chicken farm while they cross the river and make a killing as plumbers, electricians, mechanics.

This labour force is unorganised and unprotected, unlike the traditional "stoop labour" which used to come over in the spring, follow the harvest of sugar beets in Colorado, and go out to the lettuce fields of California. During the war the Mexican Government exacted a modest price for the anti-Axis alliance with a treaty dignifying the miserable wanderings of these people with a minimum wage scale, some rudimentary housing laws, sanitation, showers, the paid repatriation of pregnant mothers, and other concessions to what the ranchers from here to the Salinas Valley called "communism."

The same cry is heard again as fewer and fewer Mexicans, however lowly, agree to work for the old starvation wages. "It isn't enough," roared one old Anglo, "that the Mexicans gouge you for bad work; now the labour unions are raising hell about the wage differential."

The case of the bankrupt tomato farmer is simpler and grimmer. And Niland, California, until lately "the winter tomato capital of the United States," has to be seen to be believed. It lies just east of the Salton Sea in the great Imperial Valley, that bleak desert coaxed into raging fertility these thirty years by the waters of the All American Canal. As recently as 1957 over three hundred farmers planted 4700 acres in tomatoes, whose harvest collected more than $4 million a year.

To-day the roads to the abandoned tomato fields are grown over with weeds, like the lawns of the farmers. Thirty-nine men are left struggling with a bare two hundred acres. Three-quarters of the town's shops and stores are nailed up and the windows plastered with court orders to foreclose.

A thousand people have gone from the town and less than two hundred remain. Of these the most prominent is Paul Hobbs, the president of the local farm bureau association. His neighbours subscribed the money to send him to Washington. Five years ago he was making £25,000 a year. To-day he has lost all 640 acres, his investments, his house and home.

The cause is uncomplicated. The Mexican labourer gets eight cents an hour, the American labourer $1 an hour. Air freight plus cheap labour has replaced Niland tomato with the Mexican tomato in the refrigerator, if not the favour, of the American housewife.

It is hardly surprising that mooching round this depressed corner of the country one hears little of the United Nations, the Russians, Red China, the Dominican Republic, or anything else that does not bear on the crop you live or starve by.

Alistair Cooke

TEXANS FIND A NEW HERO

In the Dallas Airport there is a bronze statue of a Texas Ranger. He is about ten feet tall, has shoulders like the Parthenon, and leans very slightly forward, not (heaven forbid!) from fear but from his God-given instinct to smell an Indian or a Mexican on the down wind at thirty miles. His role as the protector of the South-west frontier is celebrated in the legend: " One riot, one Ranger."

Political wags in this always rambunctious State have suggested that the Ranger should be replaced with a symbol more appropriate to the political ferment that is presently exciting the South-west. The only question is whether it should be an elephant in a ten-gallon hat or a general on horseback.

The first of these emblems has actually been adopted by Democrats who are rebelling against their traditional family ties to a party that seems to them to represent nothing more than a mule proceeding at a steady gallop down the primrose path of socialism. They want to cast off the hypocrisy of the One-party South and regularise a revolt which has, after all, moved Texas to vote twice in the last three Presidential elections for a Republican.

These people have so far held fiestas in eleven of the biggest counties (there are still 243 to go) to stage " resignation rallies " at which unabashed Texans publicly take the pledge to secede from the Democratic Party and to work while God gives them strength for the welfare of the Republic and the Republicans. It is a boisterous but healthy movement, for the curse of the Democrats' hold on the South is that it rewards mere longevity in office with patronage without regard to the ability or convictions of the office-holder.

The other movement is frankly a Texan tribute to the Fanatic Right, or what General Eisenhower has better called the " super-patriots." Its local sponsor is Mr. Ted Dealey, the editor of the *Dallas News*, the Texans' family Bible. He is the man who walked out of a White House luncheon after telling President Kennedy to his face that he was moving " on Caroline's tricycle " and that what the country needed was "a man on horseback."

Luckily, the proper candidate is to hand, in a native Texan. He is General Edwin A. Walker, who was relieved of his command in Germany after the army decided he had, against its regulations, publicly attacked Government officials, tried to influence the absent votes of his troops, and engaged in partisan politics. The evidence was thoroughly substantiated by the army but, it should be said, only after Walker had been relieved, resigned in a fury, and forfeited his pension.

To-day General Walker is housed in the offices of an oil firm on the seventeenth floor of a Dallas building. He awaits the call to a crusade for the salvation of America from the Communists, and from such naïve or unwitting agents of the great conspiracy as Mr. Roosevelt, Stevenson, Ed Murrow, and Harvard University. On Tuesday evening he will be the hero and main speaker of a rally in the Dallas Memorial Auditorium. Delegations from many Texas cities and neighbouring States are promised. He will be introduced by a former Governor. At his right hand will be Senator Strom Thurmond of South Carolina, who ran as the Dixiecrat Presidential candidate in 1948 and who interprets Senator Fulbright's famous memorandum, recalling the constitutional limits of military interference in politics, as a Left-wing attempt to " muzzle " brave soldiers in general and noble Walker in particular.

General Walker is a tense man, an intense and incoherent speaker, a leathery-faced man with a turkey-gobbler neck, an upright bearing, and the liquid, penitent eyes of a man who has just recovered from a towering rage. He was a champion polo player and is by every account a daring and first-rate soldier who was as ruthless with himself as he was selfless with his men. The trauma which seems to have precipitated the martyr element of his character was the shocking proof, in Korea, that the new men cracked in the face of disorganised Chinese hordes; and the subsequent ease with which American prisoners of war were brainwashed into listless " confessions " of disloyalty.

Everyone who knows him well says that thenceforward he was a disheartened man who never regained phlegm and ambition until he visited President Benson of Harding College in Arkansas, a man who has dramatised in several documentary films (e.g. *Communism on the Map*) his fiery conviction that communism is everywhere sapping the roots of American life. General Walker was exposed to this propaganda when he was uneasily commanding the Federal troops that occupied Little Rock in the segregation crisis of 1957. From then on, evidently, he found his mission. He believes, with an absolute lack of humour or misgiving, that he is fated to be Mr. Dealey's man on horseback.

When he is asked where the money is to come from to finance his bid for power, he declares that " America is bigger than money," but meanwhile displays dollar bills and crumpled cheques pinned to a pack of letters, many of them illiterate, from Texas, Arizona, California, Louisiana, and Arkansas. No one here is deeply concerned about his lack of funds or the loss of his $12,000 a year pension, if only because he has the sympathetic support of Mr. H. L. Hunt, a Texas oil man, who conservatively figures his daily income at $220,000.

There are those who look to Tuesday as the dateline on a new lease of " the American way of life." There are others who think that General Walker is a morning glory who will shine for a night and a day and collapse unless the U.S. suffers some massive humiliation outside its own borders. There are un-ruffled, practical men, like a veteran Washington reporter who has followed Walker and simply concludes: " He might be trouble, but he won't be. By the grace of God, he is the worst speaker in the U.S."

Norman Shrapnel

A WINNING TECHNIQUE

The suggestion made in the Commons yesterday that Mr. Macmillan's supposed television broadcast was in fact made by an actor from *Beyond the Fringe*, rather misfired.

Everybody knows, or ought to know, that the Prime Minister is quite capable of imitating an actor imitating the Prime

Minister, and of thinking up several touches to make the performance far more realistic than any parodist could rival.

There could be little doubt that it really was the Prime Minister we saw at the dispatch box yesterday, answering questions with the air of purposeful relaxation he has lately brought to something like a fine art. Question time grows more and more important as a focus of Parliamentary interest and a testing-ground of policies, and the technique recently developed by Mr. Macmillan in coping with his share of it—now, more often than not, a full fifteen minutes—is worth more attention than it usually gets.

It is no easy matter, even for so subtle and experienced an operator as Mr. Macmillan, to cope (as he did yesterday) with ten main questions and twice as many supplementaries on subjects ranging horizontally from the Common Market to man-made fibres, and vertically from the Governor of the Bank of England to Mr. Khruschev. Most of them, needless to say, are aggressive rather than inquisitive, and the Prime Minister has mastered the full scale of rejoinders from the basic " no, sir " to the hundred-word brush-off.

Yet there is more to it than that. Saying little or nothing without seeming to withhold anything is only a part of the technique that Mr. Macmillan plays very cleverly indeed. Above all it is a matter of tone and mood—of keeping the House interested if not informed, quietly amused if not actually breaking into roars of unseemly laughter, and of staying superior while not goading too many frustrated backbenchers into losing their tempers.

Precariously in control, sparing of gesture but not disdaining it when a crescendo is unavoidable, he conducts his ragged orchestra secure in the knowledge that it cannot in the nature of things have been properly rehearsed. He must beat it in the end.

The off-beat surprise, the casual touch of the unexpected— Mr. Macmillan is particularly good at these. When Mr. Donelly was downright rude to him (and how much ruder can you get than talking about "arrogant soporifics?") Mr. Macmillan looked bored, and coldly turned the other cheek. And when Mr. Emrys Hughes rather coyly, naming no names, raised the question of whether it was right for members of the Cabinet to benefit financially from mergers or take-over bids, Mr. Macmillan reproved him for not being man enough to come out into the open.

"You are making a reference by innuendo to the Home Secretary," he declared with the scorn of one who likes to call a spade a spade. It was unworthy of Mr. Hughes. Everybody knew Mr. Butler's long family connection with Courtaulds, and whenever the I.C.I.-Courtaulds affair had been discussed in the Cabinet or at other ministerial meetings, Mr. Butler had always absented himself. As it happened he was doing so now, and the House was led into a feeling of something like commiseration for the absent Home Secretary over whatever gains his estate may have sustained as a result of the proposed merger.

Other things Mr. Macmillan always knows are how to line himself up for Sayings of the Week ("A meeting with Mr. Khruschev is always an interesting experience"), and how to turn an occasion to political advantage when provoked. Thus, when Mr. Shinwell, reinforced by Mr. Gaitskell, suggested that the chemical and man-made fibre industries should be taken over by the public—a vision greeted with a long, loud Labour cheer—the Prime Minister produced one of his own. He looked to the time when the Labour Party may be able to give us "the new text of the revised version of clause 4." Parliamentary jokes, like music hall ones, tend to the conventional, but at least they are impromptu. Reasonably so, anyway.

Michael Frayn

POLITICALLY SPEAKING

The news that the statue of Nkrumah in Accra, which was
damaged by an explosion, bore on its side the inscription,
"Seek ye first the political kingdom and all the rest shall be
added unto you," has touched off a great deal of speculation.
Where does the quotation come from? I have heard both the
Book of Amazing Free Offers and the Second Book of Un-
solicited Testimonials suggested—even the Book of Fub.

In fact, it comes from the Book of Usually Reliable Sources,
and was reprinted in that very handy little devotional work for
these troubled times, "Selected Wisdom from the Improved
Version." In case you are unacquainted with the range and
usefulness of this book, or are looking for an inscription of your
own, here are a few more extracts:

> Out of the mouths of babes shall come statements of opinion;
> out of the mouths of princes and counsellors, maid-servants
> and players of the lute and tabor; and each shall be harkened
> unto according to his purchasing power. (*Majorities xii.* 15.)

> The wise king holdeth his tongue before his people, and
> maketh his servant to speak on his behalf unto the multitude.
> For if the multitude find fault with his servant's words, then
> shall the king make public sacrifice of him. And the king
> shall gain great credit thereby. (*Parliamentarians vii.* 6.)

> And there was heard the voice of one crying in the metropolis:
> Come ye to have a drink and meet Rock Richmond, who
> maketh glad the people with his lute. And this same prophet
> had an coat of camel's hair, and his meat was oysters and

champagne. For he who goeth before must be as empty as the oyster-shell, and his tongue must be soft with wine, that he may become a vessel of smooth and vacant speech. (*Fub ii.* 18.)

If a prince seeketh to increase his army, he summoneth not the servant from his master nor the husband from his wife, lest he maketh them wroth. Rather shall he grind the faces of those warriors he hath imprest before, causing them to toil by night even as by day. For these are already wroth, and their labours will not increase the number of the wrathful, nor doth the law permit them to make known their burden in epistles to the Press. (*Majorities v.* 20.)

Seek not to share misfortune evenly among the people; but let it bear heavily upon the few. For howsoever sore afflicted they may be, if they cry out thou mayst rebuke them, saying: Ten thousand thousand are them that praise me, and are rich with the blessings I have brought. What are ye few against this mighty host? The voice that crieth out in you is the voice of devils, yea, and chastisement shall be added to your afflictions. (*Majorities v.* 23.)

And he that had mocked the king was brought before him. And the king saith: Mock me again, that I may enjoy that which even the humblest of my subjects hath enjoyed. And the man did as he was bid, and mocked the king, and they that stood about him were sore afraid. But the king betook himself to laughter, and they that were about him did like-wise. Then saith the king: Thou shalt have riches, and stay with me, and mock me all the days of my life, that I and no other may have the enjoyment of it. And I shall taste the sweets both of power and of the mockery of power. But when he heard these words, the man was troubled in his soul, and went aside and hanged himself. (*Jokers xiv.* 2.)

What shall it avail a man, if he keepeth his own soul but loseth his ministry? (*Parliamentarians ix.* 3.)

Sweet is music, and sweet the playing thereof, yet not so sweet as to be honoured in its playing. To be virtuous is worth more than gold; but to be known is more precious than rubies. For all the goings in and the goings out of such an man shall be reported. And his wife shall partake of his glory; yea, and his concubine and his dog. And their opinions shall be sought and prized above the judgments of Solomon. (*Celebrities iii. 9.*)

He that findeth old words for new teachings: he is the friend of merchants and the comforter of princes. (*Adverbs i. 1.*)

Michael Frayn

MIXED COMPANY AT ST. SWIZ'S FESTIVAL

Last week, you may remember, I tried to offer a helping hand to my friends in the advertising industry by announcing (free of charge) the order of service for the advertising men's Harvest Festival at St. Swiz's. I'm sorry to say that it was not too well received.

The hardest things of all were said by Mr. Mark Chapman-Walker, a director of Television Wales and West, about the extract from the article which later appeared on B.B.C. Television. It was, he said, " so staggering in its irreverence, bad taste, and general unfunniness that I am not surprised that a large number of people complained."

Mr. Chapman-Walker is also a director of the *News of the World,* so his views on matters of taste command respect. In fact I have decided that the best thing I can do is go right back to the beginning and give the details of the service in St. Swiz's

with an attempt at the reverence, good taste, and general funni-
ness which in the good old days made Mr. Chapman-Walker's
paper the trusted and respected companion of eight million
families every Sabbath.

THE VICAR AND THE WOMAN IN THE FRONT PEW

What a vicar alleged he saw going on quite openly in his own
church at Harvest Festival was described yesterday when Michael
Frayn, a journalist, of 29 Tregunter Road, Screwe, was found
guilty on three charges of irreverent staggeringness, gustatory
badness, and general humourlessness.

The Reverend Harold Admore, vicar of St. Swiz's, said that
he held a Harvest Festival for advertising men. But his first
reaction to what met his eyes on entering the church was one
of disgust. In answer to a question, he replied that it was the
smallness of the congregation that had disgusted him.

Sex Mix-up

Admore said that besides the men there were a number of
women present. The sexes were mixed. He thought that
some of the women had been brought by the men, but that
others had " simply walked in on their own from the street."
Many of the women were wearing make-up and high heels.

Associated with coloured man

Admore stated that he took as the subject of his sermon man's
quest for good, likening it to the skilled tracking which was
associated with the Red Indian. His intentions throughout the
alleged incidents, he said, had been entirely honourable.

Miss N. Grewsom said that she had been sitting in the front
pew all the time that the events mentioned were alleged to
have been taking place. She agreed that the vicar had used
certain words. They were clearly audible from where she was
sitting. She also saw him make certain gestures.

Shocked

She recalled distinctly that at the end of the first hymn, and on several other occasions, the vicar had used a four-lettered word. It had stuck in her mind, she said, because of the tone of voice in which he had uttered it, and because it seemed to be constantly on the lips of everyone present, women as well as men.

Under cross-examination, Miss Grewsom admitted that she had been shell-shocked while serving with the A.T.S.

Not His Baby

Mr. P. J. Nunbetter, a church warden, gave evidence that he had heard Admore make a certain suggestion to a younger man. As a result of this suggestion, the younger man had played the first hymn.

Nunbetter said he did not remember which hymn it was, since the musical side was " not his baby."

Nothing On

In a statement, Admore was alleged to have admitted being a miserable sinner, but to have added: " The police have nothing on me." His wife gave evidence that he had always behaved perfectly normally, so far as she knew.

As stated, Frayn was found guilty on all three charges and sentenced to five years' corrective reading of the *News of the World*.

Alistair Cooke

SUGAR RAY'S DOWNFALL

As no lover of music this morning will fail to bow his head
before the memory of the great and humble Bruno Walter, so
no lover of boxing in its squalid decline will fail to yield the
passing tribute of a sigh to Sugar Ray Robinson, the one incomparable fighter of our time, whose head this morning was
both bowed and bloody.

He was thrashed last night in Madison Square Garden as he
has never been beaten before, by Denny Moyer, a game and
supple twenty-two-year-old who fought always at a driving
angle from the centre of the ring and had Sugar Ray wheeling
around in a spry but hopeless outer circle, his back flipping the
ropes from time to time like the wrists of a clumsy guitar
player.

Before the fight Sugar Ray had said, with no bluster at all,
that he was in better condition than at any time since he regained
his middleweight championship. He was probably correct, but
he was still in no condition for a ten-round battle with a ripe
and crafty youngster who had, and exploited, a nineteen-year
advantage in muscle tone, respiration, reflex response, and the
ability merely to grunt and not expire when a piston hits the
navel.

What was charming about Sugar Ray in this, his inevitable
farewell to the big time, was that he did not snarl, pout, or
claim he was being smothered in the clinches, or indulge in any
of the self-pitying bravado that disfigures most champions in
eclipse. He was simply puzzled. He kept coming on with that
famous left jab, which punctured Moyer's nose in the first
round and kept it bleeding to the end.

The youth has springs of blood to spare, and Moyer acted as if the leeches had been put on him to rid him of some plaguey infection. Robinson would dance in again and try his old left-right-left flurry of jabs and little uppercuts. Moyer tossed his blond head with the gesture of a man blowing a hair out of his eyes. And Sugar Ray was truly baffled. Nothing that he knew, no feint or arms thrown wide in that fake invitation to suicide, was any use against this weaving, erect young man.

For only three rounds, and those the first, was Sugar Ray able to weld the memory of his greatness with its current parody and to dazzle, or at least intimidate, young Moyer with it. After that, Moyer heeled at dead centre and radiated every punch in the book around a widening circle. He never grew careless or cocky or was caught moving off balance. In the last four rounds, every punch he delivered ran as fast as a seizure clean from the ball of the forward foot, up through the calf and thigh and shoulder blade. In the ninth, a dreadful right caught Sugar Ray and for a fraction of a second he rocked and saved himself by falling around Moyer's middle.

When it was over Sugar Ray flexed his calves for the last time and did a little hobbling dance over to embrace the victor, who was pink and sweaty and very happy, identifiable on the score card as Denny Moyer of Portland, Oregon, but on closer inspection was that bearded figure with a scythe Sugar Ray had dreaded to meet.

Denys Rowbotham

BENAUD AND HIS MEN

Benaud and his 1961 Australians not only realised their ambitions but, in doing so, triumphantly vindicated their principles. They kept the Ashes by winning the Test series 2–1 and had a moral victory in the final drawn match. They promised England attractive, significant cricket, and provided it. And in the process they defied the old adage that bowlers, not batsmen, win matches.

Memory cannot recall an Australian side weaker in bowling. Kline and Quick, left arm wrist and left arm orthodox spinners, were too unreliable to win a Test place. Gaunt, the likeliest of the three new seam bowlers, was so handicapped by injury that only for the fifth Test was he fit and then, not surprisingly, lacked control. McKenzie and Misson were always lively and persistent but woefully and consistently erratic in length and direction. None of the five, indeed, could have been certain of a regular place in half a dozen or more English first-class county sides.

There remained Simpson and the veterans, Davidson, Benaud, and Mackay. No Test match wicket, even Old Trafford's, was quite hard and fast enough for Simpson, who lacked Benaud's accuracy, shrewd variations of flight and pace, and tactical acumen when he could not beat the bat by sharp turn. Davidson still rose to greatness on occasions, but to do so this time usually needed some help from the wicket. When he was resisted, control and devil alike seemed to leave him. Of a sudden he would look grey and old and a hand would creep to the back which finally at the Oval let him down.

Benaud himself was so plagued by his shoulder injury that

he could only turn an arm over at Edgbaston and Headingley and had to miss the second Test at Lord's. The Oval wicket ideally was too slow for him so that only at Old Trafford did conditions and his fitness conspire and allow him to exercise all his tantalising arts. Mackay, whose possibilities in England Benaud anticipated with rare cricketing insight, used the seam with sufficient accuracy and cunning to take sixteen Test wickets. But he lacked hostile pace and lift to test reflexes and should have taxed only England's patience. Pace and right arm wrist spin apart, there was nothing.

England's bowling, indeed, was individually more skilful and tactically searching, and collectively the more varied for all conditions. Yet Australia won the series so convincingly that only on a difficult wicket at Headingley were they outplayed in every department. How did they do it? Certainly it was not because their batsmen were incomparably the more accomplished. The difference between the combined efforts of Lawry, Simpson, Harvey, O'Neill, Burge, McDonald (in three Tests), and Booth (in two) and of Pullar, Subba Row, Dexter, May, Cowdrey, and Barrington was in aggregate 111 runs in England's favour and in average less than one in Australia's. All told Australia's batsmen made 2330 runs at an average of 31.49, England's 2479 runs at an average of 29.51.

Outstanding individual performances were comparably balanced. Two bad wickets challenged not only nerve but the highest, most sophisticated arts of batsmanship. Lawry's century at Lord's won Australia the second Test. Yet Cowdrey's ninety-eight at Headingley tapped reserves of judgment, subtle technique, self-discipline, and cool courage and unfurled a range of daring, imaginative, opportunistic shots as did no other innings by anyone in the series. On the good wickets Harvey, O'Neill, Lawry, Burge, Booth, and Davidson (at Old Trafford) played between them a dozen memorable innings. But none transcended the glory of Dexter at Edgbaston and Old Trafford, the more restrained and elegant yet no less ruthless command of May twice, or the workmanlike doggedness of Subba Row, fitfully Pullar, and finally Barrington.

What mattered, indeed, was not that Australia's batsmen were the better or even potentially the more prolific but that they scored their runs when and how they were wanted. They were not so much better batsmen as better cricketers. Unlike England's batsmen far too often since the war, they never lost sight of the game's basic object—that of seizing, consolidating, and clinching the advantage—and from that almost everything sprang.

Australia's batsmen looked tough and assertively self-confident. They expected to bat long and make runs. They believed attack their best guarantee of survival, calculated aggression always a justifiable risk, since every forced faltering in bowling accuracy eased progressively their problems of defence. So they used their feet not only to punish every loose ball but increasingly to restrict the area of good length. They scampered their singles no less eagerly deliberately to upset cramping field placings.

Merely to endure and to accumulate was never enough for them. Their aim from the outset was domination, to fashion an innings, through footwork, strokeplay, and swift running, which would create a situation of tactical advantage to the side. They concentrated, moreover, on establishing this advantage as early as possible. So in three Tests not only did the weight of their first innings' total preclude defeat but the rate of its scoring left their bowlers time, had they been good enough, to achieve victory. Even at Headingley, in defeat, they scored more in the first innings than in the second. Only at Old Trafford did Statham sabotage their policy; then they recovered with such steely aggression that Benaud was able to reward them with the Ashes.

England's batsmen lacked just these virtues. Their utmost of confidence looked like hope. They might attack sometime, one felt, if they survived. Calculated aggression seemed so hazardous to contemplate that often they did not hit full tosses and half volleys. They allowed the lengths of even erratic bowlers to restrict their footwork and Benaud's field placing to dissuade them from running. They could respond to a tactical situation but not create one.

So, Cowdrey at Headingley and Dexter and perhaps May at Old Trafford apart, their best innings were match saving, not match winning ones. Never did they succeed when batting first and when, batting second, they had a first-innings advantage at Old Trafford they failed through overcaution to consolidate it. They had determination, but when it mattered only Cowdrey, once, had Australia's decisive conviction.

The series, in short, was decided less by innate quality and acquired technical ability than by character and tactical outlook. The captaincy reflected this and probably conditioned it. Benaud beat England in four and a half days with an attack which could not win half its county games in three days. He encouraged, suggested, sometimes exhorted. He planned. If his plan failed he immediately experimented. If experiment failed he tried bluff. He used his limited resources to play on the strength, weaknesses, and anxieties of England's batsmen with a pragmatism as alive to the psychology of human frailty as to the logic of cricketing tactics. May, by comparison, too often seemed lost and detached, inflexible and inscrutable in a cold abstraction of preconceived theory.

The last day at Old Trafford epitomised much. Benaud actually conceived victory in the morning. When later Dexter was in full cry he brought on Simpson instead of Mackay—a piece of daring, as Subba Row might vouch, matched only by its devilish subtlety. Then he foxed Dexter with a stratagem so audaciously simple that the thought of it must anger Dexter still. It was great cricket because it was such human cricket. And this was the message, more valuable even than their achievements, of Benaud and his great-hearted side. Significant cricket is ruled not by technique or abstractions of theory but by men exercising their wills, spirits, minds, and wry humours.

234

Gerard Fay

JUSTUUAITANSEA!

William Barkley has established a new custom which I hope
will spread. He has written a book, had it published, and has
reviewed it himself in the most prominent position in the newspaper he works for, the *Daily Express*. I look forward to a
great extension of this labour-saving device: it reduces the work
of a literary editor to a mere choice of books and allocation of
the space available among their several authors. I had thought
of giving Mr. Barkley the chance to do something else unusual:
I was going to ask him to translate this particular edition of
This Column which is mostly about his book into his own simplified spelling. But I decided it would be unkind; it would take
too long to render the subtleties and felicities of this particular
style even with such a subtle and felicitous method as Mr.
Barkley (hereinafter referred to as Barcli) has invented.

For his book *A Last Word* (Pitman, 7s. 6d.) is neither more
nor less than a proposal for simplified spelling. Barcli has an
open and manly style. He conceals nothing. In a short space
he makes a clean breast of it and admits not only to being a
shorthand writer but to being a Scotsman as well. The combination has, of course, a pronounced (*pronounced*, get it?)
effect on his attitude to phonetics.

Everybody knows that in these islands the only people who
cannot speak the language properly are those who gave it its
name. The Irish, the Scots, the Welsh all spikka da English
puffick: only the poor English do not know how to pronounce
it at all, at all. Therefore Barcli is dead right when he uses the
same letters for the th in thin as for the th in the (and he might

have added the th in although). His argument in favour of the th sound is convincing. Much more so than the argument, if any, which can make it possible for the forty-three-letter alphabet now being foisted on some unfortunate children to use the same symbol for the o in to, the ou in should, and the u in full. The passage in question was in the *Sunday Times* and may not have been compiled by an expert, but I'll bet he was a Scotsman. I hope later on to hold a competition on the forty-three-letter alphabet with particular reference to the towns where it is being tried: for instance, I shall offer quite a large number of penny stamps to whoever can tell me how to represent the sound of l in Owdham or alternatively the w in Oldham.

Let me make it clear that I am pro-Barcli. I approve, with certain reservations, for instance, of this:

To be, or not to be, that iz the cwestion.
Whether 'tiz noebler in the miend to sufer
The slinz and aroez ov outraejus fortuen.
Or to taek armz agenst a sea ov trublz.
And bi opoezing end them? . . .

I am a lot more willing to hand over our language to that sort of treatment than to anything thought up by the Pit-avians. Of course, it has always seemed to me ridiculous that anybody should *want* to simplify our spelling. I have never had eny dificulty I mean with words like cieling or recieving or acomodate or lonliness or convalecscent or curicullum or gahstly or giudance or even phthisis. You see speling comes natural to me, like grammer. But I sympahtise with the people who have dificulty and I aplaud the efforts of people like Barcli (and his understrapper, Beverbruk) to make it easier. But I have badd neus for themm.

I have been paeing attenshun to this cweschun for menny menny ears now and I have arivd at a treu fynall soleushun. In abowt as short a tiem as it wood take Mr. Marpulls to bild a motrway from Lan's End to John o' Grotes I am going to perfekt my desimal letter-numeral sistem which will rejuice the three Rs to one. Breefly the idea is that the alfabet will contain ten symbols. The same cymbals will serve as figgers so that reeding, riting, and rithmetic will bikomm a singl ntiti. Simpl, izntit?

Ov corse ue shal v to gett sumelp fromm the teechers but thatllbeeeezi. Uith onlee tenn leters ue shal v to putt upp uith feuer ideeas: but modn edduecashun maiks that pretty simpl becaws thr r feuer ideeas tew bee xpresd. If ue awl doo les thinnkink their wont bee thee saem demahnd fr awl thoes wurds that cluter upp the langwidge noeadaes. Abowt a thowsand uerds awt to surve awl awdinary perperses, uith a fue doesn xtra wuns for peepl who rite in neuspaprs or tawk in parlimnt or apeer on the tely. Goe tue itt Bill Barcli: I uill katch upp onn eu in thee nd.

Oh, an bi the ua. I uender iff Barcli nd Smoekr an Pittmann nd awl the uthersv noetisd that a gi cawld Neuly in a sho cawld " Stop the uerld I wannagettoff " az ritn a songg cawld thee ABC songg? Taz noe uerdz orrather the uerdz r theez: ABCDEFG HIJKLMNOP QRSTUV WXYZ. Uot doo ue need uith awl theez uerdz? Thatz uor Ill preuv uen Iv got thee alfabet doun too tenn leters. Justuuaitansea!

Peter Lennon

SHELTER FROM FALL-OUT

I think it is remiss of the French to have only 114 fall-out shelters for fifty-five million people; remiss and untoward, and I said so loudly in this bar in Montparnasse, where some persons turned and said: " *Ce Brittanique? Il est fou-non?* "

" It does not matter if we are mocked," I told my Parisian friends, one of whom came from Los Angeles and the other from Bordeaux. " We have a right not to be mocked because of the high personal estimate we place on survival."

" Man," my L.A. friend exclaimed, " you're comin' on too strong. I want to LIVE, man. Survival—that's for the store owners, the State Department, hicks. Dig? The riddly-rad-rad bourgeois. Riddly rad-rad. Rad. RAD. . . ." And he began to sway, finger-snapping on the stool. (He is not too strong on concentration.)

" What we need," I insisted, turning to Jean-Pierre Claude, " is a firm, functional, practical, and genuinely applicable survival policy which would be susceptible of implementation. We also," I said, my voice growing warm, " should nourish in ourselves a deep love of humanity. We must hold fast to the conviction that even if people start slinging around destruction of a deep penetration and wide range we can still love humanity.

" What, after all, are cancer, leukaemia-provoking weapons, radioactive scalders? We know that they are all in their obscure way an expression of what is human in 'anity. As for genetic changes, we don't even have to worry about them. They will be the concern of a new generation better equipped to provide *total* love for this new kind of humanity since they will be pretty well carcinomatised themselves."

I was struck by a beautiful realisation: we are all in our little way helping to make the world fit for carcinomatised lovers! . . . (It is foolish of me, I know, to be so easily moved.)

" I can think of no more touching example of this will of ours to adjust to our new condition," I told Jean-Pierre, " than the advice given by a British ladies' journal on how to spend those last moments: ' During those last precious moments . . . ' "

" *Baise bien ta petite amie?* " said Jean-Pierre.

" No, no," I protested. " That's not what the ladies' magazine said. They said: ' Try to spend those last few moments alone with a loved one.' "

Et alors!

" I have read up on this," I informed him. " I can show you clearly how we must adjust. . . . What effect would the

238

explosion of a twenty-megaton bomb, half of whose energy comes from fission (and half from fusion), have in, say, Greater London? The whole area of 540 square miles," I said impressively, " would be contaminated."

" *Tant mieux,*" said Jean-Pierre.

" People," I said, " would be getting doses of 3000 Rads within the hour when all that is really required to perform the same service is 540 Rads. And what lesson do we learn from this? We learn that the big bombs will be dropped on the cities. So get the people out of the cities! Out! Out! Everyone! Only in this way can we *begin* to lay the foundations for our new society; can we begin to set in motion an efficient defence programme. . . . This briskly practical advice must convince you, Jean-Pierre Claude, that I am no Romantic. I am a Realist. . . . A Romantic-Realist. Realist because I know that no time must be lost in getting the people out of the cities! Romantic, perhaps, because I dream dewy dreams of our New Society of scattered, microscopic communities springing up in—if I may say so—sheltered places through France, and England. And America, too," I added kindly for the benefit of my L.A. friend, but he seemed a little oblivious.

" Has anyone ever thought out, as I have thought out, the pattern of our new way of life lived in shelters, and what must be done to prepare? We should all begin by spending at least £100 (1370 Nouveaux Francs) on a shelter. Not, regretfully, a red-bricked shelter, since they are no good, but a two-inch thick concrete shelter. If we could spare a little more of our life savings, we should erect a steel shelter which would reduce the danger by a factor of eight.

" Then—according to this scientist I read—we must all find a ' careful housekeeper ' who would spend another £100 on canned food. The same C.H. could then provide little homely touches by whitewashing the steel windows and oiling the hinges of the door for a fast slam when the first bang is heard."

" Say they invent a silencer for the bomb, man," put in my evil L.A. friend. " Diabolical, eh? You open your mouth to say something and before you know it you are as full of Rads as a bourgeois. Then the big wheels—the few that are left—step in and put your $300 shelter up for auction. Unused. Going cheap!"

"*Et qu'est ce que tu va faire avec tes abris?*" demanded Jean-Pierre.

"What will we do with our shelters? Why, use them, of course, when the bombs go off. Having set up beautiful little shelters all over the world with people hanging around ready to scuttle into them, you don't imagine someone won't drop bombs on them just to see if they work? I'd be tempted myself," I said, with a gay laugh.

"But what would life be like in the shelters after the bomb goes off? Well, we would all be living in tiny, separate, independent communities. No television—no one would really want to see what's going on outside. We would be—and this is significant—thrown back on the primordial devices of home entertainment. We would talk. We would sing. We would invent games. We would have new social classifications. The old, useless people would be put to hastily filling pillow-cases with earth in case the door is blown down.

"There would be the bards. The singers. A singer would be highly prized: he would be given the place nearest the filtered air. We would deal with criminals in the community by inviting them to ingest some contaminated foodstuffs. How closely knit our family units would be."

"Say you ain't home when the blast goes, man? You're wandering the streets. Your chick's out of town."

"Ah, indeed yes," (and here I had to call on all my capacity for honest, realistic thinking), "it is true that one might not be fortunate enough at the time of the relevant explosion to be standing a few inches from one's loved one. Nor," said I, hastily anticipating Jean-Pierre, "might we be presented with the opportunity of plucking a potential loved one off the pavement. I admit the possibility of, in the scramble, finding oneself locked in with a seventy-five-year-old concierge, a member of

*"EUREKA!! THE ANTI-ANTI-ANTI-
ANTI-ANTI-ANTIMISSILE
MISSILE"*

the Corps Républicain de Securité, and an infant child with the
measles. Not, admittedly, a useful community. But it is here
that our brave and adventurous spirits must guide us. What
one must do is, at a decent interval after the bang but *before*
fall-out has time to settle, burst out and run for another shelter
—preferably one in the fashionable section of St. Germain
des Pres.

"What I would do is guess and calculate wind directions and
speeds; guess and calculate fall-out decrease possibilities—based
on the approximation of 22/7 to *pi*—and burst out and start
running.

"I admit the possibility of a miscalculation. I might simply run in the wrong direction. But I am leaving a community which, as I have said, is not useful—I have a duty to run. Perhaps I am mistaken. Perhaps after a few hundred yards I am already a prey to nausea, sickness, and blood changes, but I make an about turn and race for a new home, a new community where I might live for at least thirty-nine hours. Who knows, I might stumble on a girls' school!"

"*A ce point là*," Jean-Pierre said despondently. "*Même une école de garçons....*"

Erika Fallaux

GRASPING THE LIFE LINE

"It is expedient," says Mr. Khruschev, exploding his monster bomb in a last violent effort to extort the peace he wants on the terms he wants, "that some shall bear idiots, shall die of bone cancer and blood disease, shall be born deformed, so that the rest may live."

Is this criminal lunacy? Or plain cold realism? We cannot be sure. We have never understood the manœuvrings of this politician: we no longer understand the manœuvrings of our own. When Mr. Macmillan informs us that we in our turn may have to damage unborn children in order to maintain the balance of power, we can only stare at him aghast—reminded of nothing so much as of the child sacrifices for the appeasement of the ancient monster gods, whom we had long thought to have put behind us for ever.

Only one thing seems clear. Retaliation in kind would be intolerable: would simply lead to more disease, more neurosis.

more fear, and—since we already possess the means of total destruction—to no clear gain at all.

From the moment when the first of the nuclear bombs was dropped on Hiroshima, sixteen years ago, we have been caught and held in the iron grip of our own invention. Neither East nor West, neither Governments nor individuals, can see how to extricate themselves from it. That is why the experience of any single human being might be of value in illuminating the total appalling human situation: why my own small experience of oppression—which consisted not simply in a certain restriction on civil liberties, in economic inferiority, or even in hunger and homelessness, but in daily bodily and mental and—literally—mortal fear, is not entirely irrelevant.

My political life—by which I do not mean politics as something professed or read about in newspapers but as something lived and experienced—began in March 1938, in Vienna. I was ten years old, ignorant, and inexperienced as only a child can be. But with a child's clear vision and purity of mind, a child's freedom from deviousness, and a child's vivid but wholly reliable memory.

It was a period when all hell had broken loose in a tiny, insignificant part of Europe—which happened, however, to be my own country, Austria. The Nazis, with their expansionist and racialist theories, had erupted out of their own country and taken possession of mine. With them, for reasons which are as mysterious now as they were then (and this the Eichmann trial fully illustrated)—equally mysterious to victim and aggressor, to psychologist and politician—came sheer, open, unexplained, brutal savagery, chiefly but by no means entirely directed against Jews.

Most people never in all their lives experience naked brutality, except perhaps by accident, during a drunken brawl. But to have had to watch, with fear in one's heart and that heart nearly torn out of the body for sadness and pity and compassion; in silence but with guilt at one's own silence; in the knowledge that one's turn was bound to come, if not that day then the

243

next—for children were spared neither sights nor sounds nor torments nor imprisonment nor death; to have had to watch while others were dragged out of their homes, their beds, their shops and offices, their hiding places, were insulted and assaulted, kicked and beaten; to have had to listen to their screams and then, suddenly, to their silence; to have had to wait, nearly frozen with terror, for parents who were late in coming and might never come back at all—that was a thing to bruise the human spirit, to mark it for ever. Even though, as in my case, the body remained whole (and I ultimately escaped to England).

Yet still I say—with my eyes open I say it—it has taken me years to see it—that I would rather live like that than not live at all: that I would choose even oppression if that were the only alternative to disease and death for myself, my husband, my (as yet unborn) children, the wider circle of those I love and know, and of humanity as a whole.

For one thing I am a Christian. And I cannot distrust the human spirit utterly. I cannot believe that the oppressed will ever totally disintegrate under oppression; or the oppressor remain completely unaffected and unmoved by moral strength.

It is true that in the Nazis I saw the madness that can seize hold of men. But such madness is a freak, a temporary, incomprehensible departure from the human norm. I do not think it exists anywhere in the world to-day. But if it did, should the world rush on its own destruction in giving battle, or should it not rather wait for that madness to spend itself? Death only is irreversible: nothing else is.

We in the West have the undoubted moral disadvantage of having been the first to drop the bomb—unnecessarily, as is now widely held, and certainly irresponsibly. It would seem that to purge ourselves we may now have the corresponding obligation of making the first real conciliatory gesture towards unlocking the deadlock.

Mr. Krushchev has said again and again that he wants

DILEMMA

universal disarmament. And this, of course, is the only realistic policy. But it takes time for trust to grow and negotiations to be started. Meanwhile war may break out—as it is bound to sooner or later—by miscalculation.

On the other hand, whatever may be said for or against one-sided disarmament, it would be an immediate gesture of unique moral distinction, and as such not easily reversible: a gesture of total trust in humanity, serving at the very least to kill the distrust that is at the root of so much of the fear and the violence in men's hearts to-day. It would certainly be dangerous; it would probably be despised rather than respected. But it could not be misunderstood.

Marian E. Davies

HOME FOR CHRISTMAS

Feeling miserably ill because I am breaking the law, and hoping that I will not be sick all over the uniforms of the two smiling Bobbies who lift me from the pavement, I am gently carried into the police horse-box. "Why can't you be a bit lighter? . . . You are not so young as some of 'em, are you? . . . Why do you do this?" Laughingly they ask me questions, politely they put me down on the floor of the horse-box next to my friend. All the way to the police station we hear cheers from our law-abiding supporters. There are twenty-one of us in the van and we all go to a police cell together, staying there long enough for the smokers to have two fags.

Then to a room where the police take down our particulars; I have to guess my height; I think my eyes are brown; I have no visible scars. I am given a charge sheet which informs me that " At 3.35 p.m. on Saturday, 9th December, 1961, you, without lawful authority or excuse, wilfully obstructed the free passage along a highway, called Princess Street, Manchester, contrary to Section 121, Highways Act, 1959." We wait in a corridor for some considerable time. The police, by now firmly established as our friends, make sure that the women have chairs. They still fire questions at us because they are interested and impressed, glad to have first-hand knowledge of how we feel and why we act as we do. " Many of our chaps agree with you, you know, though not when you break the law." And in correct order we go before the magistrate; we plead guilty; a few of us make short statements; we are fined forty-two shillings.

The police cashier's office is as efficient as the most modern bank, and fines are quickly collected, though four of the twenty-one refuse to pay and are sent into the corridor again. By now the police have discovered that I have three children. They are staggered. I must pay my fine, they say. " Lassie, change your mind, go and pay it. The magistrate will hate sending you to prison."

And she did. She tried very hard to persuade me to change my mind. Twenty-five days in prison; she " had no alternative but to give me the alternative." Twenty-five days in prison, in prison until after Christmas, I should be separated from my family at this special time of the year, wouldn't I pay my fine? I could be given time in which to pay; would I sit on one side for a moment and think about it? No? Then prison it was.

Now that I was officially a prisoner I was handed over to a policewoman, who first removed my nuclear disarmament badge and the belt of my mac (did she think I would stab or hang myself, I vaguely wondered?) and then took away what few personal possessions I had on me. I sat in a small cell with my three companions. I wept silently, feeling small and frightened when I thought I should be feeling big and heroic.

The Black Maria was uncomfortable; how much better they transport their horses than their prisoners! It was foggy, so the journey to the prison was cold and slow.

At the prison gates we entered a new world; our possessions were listed, a kindly officer explained some of the procedure and told me I could leave if I paid my fine. A doctor examined me. What was the blotchiness all over me? I assured her it was only nerves. Was I sure? Was I allergic to wool? Had I a rash? Then a dear nurse was more embarrassed than I was at having to ask me very intimate questions and to search my hair. I stripped and then, oh joy, I was given a hot bath and allowed to keep my own foundation garments. My prison clothing was passed to me over the unlocked bathroom door.

247

What queer underclothes! I smiled as I wished my two teenage daughters could see them and thought wistfully of the black nylon panties I had just surrendered. But they were clean, the cardigan was cheerful, and the shoes were enormous, which was better than being too small. Next, food and drink—but the tea was undrinkable and I didn't even sample the stodgy white bread, but this was my own fault, I was still feeling sick. More formalities, more details, maiden name, where born, husband's name, where did he live? My signature on this form and that form. And so into the prison proper.

Another official checked my particulars, assured me that I could go out whenever I agreed to pay the fine, and asked me if I would do so. Another official gave me a sheet of notepaper on which to write home, telling me that if I asked I could have another whenever I wished to write for someone to pay my fine. Would I do so?

My " room " was cream and pink, with a green rug and a green hessian bedcover. A large mug of unsweetened, unmilked cocoa awaited me. I filled my bucket from a tap along the corridor. I was locked in with a sweet " Good night, dear." So this was prison. I looked round my cell—painted brick walls and iron door, tiled floor, three plain wooden chairs and two small tables, an unmade-up double bunk, " my " single bed, buckets, bowls, chamber pots. I read, " I love Eddie," " I love Bill," " I want my mum," " Dirty rotten coppers," " I love a boy I can never have." I had my pen and ink. Should I add a Ban the Bomb sign? But no, one doesn't write on walls, one is too well brought up. But I can write home. I wonder if my husband has been arrested, I think of my children, I weep. I pull myself together and begin my letter and find this helps; I write freely hoping it won't be censored.

So to bed, chuckling over my unglamorous nightie. But no sleep. I climb up on the top bunk and look out at Manchester. The fog has cleared a little but the air is thick and smoky. I think of my beloved hills with perhaps the moon upon them and the beautiful fresh air which comes in at my own bedroom window. I weep. I pull myself together. I have got to stick this for twenty-five days.

Eventually a light goes on and I get dressed and washed and finish my letter. I sit and sit, reading the inscriptions on the wall. I reread the prison rules, but still can't understand them all. Perhaps I shall be allowed a visitor. I'll read them again to find out. But I don't find out. A bell goes and I wonder what I should do. But I can't do anything; I'm locked in. I sit. Another bell goes. I hear keys being turned and people clattering down the corridor with buckets. It's like hell let loose. What a noise! My own door is unlocked. "Good morning; you'll be allowed to empty your pail and get water as soon as the others have finished." The others clatter back past my open door. Most of them are young girls about the same age as my elder daughter. They smile at me, such welcoming smiles. I weep. Then I collect my own water, meeting the other three Ban the Bomb prisoners (as we are obviously styled) at the tap. I go to the one and only toilet. It is filthy. It will not flush; the smell is horrible.

The four of us are taken down a separate staircase to the basement to fetch our breakfast, carrying it back up three flights of spiral stairs to our rooms. I notice for the first time that we are on the top floor. But I still can't work out the geography of the place. We are locked in our cells. The porridge was unsweetened and of the coarsest kind and had no milk on it. The bread was white and stodgy, the slice of luncheon meat highly seasoned and rather dry. I could eat nothing. The tea was lovely. I sat. I wanted to go to the toilet and didn't like to use the pot; in any case I had no toilet paper. I must ask for that. Eventually the door was unlocked, the others passed back along the corridor to empty their slops. They smiled. I felt like weeping. One whispered, "Don't sit on the toilet, love. We aren't supposed to speak to you." They passed back and we were allowed out to empty our slops. I asked for toilet paper and tried to use the toilet without sitting on it. It still did not flush.

We were visited by officials. Had I considered paying my fine? I could arrange to have it paid at any time. I was brought books, the classics, *Jude the Obscure, Mill on the Floss*, and the Bible. I read, but I hadn't got my reading glasses and my headache was bad but I didn't feel quite so sick. I was allowed to stand at the door of my cell and talk to my friends, a blessed time. And then we were asked if we would like a Meeting for Worship. Three of us went to a room, the door was shut and we were watched by a warder. But it was a wonderful Meeting for Worship. I thought, "Here we sit, three Quakers all in our forties, yet the Committee of 100 is accused of being political, Communist, full of young irresponsible people." But I soon forgot such thoughts. "Where two or three are gathered together . . ." It was a marvellous half-hour.

And so back to our cells. I read. Then dinner-time. We went down three flights of stairs, separate from all the others, we came back, we were locked in, we ate our dinner. At least I ate a little. The soup was hot and tasty, but very solid; the main course was solid; the pudding was solid. I felt ashamed at the amount I was wasting, for it wasn't badly cooked. The governor came to see me. She was sweet. She was concerned about my family. She asked me to consider paying the fine. I wept. I lay down on my bed and thought it must be the middle of the afternoon, but then the wireless was put on in the corridor, very loud and distorted, and I recognised *Two-Way Family Favourites* which I knew ended at 1.30 p.m. How glad I was that, thanks to my three teenagers, I was up to date with all the latest pop songs.

I lay on my bed. I was visited by the Church Army Sister. She was one of the most marvellous people I have ever talked to. Of course she wanted me to pay the fine and of course I wept. We talked together for some time. And then I read (thank goodness for Thomas Hardy), though I wished I had my reading glasses. We were unlocked at last. And three of us were taken for " exercise." Down the three flights of stairs, into a yard, walk at the same speed, in the same direction for about twenty minutes, keep to the perimeter of the oval area, mustn't cut the corners, keep going steadily round and round. But we walked together and we talked.

Back to cell, fetch water, fetch tea—solid white bread, solid bun, but the tea was good. We were locked in. " Good night, dear," though I was sure it could only be about four o'clock. I ate little, but I read and my headache grew worse, if that were possible. The evening dragged on. From somewhere I could hear carols being sung, presumably by the prison choir; later we had *Sunday Half-hour* on the wireless. (Goodness, was it only that time?) At some time we had cocoa, still un-sweetened and with no milk. Then someone came around and, standing outside the cell door, said " Good night " to each prisoner individually. Her voice could be heard echoing round the prison for what seemed to be about fifteen minutes: " Good night, good night, good night." And so the hours passed by.

The next morning, two of the four went out, their fines having been paid by outsiders. I wept. The governor sent for me. Would I pay my fine? The 12s. I had on me when arrested would be deducted, and I should get six days less. If I paid more I should be home in time for Christmas. Would I pay? No? . . . I saw the chaplain. I was visited by a lady not in uniform, a prison visitor, perhaps. Would I consider paying my fine? No?

Out for exercise, into the workroom putting the strings on carrier bags. We were with, but separate from, the other pris-oners. How young most of them were. There was an ugly scuffle and one prisoner was removed. I tied hundreds of knots in string. It was quite soothing, almost like knitting. And I could speak quietly to my one friend who was left. Back to our rooms. Water. Toilet. It still wouldn't flush, so I put my pail of water down it. Now I had to fill my bucket again, and

251

I think I was frowned upon, though kindly. Tea, still stodge to eat. "Good night," though it was surely not dark yet. Thomas Hardy, I'd read 400 pages and at last I had my reading glasses. I could now look at the Bible with its smaller print. Another sleepless night, but I felt better, and I had drunk my cocoa and water. I'd get used to it.

The next morning the same routine, more knots in string. Then I was summoned, by my surname only, of course. Some anonymous person had paid my fine. I could go. Indeed, I must go: I had no option. But absurdly enough, I wept. I relinquished my prison clothes. After all, I needn't have washed the prison bloomers the night before and put them to dry under my mattress, for now I had back my own black nylon panties. I was given my 12s. and 4s. fare and subsistence. I was free. Bewildered, I looked at the big outside world. Was it Tuesday? What time was it? But I had only been inside four days, I mustn't feel like this. I nearly wept again, but pulled myself together and went in search of a taxi and my husband.

INDEX OF AUTHORS

254

255